# THE
# MUNICIPAL DOOMSDAY MACHINE

## RALPH DE TOLEDANO

*formerly titled*
LET OUR CITIES BURN

Green Hill Publishers, Inc.
Ottawa, Illinois 61350

**THE MUNICIPAL DOOMSDAY MACHINE**

Copyright © 1975 by Ralph de Toledano

All rights reserved. No portion of this book may be reproduced without written permission from the publisher except by a reviewer who may quote brief passages in connection with a review.

Manufactured in the United States of America

First paperback printing.

Green Hill Publishers, Inc.
Post Office Box 738
Ottawa, Illinois 61350

Library of Congress Catalogue Card Number: 75-19174

ISBN: 0-916054-31-4

# CONTENTS

Foreword, by Senator Jesse A. Helms   **1**

Preface   **5**

1   "The Seat of Government Is City Hall"   **9**

2   The Nature of Unions   **18**

3   Down with the Constitution   **26**

4   The Arsonists   **36**

5   Poisoning the Well   **56**

6   Teacher Unionism Pays—But Whom?   **67**

7   Strikes, Politics, and the Public Interest   **79**

8   Studies in Collective Misery   **90**

9   Public-Employee Unions *vs.* the People   **98**

10   Popular Sovereignty *vs.* Big Labor Feudalism   **106**

11   Above the Law? Perhaps!   **115**

Appendix I: Compulsory Unionism in the Public Sector   **121**

Appendix II: Union Campaign Contributions   **133**

Appendix III: Public Attitudes Toward Right-to-Work Laws   **135**

Appendix IV: U.S. Senate Colloquy on Compulsory Public-Sector Bargaining Legislation   **137**

Appendix V: Public-Employee Union Statutes According to States   **174**

Index   **178**

# Books by Ralph de Toledano

Frontiers of Jazz

Seeds of Treason

Spies, Dupes & Diplomats

Day of Reckoning (*a Novel*)

Nixon

Lament for a Generation

The Greatest Plot in History

The Winning Side

The Goldwater Story

RFK—*The Man Who Would Be President*

America, I-Love-You

One Man Alone—Richard Nixon

Claude Kirk—*Man & Myth*

Little Cesar—*The Chavez Story*

J. Edgar Hoover—*The Man in His Time*

Hit & Run—*The Ralph Nader Story*

Let Our Cities Burn

# Foreword

By U.S. Senator Jesse Helms of North Carolina

On the morning of March 6, 1975, eight members of the United States Senate joined in a colloquy in the Senate Chamber. Their subject involved an issue that is too often obscured in this era of multiple daily crises. But it is an issue of mounting importance to every American.

The issue: the federal government's proposed entry into the internal labor-management affairs of the fifty states and their county and municipal subdivisions.

I was one of the eight senators. The others were James L. Buckley of New York, Carl T. Curtis of Nebraska, Paul Fannin of Arizona, Jake Garn of Utah, Clifford P. Hansen of Wyoming, James L. McClure of Idaho, and Strom Thurmond of South Carolina.

Many of the issues raised that day are seldom discussed openly in public. As a rule, the so-called debate over the proposed federal public-sector compulsory collective-bargaining law is decidedly unelastic and one-sided—limited primarily to the self-serving views of professional union organizers, the simplistic solutions of a few union-suited public administrators, and the rhetoric of assorted myth-makers and less-than-omniscient soothsayers. All of them wander around in the swamps of confusion, using the industrial sector's labor policies, as embodied in the National Labor Relations Act, as their "model" for similar public-sector legislation.

One of the few voices of reason upon whom most Americans can rely is Ralph de Toledano, Copley News Service's distinguished syndicated columnist and political analyst, and author of several bestselling books. To Mr. Toledano, the "simple" solution has always been suspect, as his readers well know.

Despite the fact that labor has never been his beat, per se, former *Newsweek* editor Toledano has written often and eloquently about the power grappling and the wheeling and dealing of Big Labor. His contacts, in and out of official Washington, have continued to give him entry to facts that

1

less probing reporters ignore, or cast aside. His concern with monopolistic union power, and the abuses of compulsory unionism, is long standing, and has led him to conclude that in the public sector (as he stated in a January 1975 column), "If legislation establishing compulsory unionism and collective bargaining in government is enacted, then the one qualification necessary for employment will be a union book."

City after city, he observed, has been deprived of essential services by illegal strikes of municipal employees; and timid governments have bowed their heads. If the proposed legislation is enacted, "strikes of this kind will become epidemic, with no recourse open to the citizenry," he warned.

His files already bulging with documentation and collected research, Toledano herein spells out the issues and answers in considerably more detail than a column allows.

For two centuries Americans have recognized the imperative need for a representative, ordered, sovereign government—a government beyond suspicion of being controlled or controllable by any special interest.

Yet, the sad conclusion is inescapable: enactment of the public-sector "labor" legislation now being avidly sought by union officials would be very bad for America. This is legislation that would compel sovereign governments to "bargain" with unions as *equals;* it is legislation that would compel public servants to accept unwanted unions as their only voice in dealing with their own government; it is legislation that would permit crippling strikes; it is legislation that would make public employees, administrators, and the public interest the pawns of union organizers.

It is legislation that would create chaos out of order and serfdom out of liberty.

The intensity of the lobbying campaign that Big Labor began in the Ninety-third Congress, and earlier, was awesome in its implications. In the Ninety-fourth Congress, the pressure is greater than ever.

In the states, legislators usually have been persuaded to adopt the "orderly process of collective bargaining" from the private sector as their public-sector model. That in mind, the proposed federal law would, like the National Labor Relations Act "model," *compel,* through unneeded and unwarranted federal action (possibly unconstitutional), individual public employees to subordinate their rights to union organizers. These union organizers would be designated "exclusive" representatives of all employees in a particular "bargaining unit"—including those employees who happen to believe, rightly or wrongly, that union representation may do them more harm than good. Most likely, these same unwilling cap-

2

tives of union monopoly representation would then be forced to pay money to the union for the representation they never wanted in the first place, or lose their jobs. On top of this would be a myriad of other technical smokescreens, including unworkable antistrike provisions, which top union officials have promised they will disregard anyway.

And the model, noted earlier, becomes a model for chaos, coercion, and compulsion.

In reading this book, all Americans should keep in mind a few fundamental rules of societal order: (1) that strikes against the machinery of government cannot be tolerated in a free society; (2) that government must, by definition, be responsive and fully accountable to the people—all the people, all the time; and (3) that public employees—because of the nature of the work they perform, because of the civil service system that gives many of them extraordinary privileges—and the government's social contract with the people, are indeed different from their counterparts in industry. This is true, both by reason of the rights and privileges they enjoy and by reason of the nature of public service employment.

Instead of the simplistic, unrealistic, and perhaps even immoral "models" the American people are asked to accept, thoughtful citizens should be looking for progressive, workable alternatives. And I believe there is one; a viable solution exists *without* federal intervention! We can preserve government sovereignty and individual freedom in the public sector without being unrealistic, and certainly without being "unfair" to public employees.

In fact, such an alternative already exists. It has been tried and tested and found extraordinarily *sound* in my own state of North Carolina. In short, all public-sector "collective bargaining" is prohibited by law.

In North Carolina, we recognize, of course, that all public employees—and all Americans—are protected in their right to join lawful employee associations by the First Amendment. However, my state has rejected the notion that governments should be compelled to recognize and bargain with these associations.

This concept is demonstrably a good law. It has successfully restrained the growth of inordinate public-sector union *power* in North Carolina, while leaving open a wide range of representation options—including union membership—to all public employees.

The statute has withstood challenges in the courts. In a September 1974 decision, the U. S. District Court for the Middle District of North Carolina, upholding the constitutionality of our law, said:

3

To the extent that public employees gain power through recognition and collective bargaining, other interest groups with a right to a voice in the running of the government may be left out of vital political decisions. Thus, the granting of collective bargaining rights to public employees involves important matters fundamental to our democratic form of government. The setting of goals and making policy decisions are rights inuring to each citizen.

All citizens have the right to associate in groups to advocate their special interests to the government. It is something entirely different to grant any one interest group special status and access to the decision-making process.

Simply put, the court made a clearly affirmative and correct statement of the rights of all citizens and groups of citizens to have equal access to their own government.

While the North Carolina law puts a statutory prohibition on recognition and contract-making, it does not preclude representatives of employee associations from petitioning their government over conditions in the workplace. It does preclude the government's granting monopoly status to a particular union, trading away its own sovereignty, and depriving individual workers of their precious liberty to deal with their own government. A strict nonrecognition policy not only prevents invasions of governmental sovereignty, but simultaneously keeps the channels of redress open to all employees—indeed, all citizens. It allows government administrators to conduct their business, in the public interest, and to create and conduct responsible and effective public-employee personnel policies—a responsibility which, when subject to adversary collective bargaining, is less imaginative, and less progressive.

The attention of government administrators, under such a policy, is clearly focused, as it should be, on dealing effectively and fairly with the employees and their interests, rather than on dealing with the union and its interests. There is a vast difference.

The North Carolina experience shows that the states, if they have the courage, can handle their own public-employee labor matters without federal intervention. It seems a good place to start.

America must come to grips with the issue that faces it. We need an open, thoughtful debate; and we must consider all solutions, all "models," popular and unpopular. Ralph de Toledano has taken a giant first step in this direction.

# Preface

Government, whether in the abstract or the particular, derives its power from the people. So, too, do the instrumentalities of government—the Congress, the Executive, and the Supreme Court or their counterparts on the state and local levels. Government, as the Tenth Amendment clearly attests, is the property of the people—a property conjoined to those rights of life, liberty, and the pursuit of happiness.

A private institution, no matter how richly endowed or formidably muscled, may not deprive the people of this right of property, not even under "due process of law," so long as the Constitution remains in force. As the highest courts have ruled, the rights of life, liberty, and property are beyond the reach of the judicial process, beyond debate or cavil. Under the American system, the individual's stake in his governmental property is absolute.

This is precisely what the issue of compulsory unionism in the public sector is about—and what this book is about. Even if a case could be made that compulsory public sector unionism would be a benefit to the body politic—and the exact opposite is true—the fact and the principle would remain the same. Since government is the property of the people, no power alien to that relationship can interpose itself to determine under what terms the individual can do business with his own property or to what extent he may participate in the activities of the instrumentality he possesses.

If the AFL-CIO and the public employee unions it manipulates were to say that no person could serve in Congress, on the bench, or preside over the Executive Branch without a union card, the uproar would be tremendous. It would be argued that such an imposition would give the grand sachems of Big Labor a veto power over the elective and appointive process, and set Mr. George Meany above the President and the Constitution of the United States. Yet compulsory public employee unionism and compulsory collective bargaining differs from the inconceivable condition set forth above only in degree. Both make the process of government an adjunct of

5

Big Labor and deprive the individual of his interest in the institutions which are incontrovertibly his own.

Those who advocate compulsory public-sector unionism are proposing the overturn of the American system and encouraging a revolution which would substitute for the will of the people the dictation of a special interest group representing a small minority of all wage earners in the United States. There are, of course, other factors involved in Big Labor's assault on the Constitution and the people of the United States—factors which go to the very nature of all compulsory unionism. Robert Bork, the Solicitor General of the United States, has noted that

> Those who use or advocate coercion and disruption for political or ideological ends have a ready model in the legally sanctioned struggle between unions and management. Our labor law, and the ideology that supports and suffuses it, encourages the organization of employees into fighting groups ...

And Senator Sam Ervin of North Carolina, in his days as a member of the "world's greatest deliberative body," added:

> By sanctioning compulsory unionism, the Federal government is empowering unions, in practical effect, to compel those who labor to become members of unions as conditions of employment and to participate in strikes they deem unjust under pain of severe union-inflicted fines.

The organization of private-sector wage earners into "fighting groups" may be tolerable in a free society. But when public employees are dragooned into the service of Big Labor's fighting forces, the result is, in effect, insurrectionary—as Franklin Delano Roosevelt warned. Current efforts to unionize the soldiers, sailors, and airmen of the United States merely underscore the meaning of compulsory public collective bargaining—and for those to whom history is more than forgotten words in unread books, these efforts recall the military "soviets" of workers and soldiers which overthrew the democratic post-Tsarist government of Russia.

The question of compulsory unionism assumes another and frightening dimension when the leaders of public-sector labor organizations determine that they should decide who works for government, how he works, what he will be paid, and what government itself will do.* The long-suffering public did not elect the Jerry Wurfs or the Albert Shankers to establish a dictatorship of the proletariat. They represent but a small

---

*In this context, see 16 American Jurisprudence 2nd, section 210: "Any fundamental or basic power necessary to government cannot be delegated."

fraction of the American labor force and have achieved their present eminence by methods that would make Tammany Hall blush.

Compulsion in government labor policy, particularly where it deals with public-sector unionism, should not be reduced to irony. Its consequences are not only bankrupting our cities and destroying the civility of our daily lives; they are shredding the texture of orderly government, substituting Big Labor might for civil right, and slowly introducing us to a condition in which we will be forced to choose between anarchy and a new form of feudalism.

(One other factor, not directly germane to the theme of this book, should be mentioned here—if only as a suggestion for a separate study. I have in mind the purely political strike which is a way of life in Europe and no stranger to this country. The Allis Chalmers strike, during the period of the Hitler-Stalin Pact, was called by a Communist-controlled union. Its purpose was not to increase the workers' take-home pay but to abort the production of war materials desperately needed by the British armed forces to withstand the Nazi onslaught. For the Mine, Mill and Smelter Workers (CIO) which called the strike, fascism was "a matter of taste" (Commissar Molotov's words) until an ungrateful Hitler bit the Communist hand that was feeding him. Consider the effects of a strike by public-sector unions for political ends!)

It is with that in mind that I have written this book. The so-called average citizen who thinks that compulsory public-sector collective bargaining does not touch his life and is something for the unions and his elected officials to dispute had better understand that it is not Albert Shanker's bad manners but the future of education that is on the block, not Jerry Wurf's contrived obscenities that he must ponder but the survival of representative government in the United States.

Unions are political instruments, and given the state of the body politic, they control elections and deal in elected officials. The voter cannot match the superb organization that Big Labor has introduced into the political process. But as of this writing, one man's vote is as good as another, and union members are measurably unhappy with the power the Big Labor has arrogated to itself.

The facts are in this book. Whether the American voter—which is thou and thou—will take them to heart is something else. The materials on which this book is based are encyclopedic in scope, and I am deeply grateful to Hugh C. Newton, a Washington publicist and former newspaperman, for helping me assemble them and put them into manageable shape. For the contents of this book, I take full and confident responsibility.

RALPH DE TOLEDANO
March 24, 1976

# 1

# "The Seat of Government
# Is City Hall"

The news from Europe was ominous. On August 2, 1919, one thousand police in London and an equal number in Liverpool had gone on strike. Within days, members of the Boston police force had picked up the cue, organizing several unions. The most powerful and best financed was the creature of the American Federation of Labor. Would London's experience be repeated in the country's most proper city? Most Americans felt that it could not.

But they had premonitions of danger. For many months the nation had been gripped by a series of crippling strikes. On January 9, 1919, workers in New York harbor had walked out of their jobs. On February 6, there had been a call for a general strike in support of Seattle shipworkers. On March 12, the Public Service Railway, which served 141 New Jersey communities, shut down to forestall strike violence. Strike threats from railway workers forced the federal government to increase their pay by $65 million, a tremendous sum in 1919 dollars. On August 1, almost two million railroad shopmen quit work, while streetcar, elevated, and subway workers paralyzed public transportation in Boston and Chicago.

The unionization of Boston's police, therefore, was not an isolated instance. It stemmed from the general labor unrest as demobilized troops poured into the nation's work force, depressing wages; from the wave of revolutionary fervor that washed over from eastern Europe; from the anarchist militants who were infiltrating the AFL; and from the residue of wartime violence and the surge of postwar disillusionment.

But the question of any tampering with the process of city government seemed to have been settled in Seattle, early that year, when AFL strikers, influenced by the Industrial Workers of the World (IWW), had attempted to regulate city operations. Mayor Ole Hanson had countered vigorously with a statement that spread across the country. "Any man who attempts to take over control of municipal government function here will be shot on sight," he said. "The seat of government is the city hall."

It should be noted that the Boston police had legitimate grievances. Inflation and the high wages paid in defense industries around the city had shrunk an annual base pay of $1,100, from which they had to buy their uniforms. Conditions in the station houses were bad. But through the intercession of Governor Calvin Coolidge, the police had received an eighteen-percent increase and the improvement of life in the station houses had been promised.

But Boston, like the rest of the country, was strike-happy. A walkout of telephone workers that spring had led Coolidge to seek authority to take over the industry if the strike continued. A firemen's strike had been narrowly averted. In this atmosphere, AFL organizers saw a unionized police force itching to strike as the entering wedge that would open the door to other municipal unions. Without the cop on the beat, a panic-stricken city would capitulate to union demands. And the AFL, which counted on Governor Coolidge and his strong connections with the Massachusetts labor federation, felt that he would remain above the battle. In fact, it found encouragement in his statement to reporters: "Understand that I do not approve of any strike. But can you blame the police for feeling as they do when they get less than a streetcar conductor?"

On Tuesday, September 9, the police voted to go on strike. The balloting showed their state of mind. In a police force of 1,544, the tally showed 1,135 in favor, 2 against. That afternoon at 5:45, most of the entire force left its posts; Boston was without any police protection, as only a handful of untrained volunteers remained to maintain order. What happened that night is described by William Allen White:

> The old policemen were gone. Groups joined groups, at first hilarious, but acutely realizing that no one would bother them. Under the street lamps scores of games of craps began to operate on the Common. No one molested these games. It was evident that the new police were not interested in crap games. This emboldened the gamblers. The mob grew noisy, also offensive. Its voice changed from a mumble to a high-keyed, nervous falsetto. Sporadically, little mobs broke up and gravitated to the larger mob instinctively ... By midnight the coagulating crowds had formed one raging mob, a drunken, noisy, irresponsible mob, without grievance, without objective, an aimless idiot mad with its own sense of unrestrained power. Riots broke out in various parts of the city. Someone threw a loose paving stone crashing through a store window about one o'clock.... Sticks and bricks went whizzing into offices on the second and third floors. By two o'clock looting had begun. The situation was out

10

of hand. The volunteer police were powerless. . . . [G]oods from stores and shops were scattered from the idiot's fingers along the streets of South Boston and the north and west end, and in the downtown section. . . .*

The following morning, as another observer would report, "a sight not beautiful met the eye; lawlessness continued; license ran wild." On the streets, there were daylight robberies, and the looting continued. The volunteer police were beaten up by the raging mobs. In a futile gesture, Mayor Andrew Peters called out elements of the State Guard. The following morning, Bostonians picked up the newspapers to read:

### RIOTS AND BLOODSHED IN CITY AS STATE GUARD QUELLS MOB
Mayor Assumes Command, Calls Out State Guard—Brushes Curtis Aside—Asserts Authority Conferred on Him by Old Statute

Volley in South Boston kills two and wounds nine. Cavalry sweeps Scollay Square

Riotous mobs bent on plundering and destruction of property attempted last night again to plunge Boston into a turmoil of crime and general disorder; and only sobered down and went home after the State Guard had fired into a crowd at South Boston, killing two men, wounding nine persons, and cavalry had charged into a crowd at Scollay Square with drawn sabers, scattering it in all directions. . . .

But even bloodshed did not stop the rioting and looting. The units of the State Guard did not have the manpower or the experience to put an end to lawlessness in Boston. At that point, Governor Coolidge, who had given local authorities every opportunity to restore order, moved in decisively. No longer could he say, as he had about other political struggles, that it "wa'n't my stove." In quick succession, he issued two executive orders—the first calling out the National Guard, the second taking charge of the Boston police. He also issued a general order calling on the people of Boston to assist him and directing the police to return to work.

The violence in Boston, as White wrote, was "the dramatization required to make the people understand the principle which the Governor felt was involved, that a policeman does not strike; he deserts. The policeman's status is not that of a laborer but a defender of peace and order." Coolidge himself

---

*William Allen White, *Puritan in Babylon—The Story of Calvin Coolidge* (New York: Macmillan, 1938).

saw his contribution as being simply that he had called out the National Guard. In his autobiography, he wrote:

> To [police commissioner Edwin U.] Curtis should go the credit of raising the issue and enforcing the principle that police should not affiliate with any outside body whether of wage earners or of wage payers but should remain unattached, impartial officers of the law with sole allegiance to the public. In this I supported him.

With the militia patrolling Boston's streets and new men, including war veterans, hired to fill the jobs of the striking police, the trouble ended and the city was once more quiet. Calvin Coolidge made one more statement, which brought him a flood of mail—some seventy thousand letters and telegrams—and won him the vice presidency. When Samuel Gompers, head of the AFL, pleaded that the striking policemen be reinstated, Coolidge fired off an answer: "There is no right to strike against the public safety by anybody, anytime, anywhere." To this, President Woodrow Wilson responded with a congratulatory message, which in effect said, "Amen!"

Coolidge had galvanized the country because instinctively it realized that governments, within the limits set by constitutions written and unwritten, must be sovereign if the fabric of society is to be preserved. He had set his proscription in terms of the public safety because the shoe fitted in the instant case. But implicit in his actions and words was the further realization that the public safety is as broad as the public service. Whosoever raised his arm against the government, no matter what his grievance, had crossed over the line that divides the constitutionally guaranteed right to petition the government for the redress of actual or imagined injustice from what amounts to insurrection.

The Coolidge formulation, moreover, was not a response to the passions and the pressures of the times. Some three decades earlier, Justice Oliver Wendell Holmes, then a luminary of the Massachusetts bench, had handed down an apposite opinion in *McAullife* v. *City of New Bedford*. The case being adjudicated concerned a police officer dismissed from the police force for engaging in political solicitation and canvassing in election campaigns. Holmes spoke for a unanimous court when he formalized a self-evident proposition.

"The petitioner," he ruled, "may have a constitutional right to talk politics, but he has no constitutional right to be a policeman. There are few employments for hire in which the servant does not agree to suspend his constitutional rights of free speech, as well as of idleness, by the implied terms of the contract. The servant cannot complain, as he takes the employment on the terms which are offered him." Holmes was simply underscoring what is a matter of law and logic—that those who seek government service must accept its limitations just as a soldier who has been drafted must accept military discipline.*

Justice Holmes would have applied a far sharper cutting edge to the question had he been called upon to sit in judgment on public-employee unions that openly boast that they have broken the law, that encourage violence and sabotage, and that demand the primary loyalty of all government workers. He would have recognized that collective bargaining is meaningless unless it is armed with the right to strike, and this would have been as unthinkable to Holmes as it was to President Franklin Delano Roosevelt in August 1937.

Like others in that period when labor law was being revolutionized, Roosevelt accepted the justification of compulsory unionism, compulsory collective bargaining, and the strike as countervailing forces to the power of industry. But he recognized that if we are to have viable government there can be no force within the body politic that can set itself up as a counterforce, with one exception—the will of the people as expressed at the ballot box. In a letter to L. C. Steward, president of the National Federation of Federal Employees, Roosevelt wrote: "A strike of public employees manifests nothing less than an intention on their part to obstruct the operations of government until their demands are satisfied. Such action looking toward the paralysis of government by those who have sworn to support it is unthinkable and intolerable."

A New York State court spelled it out more precisely in a 1943 opinion:

> To tolerate or recognize any combination of Civil Service employees of the government as a labor organization or union is not only incompatible with the spirit of democracy, but inconsistent with every principle upon which our government is founded. Nothing is more dangerous to public welfare than to admit that hired servants of the state can dictate to the government the hours, the wages and conditions under which they will carry on essential services vital to the welfare, safety and security of the citizen. To admit as true that government employees have power to halt the functions of government unless their

---

*In point of fact, both federal and state courts denied that there is a common law or constitutional "right" to join a union, even in the private sector, until the Wagner Act made it a tenet of statute law in the Thirties.

demands are satisfied, is to transfer to them all legislative, executive, and judicial power. Nothing would be more ridiculous.*

The Boston police strike was a dramatic example of what monopolistic labor organization could do to the rights of the public, not to mention its threat to orderly government. The healthy reaction of the people and their support of Governor Coolidge reflected a sanity that, in the turmoil of the Sixties, was twisted and perverted. In the intervening period, however, much had happened that gave impetus to the drive for delivering the many millions of public employees into the grasping hands of Big Labor and opened the window to legal sophistries that urged the delegation of government power—indelegable under the Constitution—to self-constituted labor organisms.

Since the Thirties when, aided and abetted by a sympathetic government and its media allies, the labor movement had occupied the high ground of industrial power, the AFL-CIO and its co-religionist independent unions had employed their muscle to seize great sometimes overwhelming, political power. Through the illegal use of dues-payers' money Big Labor had captured the Democratic Party, dominated state houses, and elected a substantial number of senators and congressmen. Though it had moaned in 1947 that passage of the Taft-Hartley Act would reduce it to "slave labor," it had been able to set itself up as a species of second government, of itself entire. Close to two-thirds of the electorate could register their opposition to the compulsory unionism on which it based its power, but George Meany could still boast that the AFL-CIO, which he headed, was violating the Corrupt Practices Act with impunity.

Unbridled power knows no respect for law and creates its own logic. But in its drive to double its captive constituency, Big Labor found assistance in an executive order that ironically was widely hailed as a guarantee of free choice among public employees. It is true that Executive Order 10988, signed by President John F. Kennedy on January 19, 1962, protected federal employees who did not wish to make as a condition of their employment the payment of dues to a union. It stated flatly that "Employees of the Federal Government shall have, and shall be protected in the exercise of, the right, freely and without fear of penalty or reprisal, to form, join and assist any employee organization or to refrain from any such activity" [Section 1 (a)].

---

*Railway Mail Association v. Murphy, reviewed on other matters in Railway Mail Association v. Corsi (U.S. Supreme Court, 1945).

14

But the order codified and hallowed practices that allowed the camel to poke its nose under the tent. Its preamble struck down prior reservations of the courts and stated as government policy four fallacious propositions that experience in the private sector had amply negated. Said President Kennedy:

> WHEREAS participation in the formulation and implementation of personnel policies affecting them contributes to effective conduct of public business; and
> WHEREAS the efficient administration of the Government and the well-being of employees require that orderly and constructive relationships shall be maintained between employee organizations and management officials; and
> WHEREAS subject to law and the paramount requirements of the public service, employee-management relations within the Federal service should be improved by providing employees an opportunity for greater participation in the formulation and implementation of policies and procedures affecting the conditions of their employment; and
> WHEREAS effective employee-management cooperation in the public services requires a clear statement of the respective rights and obligations of employee organizations and agency management;
> NOW, THEREFORE . . .

That President Kennedy, a man of reasonable and informed outlook, should have put his name to that preamble bespoke considerable cynicism. For whatever the virtues of unionism, it has not and cannot bring peace or stability in labor-management relations. This had been repeatedly demonstrated in the private sector where the onset of compulsory unionism and collective bargaining ushered in an endless era of labor strife and crippling strikes. It was, moreover, contrary to fact that government efficiency "required" any relationships between management and the public-employee unions. Since the founding of the Republic, government had operated without the assistance of "employee organizations." Civil servants, moreover, had shown very little interest in the recruiting efforts of government unions. With the Civil Service Commission and the Congress constantly peering over the shoulders of executive agencies and departments, the well-being of public employees had been, for the most part, adequately protected.

President Kennedy's Executive Order 10988 did not merely bestow the "right" of union membership on government employees; it encouraged that membership and gave unions special privileges. The body of the order set up machinery for informal and formal recognition of public-employee unions as bargaining representatives, gave a union that could poll fifty-one percent of those in a given agency exclusive bargaining rights, ignoring the remaining forty-nine percent, and provided for a checkoff from wages of union dues at government expense. Compulsory unionism was not included, but only as a temporary sop to public opinion.

Precisely how much E.O. 10988 would contribute to an "orderly and constructive relationship" between government and the unions is demonstrated by union reaction to Section 2, which barred recognition of any union "which asserts the right to strike against the Government of the United States or any agency thereof, or to assist or participate in any such strike, or which imposes a duty or obligation to conduct, assist or participate in any such strike." Prior to the promulgation of the order, the American Federation of State, County, and Municipal Employees (AFSCME) had included a no-strike clause in its constitution. Once it had reaped the benefits of the order, AFSCME struck out the no-strike clause, while the government looked on benignly. Though decertification was mandatory for a union that struck, no move has been made to deprive any public-employee union of its "official" status or of the checkoff privilege.

The immediate results of E.O. 10988 were fourfold: (1) Because of the blessings bestowed upon it by the President, AFSCME and other government-employee unions zoomed in membership and ballooned in prestige. (2) Many states, some of which had in the past outlawed union membership for their employees, enacted legislation embodying much of the Kennedy order. (3) Public-sector strikes increased from fifteen a year in 1968 to 409 in 1969, with man days lost rising from 7,510 to 744,600—to the detriment of the public. (4) Legitimate employee associations, like the National Federation of Federal Employees (NFFE), were compelled to become militant trade unions in order to survive.

As public-sector unions grew in membership and financial resources, moreover, they changed from economic associations to political mechanisms. They challenged the civil service merit system and to a degree imposed union rules as a substitute. They used their political clout to undermine the authority of agency heads, particularly at the state and municipal levels, by going over their heads to the legislature. Increasingly, they set themselves up as final arbiters of wages and working conditions, in violation of constitutional precedent and practice. ("How can I vote against AFSCME," a Michigan State legislator pleaded, "when they contributed $5,000 to my campaign."*) And, by driving municipal governments to the wall, they contributed substantially to the

---

*Quoted by columnist James Jackson Kilpatrick.

16

disarray of orderly urban government and the blight of America's cities.

In 1974, as teachers' unions began to demand full control of schools and curriculums, public-sector unions made their biggest bid for ultimate power in a bill introduced by Representative William Clay, a Missouri Democrat, which would give public-sector unions a stranglehold on government, on the budgetary process, and on the lives of all government employees—a bill which insulated public-sector unions from any review of their acts by the federal courts.

The country had moved a long way from the days of the Boston police strike.

# 2

# The Nature of Unions

In the past forty years, a vast and sentimental mythology has grown up in the United States about the nature, function, and aim of the so-called labor movement. A small part of that mythology has been created deliberately by the union bureaucracy and its leaders. But a preponderance of the myths that rattle around in the American consciousness is the product of economists, sociologists, and law professors who live divorced from the realities and practicalities of union organization and the bargaining table.

The germinal myth, carefully disseminated by the public-relations machinery of every union in the land, is that "organized labor" represents the American wage earner. In point of fact, this is false, both statistically and psychologically. Union membership, even though buttressed by the compulsion of national labor policy, comprises less than one-fourth of the American work force. In the private sector, the growth of unionism has come to a virtual halt. There has been a spurt in the public sector only because, as this account will show, government at all levels has given moral support and preferential status to the more aggressive unions. Without the laying on of hands by President Kennedy in his Executive Order 10988, unionization of public employees would have remained at a standstill, as all authorities concede.

Most Americans, and this includes a majority of union members and their families, do not like unions. They suffer them because they feel there is no other alternative. An outcropping of this attitude can be discerned in the careful samplings by Opinion Research Corporation of Princeton, New Jersey, the most conscientious of the polling organizations. Its samplings disclose that seventy percent of the population believe that organized labor has too much power and sixty-eight percent oppose compulsory unionism. Sixty-one percent of union families share the view on union power and forty-nine percent oppose compulsory unionism.

In two recent instances, the attitudes of workers and wage

earners manifested themselves dramatically. In both instances, worker opposition to unionism was so great that the unions in question, to prevail, were compelled to mount campaigns of economic blackmail and labor violence against employers and workers alike—simultaneously blocking all attempts at representation elections. In the San Joaquin Valley, Cesar Chavez's United Farm Workers could not even muster a corporal's guard of legitimate pickets and had to resort to importing bodies from the San Francisco waterfront and the hippie hangouts of California's great urban centers. Defeated at every turn in its efforts to win over employees at Farah, a manufacturer of men's slacks, the Amalgamated Clothing Workers had to bring the company to the verge of bankruptcy by mobilizing a boycott effective largely because of the help it received from nonlabor sentimentalists and a misguided clergy.

The economists, sociologists, and law professors are not particularly interested in this aspect of unionism. They deal in abstractions that do not take into account coercion, which is the basis of Big Labor's power and its increasing hold on governmental and political institutions. They are in the thrall of the mystique of "economic necessity" and "orderly" labor-management relations. From time to time they are joined by a management figure who will assert, to applause, that he prefers to deal with unions rather than with an inchoate mass of employees. And, indeed, some employers do prefer surrendering management prerogatives to the unions with which they negotiate. If it means higher costs and lower productivity, they can always pass the bill to the consumer, who feebly protests against the inflation that results and blames it all on Big Business—and they avoid being pilloried by the media.

The concept that unions serve an "economic necessity" because they make labor-management bargaining tidy is, of course, untrue. It was understandable that in the Thirties, when the great push to organize was on, there should be a tidal wave of strikes. But the theory was, and it still kicks lustily, that once Big Labor had taken its place in the industrial life of the country, turmoil would subside. Yet in 1973, strikes idled 2,251,000 workers and deprived the economy of 27,948,000 days of work. To this statistic must be added the many cases when management, with a pistol at its head, agreed to "settlements" that were damaging to the country and its people, though they may have benefited a small segment of the population and, incidentally, fattened union treasuries.

Labor unions, or rather their leadership, have with increasing frankness advocated for themselves an adversary position

19

*vis-à-vis* management, the government, the public, and even their own members. That intraunion democracy is an impossible dream has long been recognized by students of the labor scene, no matter what their ideological bent may be. The individual union member long ago lost his franchise, and if he finds himself harassed or the victim of discrimination by the leadership, he has an almost nonexistent opportunity for recourse or relief. He will be shouted down or beaten up at union meetings if he raises a voice of dissent. Management will not come to his aid for fear of antagonizing the union bureaucracy. And the National Labor Relations Board has little interest in his welfare.

This has been recognized by Archibald Cox, a committed Kennedy liberal, who noted that "there are many ways, legal and illegal, by which entrenched [union] officials can 'take care' of recalcitrant members." A concerned media could afford union members a measure of protection by exposure of these practices, but the working press has become an integral part of the labor establishment and therefore has no interest in exercising its investigative talents.

Organized labor's adversary position is most manifest in its attitude towards management. Once upon a time, such union officials as David Dubinsky and Walter Reuther argued that it was not the union's function to kill the goose that laid the golden eggs. David Dubinsky's International Ladies Garment Workers realized that high wages and good working conditions depended on the health of the industry. And Reuther called for a "partnership" in the form of "industry councils" to benefit both management and organized labor. That point of view has vanished as Big Labor increasingly sees its role as one of redistributing the wealth, even if it puts any number of companies out of business, and any number of workers out of jobs. So long as compulsory unionism gives it an unchallengeable control over employment, it need not worry about its impact on industry or about the hardship on those members whose place of livelihood is shuttered.

(That union leadership is interested solely in power, as the expense of the common good, is amply demonstrated by its frantic efforts to bring about the repeal of Section 14(b) of the Taft-Hartley Act, which allows state options on compulsory unionism. Right-to-work states have shown a consistent pattern of rising wages and profits, at a rate greater than in compulsory-union states. But in right-to-work states, the labor leadership has been compelled to look to the welfare of its members, on pain of losing them. If a worker, disillusioned with or mistreated by his union, can resign and not lose his job, this puts certain constraints on the leadership that are

20

not present in a compulsory-union situation, and that it finds onerous.)

By its very nature, a union is an instrument of class war, as even the most casual reading of labor papers and literature discloses. It is not there to redress the grievances of members but to create them, not to be the link between employees and management but to be an assault force, not to bring industrial peace but to foment sufficient dissatisfaction to justify its existence. In its dealings with Congress and with state legislatures, it is no less a "special interest" than industry, except for its greater effectiveness. It takes no more than the statement of George Meany, president of the AFL-CIO, that Big Labor consistently violates the Corrupt Practices Act with impunity—or an assertion by AFSCME's Jerry Wurf that he has participated in many illegal strikes—to mark organized labor's contempt for government or its devout conviction that it is, and should be, above the law.

But the biggest myth of all is that Big Labor is an association of individuals working towards certain economic goals. This may have been true in the days of Calvin Coolidge, but it began changing with the passage of the Norris-LaGuardia Act and the Wagner Act. Today, organized labor is the single most powerful political force in the United States. In 1968, its contribution of what has been estimated at $60 million, almost won the presidential election for Hubert H. Humphrey. In 1972, AFL-CIO refusal to participate in the George McGovern campaign guaranteed his defeat and proved that Big Labor was a dominant—and domineering—force in the Democratic Party.

It is no wonder then that George Meany can boast that "we've got the finest political organization in the nation right now." The AFL-CIO Executive Council spelled this out in a report stating: "By any standard of measurement the COPE program in 1972 exceeded any previous year—more volunteer manpower and womanpower and more full-time staff assigned by international unions; increased funding . . . improved precinct-level organization."

In short, the AFL-CIO—and its activities were matched by nonaffiliated unions such as the United Auto Workers—functioned precisely like what it truly is, a political party. Dr. Herbert E. Alexander of the Citizen's Research Foundation underscored this point when, in a study of the 1968 election, he pointed out that "the contribution of labor committees . . . accounted for 61 percent of Democratic [Senate and House] candidates' funds," adding that these committees gave Democrats "almost as much money as party committees gave to Republicans." That much of this expenditure came from

21

union dues and therefore was in violation of federal law (no secret to the Justice Department) is significant only because those who similarly employ corporate funds are exposed by the media and end up in prison.

To regard this kind of political power concentration as an "economic association" concerned with wages, hours, conditions of work, and fringe benefits betrays egregious naiveté. As head of the AFL-CIO, George Meany has been involved in foreign policymaking; in the political agitation over Watergate which led to President Nixon's resignation—to which the AFL-CIO contributed very large sums of money; in trafficking with the Central Intelligence Agency; and in overseas political adventures for or against other governments.

Contributions to senators and representatives are not forgotten when Big Labor lobbyists rove Capitol Hill supporting or opposing legislative enactments that range as far afield as the confirmation of a Supreme Court justice, for which Big Labor took appropriate bows when he was defeated. Money talks, but it also creates dangerous conflicts of interest. How can a legislator vote his conscience or the needs of his constituents in labor matters under these conditions? During his first campaign, Senator Birch Bayh, an Indiana Democrat, received $70,000 in cash, as well as uncounted thousands in organizational help by full-time union officials, and it would require a superman—which Bayh is not—to resist the demands of AFL-CIO lobbyists when labor matters are up before the Congress. How can the public expect that Congress will investigate the very practice—legal, quasilegal, and illegal— that is responsible for the election of so many of its members?

The abdication of Congress and its subservience to "King George" Meany was nowhere else more apparent than in the hearings of March–June 1968 held by a Senate Subcommittee on Separation of Powers, presumably investigating the usurpation of the National Labor Relations Board, which, since set up under the Wagner Act, has ridden roughshod and carefree over the law and the intent of those who wrote it— aided and abetted for the most part by the Warren Court. So flagrant has been this subversion of law that even David Brinkley, the NBC network TV commentator whose views on Big Labor are determinedly benign, could say: "The NLRB is supposed to be an unbiased adjudicating body, something like a court. It usually behaves like a body of the AFL-CIO and is about as neutral as George Meany."

Through the NLRB, as testimony before the subcommittee amply proved, the AFL-CIO and the other labor mammoths took over executive, judicial, and legislative powers in a manner unknown on this continent since the days of George

22

III and his compliant ministers. Testifying before the sub-committee, Senator Robert P. Griffin—co-author of the Landrum-Griffin Act, which for the first time in the history of American labor laws addressed itself to safeguarding wage earners' right, rather than to those of Big Business or Big Labor—stated:

In the minds of some, any criticism of the NLRB is casually dismissed as just part of a power struggle going on between big business and big unions. Nothing could be further from the truth. More often, those who actually suffer from the distorted and twisted rulings of the Board are the individual workers, small unions, small businessmen, and the public at large.

Senator Griffin sustained his charge that the NLRB condones coercion of members by unions, citing the fines imposed by the United Auto Workers on 170 members who refused to participate in an Allis-Chalmers strike. Those fines directly violated provisions of the Taft-Hartley Act, but the NLRB upheld the UAW's violation of the law as an "internal matter." He also cited NLRB "legalization" of two activities specifically barred by federal statute: blackmail picketing to force employees to join a union and product boycotts—all in the guise of protecting union jobs. By *union* the NLRB meant the AFL-CIO. Said Griffin:

Over the years, the Board has clearly revealed a bias which works not only against individual workers and the public, but also against certain unions if their interests happen to conflict with favored unions. For example, an independent union rarely prevails before the Board if it dares to compete with an AFL-CIO-affiliated union.

Although the federal labor statute gives employees the right to request and obtain a decertification election when a majority of them no longer wish to be represented by a particular union, the NLRB has frustrated them from exercising this right and unions are permitted to fine and discipline members who try to invoke their right under law to initiate decertification procedures.

The bill of particulars against the NLRB, as an arm of the AFL-CIO, could fill a volume. But among them are examples of kangaroo-court procedures and subversion in Big Labor's behalf of statutes already tilting markedly on the side of union oligarchs. In one case, the NLRB, reviewing the testimony of 443 witnesses, ruled that all those who testified against the company told the truth whereas all those testifying for the company—and these included rank-and-file employees—were lying. Guy Farmer, a former chairman of the

NLRB, offered the subcommittee another example of the board's capricious behavior:

In Middle South Broadcasting, the union had a dispute with Middle South, operating a radio station in Chattanooga, Tennessee. The union circulated a blacklist of local firms that advertised over the station. The Trial Examiner found this to violate the secondary boycott provisions of Section 8(b)(4). He found that the publicity proviso did not apply because the primary employer, the radio station, did not produce, manufacture, or sell any products, and that the blacklisted merchants did not distribute any product produced, manufactured, or sold by the struck station.

The Board reversed. The Board held that the radio station was a producer of the products advertised over the station, including being a producer of automobiles, and that the advertisers distributed a product which the station produced.... [T]he finding that the radio station was a producer of automobiles [must have] come as something of a surprise to the station, as well as to General Motors, Ford and Chrysler.

In still another decision, the NLRB ruled that a manufacturer who planned to subcontract some of his work had to have the acquiescence of the union before he could do so, failing which the company was guilty of an unfair labor practice. Had the NLRB been given half a chance it might well have ruled that a management executive who took two-hour luncheons was violating the National Labor Relations Act because his employees were not accorded the same privilege. Though Congress very stringently restricted the NLRB's function to the adjudication of unfair labor practices, it has, as stated by Gerald D. Reilly, a former member of the board and a onetime solicitor of the Labor Department, reconstituted itself into "a maker of national labor policy" in defiance of the Congress. "Thus," he said, "we find well-intentioned members of the board telling state labor relations agencies that their respective jobs have been only one-fourth accomplished because only twenty-five percent of the labor force belongs to unions, or saying that with the great technological changes that have occurred in industry in the past twenty years, the board must now deal with a fresh set of problems: automation, hard-core unemployment, racial discrimination and the like."*

---

*It should be noted here that, through the instrumentality of compulsory unionism, the AFL-CIO was one of the most entrenched practitioners of racial discrimination—condemning blacks to the category of second-class citizens by the imposition of Jim Crow and lily-white unions, particularly in the building trades. Unions openly compelled black workers to accept wage scales lower than those of their white union "brothers"—a practice which has not been totally eradicated despite the lip service that Big Labor pays to civil rights.

The national experience since the passage of the Norris-La-Guardia and Wagner acts, and the concomitant nullification of the First and Fourteenth amendments, assumes heightened significance as Big Labor casts lustful eyes at public employees and the protection they have received under the civil service system. Fourteen million public employees and their tremendous dues potential are now the target of unions that, if allowed the license, will have the power to paralyze government, as Franklin D. Roosevelt warned, and to arrogate to themselves the functions of government as they have already done in England. It is a truism in that bedeviled country that the reins of government are held not by the Parliament or Ten Downing Street but by the Trades Union Council. In the United States, Big Labor is rapidly approaching the status of a state-within-a-state, dominated by leaders not elected by the people and independent of the needs and mandates of their own members.

Yet how many of those who argue for the right of unions to impose involuntary servitude recognize this?

3

# Down with the Constitution

In the late spring of 1973, Representative William Clay of
Missouri introduced a bill, the "National Public Employment
Relations Act," which if enacted would have been the most
massive assault on the American system in its 197-year history. Not only did it strike at the First, Fifth, Tenth, and
Fourteenth amendments to the Constitution, but it deprived
the fifty states of their right to conduct internal business and
delegated to a nonelected, nongovernmental instrumentality
powers and prerogatives held exclusively by state executives,
legislatures, and judiciaries.

The bill bore Clay's name, but it was no secret on Capitol
Hill that it was written in the offices of the American Federation of State, County, and Municipal Employees, a union
which had already demonstrated its contempt for law, both
criminal and civil, and avowed its true nature in a statement
by its leader, Jerry Wurf, that "we're political as hell." It was
referred to the House Education and Labor Committee where
such radical authoritarians as Phillip Burton of California,
James O'Hara of Michigan, Patsy Mink of Hawaii, and Shirley Chisholm of New York could guarantee it a friendly
reading.

It was the shrewd consensus of those pressing to put every
public employee into a union straitjacket that a chronically
shortsighted and timid business community would make but
feeble objection to a bill affecting the livelihood of state,
county, and municipal workers, and would accept the argument that this was none of its business. Nevertheless, the
strategy was to push for committee endorsement and congressional enactment as quietly as possible, making few waves
and counting on the massed support of those members of the
House and the Senate who owed their seats to Big Labor's financial and manpower assistance to sweep aside objections of
nonsubservient and independent-minded legislators.

Motivating Jerry Wurf was the realization that the National Public Employment Act would not only give AFSCME

irresistible political muscle but make him the single most powerful union official in the United States. Private-sector union leaders also realized that the bill would give the AFL-CIO the largest political bank account in the country doubling, by conservative estimate, its present two-billion-dollar annual dues intake—and reverse a disturbing trend. That trend was summarized by the *Washington Post* in its notable series, "The Unions," written by reporters Haynes Johnson and Nick Kotz.*

> [O]rganized labor's total membership is virtually stagnant and unions represent an ever-declining minority of the work force. Fewer than one in four American workers belong to unions.
> Many of the largest old-line unions such as the Steel Workers and Machinists are losing members, and some unions are faced with threats of insolvency. With members hard to find, as many as four or five international unions are seeking—in bitter and sometimes bloody jurisdictional warfare—to organize the same worker.
> Organized labor is painfully aware that its membership is weak in the faster-growing parts of the economy—wholesale and retail sales, government, services of all kinds and the insurance, financial, and real estate fields. Labor's strength has been concentrated in areas of the economy that have not been growing rapidly or are actually declining—mining, transportation, manufacturing and construction.
> Furthermore, labor leaders are concerned that 75 percent of their membership is concentrated in 10 large industrial states, while their membership is weak in fast-growing areas of the South and Southwest. There are more labor union members in New York State, for example, than in 11 Southern states, including Texas. . . .
> Labor leaders also are aware that their increasing minority status in the work force makes them vulnerable to charges that labor has too much power for the numbers it represents.

George Meany has professed unconcern over the decline in union membership. He has always been aware the Big Labor's power stems from its ability to buy candidates and sell issues. In his blockwide palace on Washington's Sixteenth Street, just across Lafayette Park from the White House, he told the *Washington Post,* "To me, it doesn't mean a thing. I have no concern about it, because the history of the trade union movement has shown that when organized workers were a very, very tiny percentage of the work force, they still accomplished and did things that were important for the entire work force. The unorganized portion of the work force

---

*Published as a paperback, New York: Simon & Schuster, Pocket Books, 1972.

has no power for the simple reason that they're not organized."

This view was parroted by Lane Kirkland, the AFL-CIO secretary-treasurer and, absent a shift in the organization's power balance, already handpicked to succeed Meany in Big Labor's totalitarian fashion. "In many industries, there has been a declining percentage of production workers and an increased percentage of people employed in sales, advertising, clerical, managerial, and research," he told Johnson and Kotz. "Well, these haven't been areas we've found particularly responsive to organizational appeals. Nor have we felt much compulsion to make a major effort of it."

This cosmetic "explanation" hardly fits the facts. In the first place, Big Labor has felt a "compulsion" to increase its membership and broaden its constituency, spending considerable sums of money in the attempt. It not only has failed in this but has also, as S. Frank Raftery, president of the Painters Union, glumly admitted, "lost a helluva lot of members and maybe we're organizing five or six people just to keep one." Wherever the NLRB and Big Labor, working in tandem, have not been able to rivet the worker to the union, there has been a decline in membership. That wages have increased more rapidly in right-to-work states, where there is no union compulsion, than in the stringently unionized states has not helped Big Labor's expensive organizing drives.

The Clay bill and others like it introduced in the Ninety-third and Ninety-fourth Congresses were conceived because the less arrogant and self-deluded elements in Big Labor realized that they had reached the end of the road in the private sector. Unionization of agriculture had failed dismally not because of any lack of tactical brilliance of the growers but as a result of the massive opposition of farm workers. That opposition would, of course, have been futile but for one fact: Big Labor did not have the coercive weapon of the National Labor Relations Act, which had served it so handsomely in the industrial field.

Big Labor realized that it could extend its hold only by the direct intercession of government, as it had since its initial expansion in the days of the New Deal. The logical direction, therefore, was the government itself, which the political power of the AFL-CIO could threaten via its captive senators and representatives. Government, whether federal, state, or local, controlled one-sixth of the nation's jobs.

It had taken many years to reduce or eliminate political trading in government jobs—the old spoils system—and to introduce the merit principle into the civil service. President Kennedy's Executive Order 10988 had been the first step

28

towards substituting for merit a set of trade union criteria. The Clay bill was planned as the karate chop that would destroy completely the merit system. The one hazard was the Supreme Court, but Big Labor strategists were fully aware that in labor matters the nine men, young or old, who occupied that exalted bench had long since forgotten the lesson of the landmark *Barnette* decision:

> ... the very purpose of the Bill of Rights was to withdraw certain subjects from the vicissitudes of political controversy, to place them beyond the reach of majorities and officials, and to establish them as legal principles to be applied by the courts. One's rights to life, liberty, and property, to free speech ... and assembly, and other fundamental rights may not be submitted to vote; they depend on the outcome of no election.

From its very preamble, the Clay bill was—and is in its current incarnation—as large a mouthful as the Congress and the public have ever been asked to take of indigestible hypocrisy and anti-constitutional authoritarianism. The *Declaration of Purpose and Policy* is so flagrantly violative of the Tenth Amendment of the Bill of Rights that it requires quotation in full, to wit:

> Experience in both private and public employment indicates that the statutory protection of the rights of employees to organize and bargain collectively safeguards the public interest and promotes the free and unobstructed flow of commerce among the States by removing certain recognized sources of strife and unrest. Such protection facilitates and encourages the amicable settlement of disputes between employees and their employers involving terms and conditions of employment and other matters of mutual concern.
> It is the purpose of this Act, in order to promote the free and unobstructed flow of commerce among the States, to prescribe certain rights and obligations of the employees of the States, territories, and possessions of the United States, and the political subdivisions thereof, and to establish procedures governing the relationship between such employees and their employers which are designed to meet the requirements and needs of public employment.
> It is the policy of the United States to recognize the rights of employees of the States, and the political subdivisions thereof, and to establish procedures governing the relationship between such employees and their employers and to meet the special requirements of public employment.
> It is the policy of the United States to recognize the rights of the employees of the States, territories, and possessions of the United States, and the political subdivisions thereof, to form, join, and assist employee organizations, to bargain collectively with their employers over the terms and conditions of employment and other matters of mutual concern relating thereto

29

through representatives of their own choosing and to engage in other activities, individually or in concert, for the purpose of establishing, maintaining, and improving terms and conditions of employment and other matters of mutual concern relating thereto; and to establish procedures which will facilitate and encourage the amicable settlement of disputes between such employees and their employers.

It takes no Harvard Law School education to realize that the "policy of the United States" is, in reality, the policy of Jerry Wurf's American Federation of State, County, and Municipal Employees. The policy of the United States is stated very clearly in the Tenth Amendment: "The powers not delegated to the United States by the Constitution, nor prohibited by it to the States, and reserved to the States, or to the people." The federal government may not interfere in the internal affairs of the states unless those states have trespassed on guarantees specifically cited in the Constitution. In their ratification of America's basic law, the states retained for themselves the right to conduct their internal business, to establish the rules of public employment, of marriage and divorce, of taxation, of law enforcement and the regulation of their courts. If it were demonstrated that they forcibly recruited their public employees and subjected them to involuntary servitude, federal intervention would be warranted.

To circumvent the Tenth Amendment, the authors of the Clay bill and its various progeny invoked the interestate-commerce clause of the Constitution. The expressly stated justification, possibly propounded tongue in cheek, argues that since a municipal official in California may be writing with a ballpoint pen made in New York at a desk manufactured in Michigan, he is engaged in interstate commerce. This novel doctrine, which would give the federal government the power to supersede the states in all activities protected by the Constitution, was matched by another, which struck directly at orderly government.

Repeatedly in the preamble, the Clay bill employed the phrase, in setting the scope of collective bargaining, "and other matters of mutual concern."* This catchall language clearly reflected the demands of Jerry Wurf, the AFSCME, the American Federation of Teachers, and the National Education Association that a proper subject for collective bargaining—over and above wages, hours, and conditions of

---

*The bland assertion that collective bargaining produces industrial peace and "the amicable settlement of disputes" has already been taken up. The even blander assertion that there is a constitutional "right" to organize without a concomitant right not to organize will be taken up at greater length in later chapters, along with the all-important question of sovereignty.

employment—should be government policy itself. In implementation of this view, Wurf had taken the AFSCME into the tumultuous demonstrations against the Vietnam war, and he would not have thought it beyond the parameters of trade unionism, had he been able to command them, to call a strike of State Department workers until the White House acceded to his insistence on full surrender to Hanoi and the Viet Cong.

If there were any doubt as to what the preamble meant, it was removed by Section 3(m) of the bill, which defines what "collective bargaining" included: "The duty to negotiate shall extend to matters which are or may be the subject of a statute, ordinance, regulation, or other enactment of a State, territory, or possession of the United States, or a political subdivision thereof." In other words, any enactment of the elected representatives of the people could be literally wiped out by the unions in their collective-bargaining sessions. That challenge could extend to matters that were no more than a glint in the eye of legislative bodies.

Section 3(n) also rings a warning bell. It states:

> The term "labor dispute" means any controversy concerning terms and conditions of employment or other matters of mutual concern relating thereto, or concerning the representation of employees for the purpose of collective bargaining, *regardless of whether the disputants stand in the proximate relation of employer and employee.* [Emphasis added.]

What this seems to mean is that if a union, in attempting to sign up members for a particular unit, runs up against opposition from the employees of that unit, this becomes a "labor dispute" to be adjudicated like any clash between employer and employee. The significance of this can be understood in the context of the National Public Employment Relations Commission set up by the Clay bill. Experience with the NLRB has laid open the lawless bias of such quasi-judicial bodies and the manner in which they become adjuncts of Big Labor. The NPERC, moreover, is given powers once reserved, with limitations, to the Congress and the federal courts:

> The Commission is authorized to *issue, amend, and rescind* ... such rules and regulations as may be necessary to carry out the provisions of this Act.... In order to carry out its functions under this Act, the Commission is authorized to hold hearings, subpoena witnesses, administer oathes and take the testimony or deposition of any person under oath, and in connection therewith, to issue subpoenas *requiring the production and examination of any books or papers, including those of the Federal government* or any employer, relating to any matter

31

pending before it and to take *such other action as may be necessary*. [Emphasis added.]

Since the clear intent of the measure is to bring every public employee into Big Labor's parlor, by suasion or otherwise, the NPERC under Section 4(g) can declare any resistance to unionization efforts an "unfair labor practice." It can subpoena the records of the White House, of the FBI or CIA, and of any government agency—federal, state, or local—at its own discretion. And in clear-cut rejection of constitutional and juridical strictures, it enunciates the "right" of public employees to participate in union activities—without the right *not* to do so. But as logic and the courts have repeatedly ruled, a "right" becomes compulsion unless it is coupled to an equal right to desist. Under the First Amendment, the guarantees of free speech and free association include the rights not to speak and not to associate—but these are denied by the Clay bill in the clearest derogation of the Bill of Rights since the enactment of the Alien and Sedition Acts in the early days of the Republic by a vindictive Congress.*

Under the bill, a category of "exclusive representative" gives unions so sanctified tremendous and unconscionable powers. To achieve that exclusivity, a union need not win a representation election but simply submit a request that "shall allege that a majority of the employees" in a bargaining unit "wish to be represented" and submit "credible evidence" to that effect. Past experience with the NLRB has repeatedly demonstrated that such "credible evidence" is all too often simply the allegation of a Big Labor organizer. Once a union has won exclusive representation rights, the government unit will deduct from employees' wages the dues and assessments demanded by the union, whether or not they wish to join.

If an employee has a complaint, he can take it up with a superior only if a union official is present to argue for or against him. The employee may not have at his side an official of a rival union to assist him. Once the NPERC determines that a particular union is the "exclusive representative, its ruling "shall not be subject to judicial review or other collateral attack." The determination will be set in concrete, unless the commission has a change of heart.

*Enacted in June and July of 1798 and repealed in March of 1801. Kentucky and Virginia, in 1798 and 1799, passed resolutions, drafted by Thomas Jefferson and James Madison, holding that where the federal government exercised powers not specifically granted it by the Constitution, each state "has an equal right to judge for itself, as well of infractions as of the mode and measure of redress" (Madison) and that the states "have the right to interpose in arresting the progress of the evil" (Jefferson).

Sections 9 and 10, however, go to the heart of the Clay bill's intent. Section 9(a) declares that "nothing in this act ... shall be construed to interfere with, impede, or diminish the right of an exclusive representative to engage or an employee to participate in a strike arising out of or in connection with a labor dispute"—and this may mean anything the union wants it to mean. The courts may issue a restraining order only if the strike "poses a clear and present danger to the public health or safety which in light of all relevant circumstances it is in the best public interest to prevent." Presumably, if public-employee strikers were blowing up homes and hospitals, this lone exception in the bill might have some relevance. But since the bill stresses throughout that all union activities are beneficial to the public interest, it would take more than a Solomon's judgment to condemn a strike.

The implication of the Clay and other bills and their economic impact on the American way of life will be discussed at some length further on in this account. But one aspect stares out of the large print—the determination of Big Labor and its allies in the Congress to destroy both the civil service system and the right of Americans, if qualified, to government jobs. It has not been enough for Jerry Wurf, through the instrumentality of obsequious national legislators, to attempt the imposition of an "agency shop" whereby those who do not wish to join the union must nevertheless pay full initiation fees, dues, and assessments to retain their jobs. Section 10(b)(1) holds it unlawful for

an employee organization to coerce any employee in the exercise of the rights guaranteed to him by this Act [a generous gesture, perhaps, since all the rights are to unions and none to employees]; *provided,* that this subsection shall not impair *the right of an employee organization to prescribe its own rules with respect to the acquisition or retention of membership therein* . . . [Emphasis added.]

Since an exclusive representative will have the right to bar from employment any individual who is not a member of the union, Section 10(b)(1) goes far beyond anything in the National Labor Relations Act by reimposing an outlawed closed shop. The civil service system opens the door to government employment for all qualified citizens. The Clay bill slams that door shut by allowing unions to set up their own standards of employment that supersede those of previous government statutes. A union can decide that only brown-haired males, five feet ten inches in height, who swear eternal fealty to George Meany can qualify for membership in the union. Un-

33

der the Clay bill, all government within the United States will have to bow to what the unions "prescribe"—and have prescribed in the private sector. (In the past, unions have barred blacks from membership, thereby depriving them of the right to work.)

If there is any doubt that the authors of this legislation had this in mind, it should be removed by a reading of Section 13(b):

> All laws or parts of laws of the United States inconsistent with the provisions of this Act are modified or repealed as necessary to remove such inconsistency, and this Act shall take precedence over all ordinances, rules, regulations, or other enactments of any State, territory, or possession of the United States or any political subdivision thereof.

This says it very loud and clear. The foregoing bill, and others of its kind, eliminates with the stroke of a congressional pen the accumulated experience of federal, state, and local governments. It delegates to a private association dedicated to its own self-interest the legislative and executive powers now vested in elected officials. It delivers some fourteen million government workers to the tender mercies of Big Labor. And it reduces the Constitution to a scrap of paper.

The extreme nature of the Clay bill, however, was responsible for its demise in committee. Too many irate government employees on the state and municipal level, seeing themselves deprived of their rights, protested—and their efforts were seconded and publicized by organizations such as the National Right to Work Committee and the Public Service Research Council (PSRC). Not even the dogged lobbying of the AFL-CIO could bring it to life.

But there were other bills, more subtly worded but with greater potential for mischief before the Congress. The Clay bill had applied solely to government employees in state, county, and municipal jurisdictions. So, too, did another measure introduced by Representative Frank Thompson which would subject all public employees not working for the Federal government to the National Labor Relations Act—a back door way to what the Clay bill had sought to accomplish.

Representative Edward Roybal, a California Democrat, submitted another bill creating a special public sector "labor code" which would authorize and promote compulsory union membership.

Other handmaidens of Big Labor in the Congress added their own refinements to the general drive for compulsory unionism of public employees. Representative Charles Wilson, also of California, sought to repeal the right-to-work provisions of the 1970 Postal Reorganization Act from which, after a hard battle, a compulsory unionism provision had been eliminated. Representatives from Pennsylvania, New Jersey, and Michigan offered bills which would coerce Federal employees into public sector unions. Still another bill applying to Federal employees, dropped into the hopper by North Carolina Democrat David Henderson would not impose the "union" or "agency" shop but would compel those holding government employment to accept a union they did not want as their exclusive bargaining representative.

In an election year, these bills had little chance of passage, given the widespread popular opposition manifested in the polls and in congressional mail. When President Ford successfully vetoed the "common situs" picketing bill, in spite of his initial support, because of overwhelming public opposition, the handwriting on the wall was clear. It was no less clear in the various legislatures where Big Labor lobbyists had been attempting quietly to slip through state bills to achieve what had not succeeded nationally. In Virginia, Indiana, and Missouri public sector compulsory unionism bills died in committee or on the floor after ventilation of the issue by the PSRC and local citizens' groups.

By one of those incomprehensible breakdowns of public relations sense, Big Labor further compromised its position and stirred up even greater opposition to its heart's desire. Out of the blue, the American Federation of Government Employees and the National Maritime Union proposed that the military services also be unionized. Simultaneously, there were proposals that inmates of prisons in California be allowed to form their own unions—a plan seriously under consideration by Governor Edmund (Jerry) Brown Jr., which followed the pattern of a bill introduced to the Minnesota Senate a year before.

At first blush, the military unionization proposal seemed so zany that it was considered to be some kind of a joke. The realization, however, that AFGE and the NMU were serious conjured up visions of a military establishment in which every platoon would have its shop steward—or political commissar—to determine whether or not the enlisted men had to obey the orders of their officers, in or out of combat.

Suddenly, Americans became aware that public sector unionism had less to do with wages, hours, and fringe benefits than with the ultimate control of all phases and jurisdictions of government—a kind of sovietization of industry and the armed forces which would substitute Big Labor hegemony over the traditional Constitutional organization of these United States.

# 4

# The Arsonists

"Let Baltimore burn!"\* said Jerry Wurf in throwing down the gauntlet to Governor Marvin Mandel of Maryland. The year was 1974, the Baltimore police were on strike, and there were threats that other municipal workers would leave their jobs in sympathy. Wurf's words were neither a rhetorical flourish nor a temper tantrum. He meant precisely what he was saying. Let our cities burn, let the public be damned. If Baltimore had to burn in order that Wurf's union, the American Federation of State, County and Municipal Employees, might impose its will on the people of a city and a state, then so be it. The special interest of the tiny minority he represented was of more importance than the needs of the community that paid the wages of AFSCME's members and relied on them for the orderly administration of government.

In the last analysis, the needs of AFSCME's members were secondary to Jerry Wurf's personal power drive, as funneled into the instrumentality of a growing union. In the years since President Kennedy's executive order had opened the doors to compulsory collective bargaining in the public sector, one municipality after another had been compelled not only to reduce essential services to its constituency but also to cut down on the size of its civic machinery in order to meet the wage costs exacted by Wurf. For the tough and exhibitionist president, none of this is important. The ultimate function of public-sector unions is "to grapple with the most pressing of all the issues facing the world and mankind today"—which led him to participate in the riotous demonstrations over Vietnam.

In the case of the Baltimore police strike, Wurf was out to

---

\*Jerry Wurf, through his attorneys, has vociferously denied having made the statement attributed to him by Governor Marvin Mandel of Maryland. Mandel has refused to retract his allegation. Wurf has threatened libel action and asserts that he has included Mandel's use of the alleged quotation in a suit against the governor for unfair labor practices.

ram home to the citizenry the power of his union and to demonstrate that only total capitulation by municipal and state authorities to his demands would be acceptable. It was his belief that a frightened populace would pressure these authorities to grant AFSCME the status of a co-equal branch of government which would determine both wages and government policy. What he succeeded in doing was to raise the question, among the people of Maryland: "If the police become part of a militant union, how can they protect the city from the depredations of their fellow unionists if strike violence erupts? Can a police officer, in pursuance of his duty, cross the picket lines of any union without courting disciplinary action? Is a police officer's primary loyalty to the people he is sworn to guard or to Jerry Wurf?" The Baltimore strike answered these questions.*

"The clenched fist, the symbol of militants that police often confronted on the picket lines of protesters," the *Washington Post* reported on July 14, 1974, "now belongs to patrolmen in Baltimore, too, as they march the streets in their first strike." This was the least of what the city had to endure after striking police, insisting on wage demands that the city could not meet, rejected a counteroffer of six percent in pay and fringe benefits. In many ways, it was a duplication of what Montreal had suffered on a single day of violence by striking police, during which time downtown stores were smashed, looting was rife, one nonstriker beaten to death, and officers hijacked police cars of the Quebec province police force, which was attempting to maintain order.

The Baltimore trouble had begun on July 1, when three thousand sanitation workers, jail guards, and other nonpolice city employees had gone on strike. At first, the police had not joined the strikers, but they had done their best, under the tutelage of AFSCME "experts" sent up from Washington to obstruct or paralyze law enforcement. As the *Washington Post* reported:

> Police in Baltimore ... observing a law that requires reporting found objects of value, turned in lengthy reports on pennies found along the sidewalk, or transported obvious pieces of tobacco to the police lab for drug analysis and ticketed as many as ten times the number of cars as normal for rarely enforced parking violations.

When AFSCME decided to join the strike of municipal workers, what had been a nuisance descended into the kind of situation that had obtained during the 1919 Boston police

---

*What follows is drawn not from antilabor sources but from the *Washington Post* and the *New York Times*.

37

strike. Patrolmen picketed station houses, attempting to close them down to nonstrikers. Striking police shouted "pig" and "scab" at those fellow officers who continued to work. In the city jail, the thin line of nonstriking guards were attacked by inmates. Two were injured and one suffered a heart attack.

Several thousand young people rampaged through Baltimore's commercial district, smashing windows and looting. In a neighborhood where tension existed, there were incidents of racial violence. An eleven-year-old white girl was shot as she sat on the steps of her house by a black man who drove through the streets firing at random. Fires ran 150 percent above normal. State troopers helping to patrol the city were harassed by striking police. Looting, shooting, and rock-throwing were, according to the *Washington Post*, widespread.

And it was all according to plan. Back in May of 1969, Jerry Wurf, presuming to speak for America's public employees, had threatened: "They do not want to engage in strikes, but they will if that is the only answer. They do not want to engage in *civil disorder*, but they will if that is the only answer" (emphasis added). And a year before that, he had boasted: "To win or reinforce bargaining rights for public employees, [AFSCME] has staged 75 illegal strikes in the past two years."

The police strike, as Maryland Judge James W. Murphy stated, had caused "a terror in the community." That terror would have continued indefinitely except for the strong stand taken by Governor Mandel and Police Commissioner Donald Pomerleau. Some of the police ringleaders were fired and others were demoted or otherwise disciplined, in spite of AFSCME's threats of vengeance.

But what did it cost the city of Baltimore? In order to get its employees to return to work, it granted them increases that it could not afford. And as a result of these increases, it was compelled to reopen negotiations with nonstriking union, and city and state officials. To meet the cost of the on the city—as well as open warfare between Jerry Wurf's union, and city and state officials. To meet the cost of the strike, these officials immediately huddled to increase taxes.

Wurf and the AFSCME believe in pulling out all stops. Part of their strategy is to impose statewide negotiation. If the police in one city go on strike, then pull them out all over the state. In time, he also hopes to make that strategy nationwide. While Baltimore was, in part at least, burning, the AFSCME was at work to "shut down the state of Ohio." The strike called by Wurf's lieutenants hit at the Lebanon Correctional Institution, but that was merely for starters. As the

38

*New York Times* of July 16, 1974, reported, "Since then employees at five other penal institutions, five mental health facilities and a facility of the Ohio Youth Commission have walked off their jobs in protest because the Ohio General Assembly did not pass a wage increase for state employees."

Also included in what another age would have called insurrection, were strikes at state universities, state liquor stores, and "other state-run businesses and institutions." With true Big Labor piety, Owen King, communications director of AFSCME, announced to the world that "our members hope by shutting down the State of Ohio, which is their intention, we will produce a public outcry for justice." Two days later, the Associated Press could report:

> Strikes involving prison guards in Rhode Island and 4,000 state employees in Ohio were settled, but almost a quarter of a million other Americans were off their jobs because of labor disputes. . . .
> The remaining strikes interfered with activities ranging from transit operations to hospitals. . . . Supervisors and volunteers worked to keep a San Diego hospital and three clinics open in the face of a walkout by 680 nurses, technicians, clerks, and custodians. . . . Los Angeles officials were worried over a walkout by 5,000 employees of the Department of Water and Power who struck at 12:01 A.M. yesterday.

For calling the illegal strike in Baltimore, the AFSCME was fined $10,000—but none of the leaders was sent to jail, as could have been done under the law. The sum, of course, meant less to the union than the ten-dollar bill a girl will often tuck away in her purse as "mad money." It was, moreover, but a tiny faction of what the strike had cost Maryland taxpayers. But though public-employee unions regard fines for violating the law as part of their "organizing" expenses, and cheap at the price considering the propaganda mileage they get out of it, Wurf and his lieutenants screamed from the rooftops that they had been betrayed. They insisted that part of the settlement package had included a promise that no reprisals would be made against the union—common enough in other public-employee strike settlements. To bolster this claim, AFSCME issued to the media what it claimed was the transcript of the tape-recorded conversations with Governor Mandel and other state officials. When reporters asked to hear the tape, the union lamely admitted that the "transcript" was nothing more than the "recollections" of AFSCME leaders.

The illegality of the AFSCME labor arsonists in Maryland, Ohio, and points north, east, south, and west, is part and parcel of political illegalities designed to use union money to elect candidates for Congress and for state office who will do Jerry Wurf's bidding. To his credit, it should be noted that unlike other labor leaders, Wurf has not attempted to weasel on these activities. He had laid on the line his defiance of state and federal statutes against strikes by public employees and has felt no qualms about proclaiming that AFSCME is "political as hell." Politics being the handmaiden of public-sector collective bargaining, a written deposition he submitted on July 26, 1973,* assumes major pertinence. In it Wurf said:

The American Federation of State, County and Municipal Employees, AFL-CIO (hereinafter AFSCME) receives revenues in the form of per capita tax payments. . . . Per capita tax revenues so received are co-mingled in the general fund of AFSCME and used for its programs and activities, including *political action* and legislative action programs. . . .

In carrying on its political action programs and activities AFSCME utilizes its officers and salaried staff personnel. *A portion of the salaried time and reimbursed expenses of staff personnel and of the cost of office space, office supplies, telephone and telegraph, printing and general overhead and administrative expenses of AFSCME are either directly related to its political action programs and activities or provide administrative support* for such programs and activities. . . .

In recent years, the political programs and activities of AFSCME have been closely related to one of the major political parties, particularly at the national level. *Some AFSCME officers and staff personnel* hold official positions in that party at the national, state, or local level, and *participate in the election campaigns of candidates of that party.* Through coordination with other international unions and their state and local representatives AFSCME and its PEOPLE Committee assist in *providing financial, organizational, and manpower resources* for voter registration drives, preparation and dissemination of campaign literature, and get-out-the-vote activities *in support of candidate campaigns.* . . .

*Contributions are made from the general funds of AFSCME to candidates* for state and local offices where such contributions are not prohibited by law and where AFSCME has determined that such support is in the interest of public employees. . . . The expenses of voluntary fund-raising activities of the PEOPLE Committee, including staff salaries and expenses and use of physical facilities, are to the extent legally permissible, paid for from the general funds of AFSCME. [Emphasis added.]

The reservation that AFSCME makes political contributions where "not prohibited by law" and dips into general funds—members' dues money—"to the extent legally permis-

---

*Mamie Adams, et al.* v. *City of Detroit, AFSCME Council 77, et al.*

sible" can only have been *pro forma*. Neither AFSCME nor the candidates who receive its largesse make any secret of those contributions, though they are illegal. And, as has been already noted, both the Congress and the Justice Department determinedly shut their eyes to violations of the Corrupt Practices Act by Big Labor. The act is enforced only against hapless businessmen and corporations whose relatively small contributions nowhere approach the magnitude of Big Labor spending.

That Jerry Wurf and the AFSCME should so boldly proclaim their illegal actions is not unusual. Back in September 1966, in an interview with *U.S. News & World Report*, Wurf described a public-employee strike, excoriating the "employer" for abiding by statutory restrictions on his negotiating power.

Q. When they went on strike, were they violating a State statute?
A. Oh, yes.
Q. Did they win the strike?
A. Yes. They always do . . .

Wurf's reasoning is that the Corrupt Practices Act is bad. Therefore, he does not have to obey it—and neither does his union. He believes that restrictions on the political activities of government employees are "nonsense"—so that they don't have to conform to the law. He believes in "civil disobedience" for public employees—which is his right as it was Thoreau's—but he insists that union members who take up arms against the law should be granted immunity from prosecution, which was not what Thoreau argued. He comes by this position honestly, as a product of the left-wing socialist milieu in New York where he first won his spurs as a union official. He is convinced that only the troublemaker succeeds, which has made him one of the most detested members of the AFL-CIO Executive Council. Only the fact that AFSCME is sixth in size of all AFL-CIO international unions protects him from the wrath of his fellow vice presidents—a wrath which is motivated not by ideological differences but by personal animus.

In the *U.S. News* interview, Wurf stated with equal frankness his opinion that public-employee unionism was a "revolutionary" change, that the "old concept of government sovereignty is fast fading away," and that unions were "coequals" with government in the ordering of public affairs—a kind of fourth branch on a par with the executive, legislative, and judicial branches.* At the time, AFSCME claimed only

*See chapter ten.

305,000 members—out of a total of 7.5 million people in state and municipal public service—so Wurf was a little more cautious in discussing public-employee strikes. He had been head of his union for about two years—after having carefully maneuvered the ouster of Arnold Zander, founder and president of AFSCME, who had been his friend and sponsor—and the reins of power were not yet completely in his grasp. So he made it a point to underscore the fact that under the union's constitution, "We forbid [police unions] to strike or take strong positions or demonstrate. . . . People who work for agencies like prisons—any law-enforcement group—are forbidden by our union constitution to take any step that might result in an interruption of work."

And he was cagy in discussing AFSCME's position on strikes by other public employees:

Q. Are all others in your union free to strike?
A. The situation is this: Consistent with our constitution, the national union cannot call a strike. The national union cannot end a strike, unless it's a law-enforcement group, where the international union will take the most drastic measures to stop the strike.

In other cases, the national union takes the position that the decision to strike or not strike resides with the local union. . . .

It is perfectly legal in our union for a local union to have a clause in its constitution stating that it will never assert the right to strike, and never strike.

It is equally legal as far as the national union is concerned, for a local union to strike if it finds no other way to get redress for its grievances.*

But Wurf was not at all modest in discussing where and how public-employee unions got their clout:

[The] main interest [of people who make the management decisions in government] often is their public image because motivation in politics may be different that in private industry.

With that fact of life present, we would be less than sensible if we didn't use public relations techniques. . . .

There is another thing—
Q. Lobbying?
A. Right—not merely lobbying, but accompanied by political action. . . . The cold facts of life are that—with thousands of unionized public employees no longer fearful of political reprisal—if they take a position for or against a public official, they're bound to have an effect on his decisions. . . .

---

*At the time of this interview, AFSCME was already engaged in collective bargaining with federal agencies. Yet the Kennedy executive order that, as Wurf admitted, has given AFSCME its great impetus, expressly prohibited bargaining with any union or local that asserted the right of public employees to strike.

You know, a politician only reacts in terms of the pressures you put upon him. . . .

Q. How much is all of this going to cost the taxpayers?

A. I haven't the slightest idea. . . †

By 1970, Jerry Wurf was no longer playing down the strike weapon at the disposal of AFSCME and other government-employee unions.** It had, in fact, become almost axiomatic that the moment a public-sector union achieved recognition or exclusive bargaining status, or both, it struck. ("What the hell," one union official said, "that's what unions are for—to strike. That's the only thing those management bastards understand.") To him, this process was called "the revolt of the public workers" and in jurisdiction after jurisdiction his four-letter-word approach to union-management discourse became notorious. His idea of "labor peace" was summed up in an article he wrote for the *Progressive*:

> In Washington, D.C., after twelve months of unresolved grievances, 1,700 union sanitation workers walked out on strike. . . .
> In San Diego, city firemen and bus drivers left their jobs in a wage dispute; an unprecedented slowdown by police disrupted public services. In Rapid City, South Dakota, the city's entire fire department resigned after the firefighters' strike was blocked by an injunction.
> In Los Angeles, Boston, and Newark, unionized school teachers withdrew their services . . . adding to the national figure of 131 teachers' strikes in 1969. In San Francisco, a three-day strike of nearly 20,000 city employees ended with . . . higher wage scales.
> In New York City, the first major strike in the 195-year history of the postal system caused President Nixon to send in Federal troops.
> And back in Washington, D.C., the daily *Congressional Record* reached Senators and Representatives days late after ninety percent of the 1,200 union typesetters in the Government Printing Office "called in sick."

---

†Interestingly, Wurf was not asked what effect "all of this" was going to have on union members themselves. It was his position that if state and local governments could not afford to pay the wages he was exacting, they could get the money by cutting down on other expenditures —not building a "convention hall" is how he put it. Municipalities were willing, in order to maintain "labor peace," to cut back on some essential services until recession and inflation struck the economy. Then, with no funds available, they were compelled as in New York City, a fiscal shambles because of union raids on its treasury, to resort to wholesale firings in order to keep their heads above water.

**AFSCME amended its constitution to allow strikes by police and other law-enforcement locals.

Three years later, Wurf would boast to *Time* magazine of a strike by Maryland road workers that lasted 365 days, probably the longest public-employee strike in United States history, under the aegis of AFSCME. He also noted with pride the sixty-five-day walkout of sanitation workers in Memphis, an action which, as *Time* put it, "indirectly precipitated the assassination of Martin Luther King." In all of the battles to impose Big Labor's "right" to bargain exclusively for public workers, thousands, having no interest in the union and feeling adequately protected by the civil service merit system, were forced into membership and warned that henceforth they were bound by union rules—meaning "pay up or get out."

In the executive agencies of the federal government, by a kind of statistical inflation, unions employed a Civil Service Commission study to "prove" that a majority of all United States government employees favored unionism. Once a union attained exclusive recognition, which in practice does not require a majority of employees to join, the entire unit was lumped together to arrive at the number "represented" by the federal unions. By that system of statistical jujitsu, the American Federation of Government Employees could give the impression that it had 482,000 members; the United Federation of Postal Clerks, 310,000 members; the National Association of Letter Carriers, 203,000 members; etc.—though this was not the case.

But the size of a union is no gauge of its ability to let our cities burn. What Lenin called a "strategic minority"—a small group so situated that it has controlling force—can be as devastating in what the *New York Times*, describing a public-employee strike, called "the exercise of economic blackmail" as most any majority. In the Auto Workers strike of 1936, led by Walter Reuther, the strategic minority could be the one man who threw the switch that halted the assembly line. A public-employee union is a strategic minority not only because its members are involved in a vital civic function but also because they can bring organized pressure on the lever of political power. That the latter power is mercilessly operative was demonstrated in two public-be-damned strikes in New York City.

On January 1, 1966, the Transport Workers Union, AFL-CIO, and the considerably smaller Amalgamated Transit Union—representing 34,800 workers in a population of some eight million people—struck the New York City transit system. Leading the strike was Michael J. Quill, a tough, shillelagh-wielding Irishman, former member of the city council, and a power in the city's political structure. The strike had been called when the New York Transit Authority rejected Quill's outrageous demands for a thirty-percent pay increase; a four-day, thirty-two-hour week; and six weeks of vacation after one year's service—a $700-million package.

Clearly unlawful under the state's Condon-Wadlin Act, which prohibited public-employee strikes, the walkout created immediate chaos in New York, a city heavily dependent on public transit. Commuters from the outlying boroughs took to their cars, with resultant traffic jams of incredible dimensions at the city's thirteen bridges and tunnels. By the fourth day of the strike, New York's normally frustrating morning rush had stretched out to six and one-half hours, starting at 4:45 A.M. with those who hoped to beat the traffic. The evening rush began at 3:15 P.M.

Calling the strike "an act of defiance against eight million people," Mayor John V. Lindsay announced that the city would "not capitulate before the lawless demands of a single power group. . . . The paramount issue confronting us today, the one that threatens the destiny of our government, is whether New York City can be intimidated." Quill and three other TWU leaders were jailed on January 4 for their defiance of a court order to call off the strike. ("I don't care if I rot in jail," Quill said. "I will not call off the strike.") And a suit for $382,000 a day in damages was filed by the Transit Authority against the unions.

The Condon-Wadlin Act was very precise in defining the penalties to be imposed on public employees who went on strike. An employee who violated the no-strike clause automatically terminated his employment and could be reemployed only if his compensation in no case exceeded the salary he received before going on strike. That compensation could not be increased for three years after reinstatement. The striker, moreover, would be placed on probation for five years, serving "without tenure and at the pleasure of the appointing office or body."*

Mayor Lindsay's course, therefore, was clear. But he did not count on extralegal factors and pressures. When President Harry Van Arsdale of the New York Central Labor Council, the single most powerful labor leader in the state, huddled

---

*The federal statute states: "It shall be unlawful for any individual employed by the United States or any agency thereof including wholly owned government corporations to participate in any strike. Any individual employed by the United States or by any such agency who strikes shall be discharged immediately from his employment, and shall forfeit his civil service status, if any, and shall not be eligible for re-employment for three years by the United States or any such agency." Needless to say, this cause has been a dead letter.

45

with Governor Nelson Rockefeller, the stage was set for the capitulation Lindsay had adamantly disavowed. Under pressure from Rockefeller, Lindsay offered the striking transit workers a pay-increase package that would cost New York $25 million. This was rejected out of hand by union bargaining agents. Thereupon a panel was set up that granted the union a fifteen-percent increase, costing the city's taxpayers $70 million. It also made inescapable an increase in the fifteen-cent fare on buses and subways. (The fare has risen to fifty cents, with another raise in prospect.) This fare increase struck directly at every low-income family in New York.

That ended the strike. Quill was released and the Transit Authority's suit against the unions was dropped. There was only one flaw. The settlement was a clear-cut violation of the Condon-Wadlin Act provision barring pay increases to strikers for a three-year period. A citizen's suit was filed, and the New York State Supreme Court upheld the law and ruled that the settlement was illegal. The unions cracked the whip, threatening to go out on strike again—and at Rockefeller's behest, the state legislature amended Condon-Wadlin to exempt New York City's transit workers from its penalty provision. The only penalty suffered by the strikers for their twelve-day disruption of New York and for their defiance of the law was the wages they lost during their absence from work.

The strike had cost New York an estimated one billion dollars in lost wages and income, with 185 million man-hours of employment also lost. To soften the economic blow, Rockefeller, "discovered" that he had $100 million that he could, and did, turn over to the city—thereby making the burden of the settlement statewide. President Johnson, who had remained silent throughout the strike, suddenly found his voice, castigating Lindsay for exceeding the antiinflation guidelines laid down by the federal government.

The end of the New York transit strike marked the beginning of a new drive to modify the New York labor statute as it applied to public employees. There was a loud outcry that the Condon-Wadlin Act "did not work"—though, in fact, it had not been allowed to work because of the pressures exerted on timid politicians by the trade unions. One flaw was discovered in that act, however. It invoked penalties against individual strikers, but none against the unions.

Proponents of union power argued that since a law prohibiting public-employee strikes had not been properly enforced, the fault lay in the law and not the agencies of enforcement. For them, the solution was simple—grant public employees the right to strike as a means of preventing future strikes. Few cared to admit that the fault lay in a collective-bargaining process developed in the private sector, a process which could not apply to government management since it involved the legislative process. Even fewer cared to confront the simple fact that, since public-employee strikes are intolerable and anarchic, the usual machinery of compulsory collective bargaining could not possibly work. If, under such compulsory bargaining, the parties disagreed, what then? To submit the dispute to compulsory arbitration would delegate to a third party, independent of the body politic, powers which inhere only in the state—an equally intolerable situation.*

The Taylor Law, drawn up by Professor George W. Taylor and a committee appointed by Governor Rockefeller, was no improvement over its predecessor. For while it continued the ban on public-employee strikes, it invited such strikes by increasing union bargaining "rights" and authorizing fact-finding boards that could make recommendations not binding on either party in a dispute. Its only recognition of the inevitable consequences of collective bargaining was a semantic one of eschewing that expression and renaming the process "collective negotiations." Compulsory collective negotiation, moreover, continued to be enshrined as a sacred duty of government.

The Taylor Law faced its first and disastrous test early in February 1968, when the Uniformed Sanitation Men's Association, headed by John J. DeLury, demanded a ten-percent pay increase on threat of striking. When Mayor Lindsay, justifiably arguing that the city's resources were already overcommitted, refused to "pay blackmail," DeLury ordered his men out. In a demonstration before City Hall, he told union members:

> Your sentiments before was go-go-go. I'd accept a motion for go-go-go. [Cheers.] All opposed. [Boos.] I didn't come here to bargain. I took a firm position with the city. I gave the members a final offer of this union. Now I want to show discipline here this morning—or this afternoon. I don't want to show where there is confusion in the members. You got a job to do at the locations to see that this is 100 percent effective. [Cheers.]

---

*In attempting to deal with the problem, Theodore W. Kheel, a labor lawyer of considerable standing who has been called in on many occasions to arbitrate labor-management disputes, rejected the viability of arbitration in this context and squirmed to an advocacy of a "limited" right to strike for public employees—a concept on a par with a belief in "limited" pregnancy.

That same day, New York City obtained a temporary restraining order from the state supreme court under the Taylor Law. In granting it, Judge Saul S. Streit said, "It's not really a strike. It's blackmail, it's extortion." Four days later, on February 6, DeLury was sentenced to fifteen days in jail and fined $250 for criminal contempt. The union was fined $80,000 for criminal contempt, because of its failure to honor the injunction and to order the sanitation workers back to their jobs.

With garbage piling up in the streets at a rate of 10,000 tons a day—a serious threat to the city's health—and untreated sewage pouring into the Hudson River, Mayor Lindsay declared a "limited emergency" and directed unionized hospital workers to drive sanitation trucks so that the garbage could be collected. They refused, putting their commitment to unionism above their duty to the city. An order transferring these workers to the Sanitation Department was also rejected as "strikebreaking." Fires began to break out in trash piles.

On February 7, Lindsay broadcast an order to the strikers that they return to work. If they did not, the mayor said, he would ask Governor Rockefeller to call out the National Guard. This, of course, the governor refused to do, citing the curious reason that it would involve "very real risks as far as the stability and structure of organized labor" was concerned. This was to be expected, and it starkly demonstrated the dual role of an elected official when confronted by union power. DeLury and the Uniformed Sanitation workers were known to have one of the best-organized political machines in New York—and one that was an integral part of the Rockefeller political apparatus. DeLury had endorsed Rockefeller's gubernatorial candidacy, moreover, and was expected to support his quadrennial bid for the presidential nomination.

Ignoring the union's violation of the strike prohibition in the Taylor Law, Rockefeller appointed a five-man mediation team that quickly proposed substantial pay increases to DeLury's sanitation workers, retroactive to July 1967. When Lindsay rejected these recommendations, again characterizing them as "blackmail," Rockefeller announced that he was taking over the Sanitation Department and granting the union the pay recommended by his panel. He ignored Lindsay's protest that the union was being "rewarded" for violating the law and that the settlement would lead other municipal unions to raise their demands to "unmanageable levels." But legislative sanction was needed for Rockefeller's "settlement"—and this was not forthcoming. After nine days the workers returned to their jobs on the guarantee that the dispute would be submitted to binding arbitration. The union, of course, got most of what it had gone on strike to get.

The award to the union made a sour and retroactive joke of what Judge Streit had said in fining the Sanitation Men's Association: "If there is one thing that the people are entitled to expect from a civil service to whom it gives life tenure, vacations, sick leave, pension, and the right to bargain collectively, it is a respect for law."

But the lesson of the sanitation strike—that collective bargaining with public-employee unions is an act not of law or economics but of raw politics—was not lost on Mayor Lindsay. He quickly made his peace with AFSCME and with the other municipal unions—even to supporting them in their demands for the taxation without representation of the agency shop—and, after a campaign for reelection in which he was rejected by both of New York's major political parties, won.

By 1974, the results of this accommodation were more than apparent. New York City was not burning. It was simply dying of economic strangulation and elephantiasis of the municipal budget. With crime on the rise, city hall was compelled to reduce the number of police and to cut back on other essential services. The question for those municipal workers who were fired might well have been, "What price Jerry Wurf?"

Such was the situation that the hitherto Big Labor—oriented *New York Times* felt constrained to editorialize in terms which but a few years earlier it would have indignantly deplored:

> The city is staggering out of its budget crunch with one thing clear: New York is working for its unionized civil service workers, not vice versa. The real power in the city is held by the municipal unions. Last week's illegal sanitation strike, a wretched charade in which every step was apparently orchestrated by the union leadership . . . was the end product of three decades in which one New York mayor after another systematically fostered the growth of centralized union power. The rationale always was that strong, secure unions would bring cooperation for a more efficient civil service. Instead, it delivered into union hands ironclad control over every essential civic department, with a precipitous increase in personnel and payroll and a steady shrinkage in standards of performance.

New York City, of course, did not stagger out of its "budget crunch"—nor could it with the albatross of unyielding public employee unions on its back. By mid-1975, the city was in a state of virtual bankruptcy—unable to guarantee from day to day the continuation of essential services or the payment of municipal salaries, and with the constant threat of defaulting on the municipal bonds which had helped satisfy the inordinate demands of public sector unions. Complete fiscal collapse was averted by massive Federal aid, delivered only because the approaching national elections gave political muscle to the pleadings of the nation's mayors that their cities would follow suit if New York was submerged.

But the year 1975 brought the nation more than the mounting statistics of millions of school children deprived of an education by striking teachers or of the man-hours and tax dollars lost in the tidal wave of Big Labor's public sector militancy. Two major strikes, in San Francisco and Kansas City, brought home to otherwise complacent Americans the seriousness of what the *New York Times* would call the "death knell of democracy" being sounded by public employee unions.

The San Francisco police strike was, in a way, a landmark case. The people of the city and their government prided themselves on being perhaps the most pro-union in the country. In some cases according to the city's charter and in others by tradition, San Francisco paid the highest municipal wages in the state of California. As a result, as the *Washington Post* reported, almost 70 percent of the city's budget went to wages and fringe benefits. All other expenses, from the maintenance of city streets to welfare to the acquisition of textbooks for the schools, were squeezed out of the remaining 30 percent.

But this was not enough for San Francisco's police force. At a time when "stagflation" hit the city, they demanded a wage increase of 13 percent. When the Board of Supervisors, San Francisco's governing body, and Mayor Joseph Alioto explained that the city could not afford the $13 million price tag in wages and fringe benefits, if it was to avoid the catastrophic road taken in New York City, the police on August 18, 1975 went on strike. More than 90 percent of the city's 1,900-member force responded to the Police Officers Association call to "hit the bricks," rejecting an offer of 6.5 percent.

In the early stages of the strike, Mayor Alioto took a firm stand against the strike. "We'll do whatever is necessary to vindicate our basic belief that policemen don't have the right to strike," he told his fellow citizens. To the police, he added, "To put it as bluntly as I know how, you're going to be fired." On August 19, at the request of the city attorney, Judge Robert Drewes issued a restraining order against the union and the striking policemen and ordered them back to work.

San Francisco has no local income tax and more than 30

percent of its income comes from property taxes. To meet its needs it had already increased property evaluations by an average of 22 percent—in some instances as much as 100 percent—thereby taking a bigger slice from the pocketbooks of home owners and home renters alike. It was paying plumbers $24,000 and street cleaners $17,000—not counting the cost of retirement plans and fringe benefits.

The striking police nevertheless refused to consider the financial bind in which the city found itself. Picket lines were thrown around police stations. Strikers broke into the key cabinet at the police parking garage and stole the keys to most of the 200 patrol cars, then let the air out of the tires of two cars, blocking the entrance. The traffic light system was sabotaged, and the tires of those patrol cars being driven by non-strikers were slashed. When a city investigator tried to serve Gerald Crowley, head of the POA, with the court order prohibiting the strike, he was roughed up and thrown out of union headquarters.

Mayor Alioto tried to show that the city was still safe by taking a walk through one of the tougher districts arm in arm with "Marsha" Pistol, a drag queen. But he refused catagorically to request police aide from Governor Edmund (Jerry) Brown Jr. The city was far less impressed by Alioto's stroll than it was by the knowledge that police were walking police lines carrying their guns, that frequently they were drunk, that they roughed up those who attempted to cross picket lines, and—as a number of people reported in somewhat more pithy language—were defecating in parked cars.

The issues were clear. The police were illegally striking not because they were underpaid but because they insisted on a scale superior to that of any city in California, or the nation. They could act with impunity because the mayor, for all of his tough talk, feared to take any action against the strikers though he had the backing of the Board of Supervisors which held that inaction "will set back the cause of law and order for a decade." Alioto was a lame duck and could have moved decisively. But he had dreams of glory and nourished the belief that if he enforced the law as Calvin Coolidge had done some five decades earlier, he would have Big Labor as an enemy.

"Everybody is watching us," said Supervisor Dianne Feinstein, a candidate for the mayoralty. "Every major city in the United States is in a severe fiscal situation. And every city is going to have to learn to say 'no' and make it stick."

What the rest of the country saw instead was a veto by Mayor Alioto to a declaration of a state of emergency voted by the Board of Supervisors and a request for 200 Highway

Patrol officers to maintain order during the strike. To make matters worse, the city's 1,700 firemen voted almost unanimously to strike for a pay raise equal to the police's 13 percent—and picket lines were thrown around San Francisco fire houses and other firefighting facilities. As crime and looting increased, the American Civil Liberties Union appealed to the courts to issue an order barring police strikers from carrying their weapons on picket lines, and neighborhood associations gathered before the city hall asserting that they would not "submit to extortion by any group of city employees."

It was at this point that Mayor Alioto exhibited the calibre of his leadership and his subservience to public employee unions. Ignoring his Board of Supervisors, he went into negotiation with representatives of the illegally striking police and firemen. He emerged with a "compromise" settlement which gave the strikers almost everything they had been asking for—a package of wages and fringe benefits which gave the average officer $29,450 a year and amnesty to those law enforcement officers who had taken the law into their own hands. An enraged Board of Supervisors refused to approve the Alioto giveaway, but he blandly invoked a 1906 statute, passed during the crisis of the San Francisco earthquake, to overrule the board.

"Someone has to act with reasoned restraint," Alioto told the press in answer to charges by the Board of Supervisor that he had made himself "the first dictator in the United States" and that the strikers were "outlaws" and "hypocrites" who had violated their "sworn oath to uphold their duty to the people."

The year had seen a spate of public employee union strikes, each one encouraging the next. The *New York Times* could excoriate Mayor Alioto because "he reinforced the conviction that unions in control of vital services can compel the community to capitulate by holding a strike gun to its head," and adding that "This is not only the road to municipal bankruptcy, it is the road to anarchy ... a death knell to democracy." And the *Boston Globe* could comment on the "liberal second thoughts about some trends in public hiring and management—the introduction of collective bargaining and, in some cases, binding arbitration, in addition to the job advantages already conferred by Civil Service."

But these voices of reason could not cope with the temptation, encouraged by the militant words of George Meany and other Big Labor leaders that any invocation of the public's right was to be brushed aside in the interest of union hegemony over city, state, and Federal government. Small fry union bosses saw the public sector strike as a means not merely of making headlines but of propelling themselves into the hallowed precincts of Big Labor. The San Francisco police strike not only carved a barbaric image on a city once known for its particular charm and civilized behavior. It also led union leaders in other cities into believing that they too could strong-arm their way into the pages of *Time* and *Newsweek* and appear on the network evening news. Had Mayor Alioto stood firm for principle instead of strong for ambition in his handling of the San Francisco police strike, there is little doubt that the second major, and far uglier, Kansas City firemen's strike would never have taken place.

A striking policeman, carrying his gun and drunk on the picket line, may frighten the citizen who views it. But fire fighters who interpose themselves between a burning building and those volunteers who are attempting to control the blaze can strike terror into an entire city. And, as the *Kansas City Times* summed it up in the head of a lead editorial, "Firemen's Strike Did Needless Damage; Gained Nothing," In point of fact. it would have been a catastrophe for Local 42 of the firefighters union had W. J. Usery, then head of the Federal Mediation Service and Secretary of Labor—a man who wears his devotion to Big Labor like frontlets on his forehead—not interceded.

The issues were hard to define and narrowed down basically to the demand of the union for pay equal to that of the police. Local 42 was bound by a solemn agreement with Kansas City not to go on strike during the period of its contract but ignored its commitment. This, of course, is not unique in public employee strikes, but the manner in which the union conducted its controversy sent shock waves around the country. For one thing, striking firemen did not merely abandon their posts. They fought volunteers and police doubling as firefighters by actively opposing all efforts to maintain safety.

In the 96 hours that the strike lasted, Kansas City had 150 fires—three times the normal number—and an uncounted number of false alarms which kept skeleton crews on the run. There was considerable evidence that many of those fires were the result of arson. Striking firemen threw picket lines around burning buildings. Though they had no grievance against private contractors, they surrounded construction sites in order to halt work. In several instances, fire extinguishers were filled with gasoline and other flammable materials, which could have lead to the deaths of volunteer firemen and which increased the damage to burning buildings. Nearby communities, which had mutual aid agreements with Kansas

City, refused to send in their equipment to help extinguish large and dangerous blazes.

The major difference between the San Francisco police strike and the Kansas City firemen's strike was in the attitude of Mayor Charles B. Wheeler Jr. and other city officials. Far more vulnerable politically than Mayor Alioto, they nevertheless refused to bow to union blackmail, commenced recruiting a new firefighting force, and compelled Local 42 to back down by ordering its members to return to work before the city would even negotiate. Only on one point did Wheeler and the other city officials give ground. They had fired 59 strikers, but agreed to take them back as a result of Federal Mediation Service prodding. But they refused to withdraw suits for damages against the union for the losses it had caused the city.

The Kansas City firemen's strike, coming less than a month after the San Francisco police strike did have important and far-reaching effects on public opinion and, more significantly, on the media. There were some who reexamined their blithe assumptions that public and private sector collective bargaining were no different. And, to the deep concern of Big Labor leaders, there were others for whom the indignation over public employee strikes began to wash over to other activities of organized labor.

Representative of the first reaction was an editorial in the liberal and pro-union *Sacramento Bee,* the "flagship" of the McClatchy chain of newspapers. In a solemn editorial, it argued:

> The recent collapse of law and order in San Francisco, brought on by an illegal policemen's strike, and numerous other strikes and threats of strikes by various municipal employes' unions require a major re-evaluation of the relationship between public employes and the public they are presumed to serve.
>
> It is pertinent to mention that federal and state employees are performing their jobs without destructive and illegal upheavals. Why, then, have illegal municipal and school strikes spread like the bubonic plague throughout much of the nation, wreaking havoc on innocent school children, ordinary citizens and the very fabric of government?
>
> The answer is pretty clear. There has been a growing acceptance that unions representing public employes should have the right to bargain collectively with government. And with this development has come the weakening of the civil service system and the placing of union leaders in positions where they can dictate to elected officials. When this happens decisions are made not on the basis of what is good for the public but rather what will satisfy the labor leaders and their followers. New York City's present financial debacle is the end result of leaders

of municipal labor unions imposing their will on elected officials.

Recently The Bee supported a bill giving public employes the right to join together and bargain collectively. We also endorsed a bill specifically giving teachers the right to bargain collectively. It now seems clear our position in both instances was wrong. . . .

The granting of collective bargaining to public employes is not necessary and dangerously weakens the public's ability to protect its most essential services, services that should not be poker chips traded back and forth between public officials and union leaders.

When an individual goes to work for a governmental unit, he is entering into a relationship that is entirely different from one getting a job in private enterprise. Civil service gives the government employe far greater job protection. His retirement pay and other fringe benefits generally are higher than in private enterprise.

Most important, the government worker has gone to work for the people. In accepting a job as a public servant, he has accepted a public trust. The idea of firemen, teachers, public health employes, policemen or city garbage collectors going on strike is an affront to that public trust. If an individual does not feel he is willing to trade the special benefits of government employment for a commitment to obey that public trust, then he should seek other employment. . . .

Government is not in a position to successfully bargain collectively. If a private business enterprise is faced with wage demands so unreasonable that it will be forced out of business, the private business can say no, even if it means a strike. But government is different. Often unreasonable demands cannot be turned down by government because the public cannot tolerate the loss of essential public services.

The man negotiating for the public is not like the representative of a private company. He is a public servant, subject to political pressures. There is nothing to prevent him from caving in to threats. And when he does, he does not pay the bill. The bill simply will be handed on to the taxpayer who had no effective voice in the negotiations.

Generally, public employes have earned the respect of the public they serve. This is true whether you are talking about the city garbage collector, the state highway patrolman or a forest service ranger.

It would be tragic if the inevitably destructive consequences of collective bargaining are permitted to jeopardize the best interests of public employes and the public they serve.

The time is late but the issue is critical. The Bee believes the public, elected officials and public employes should pause before they turn their fate over to collective bargaining and labor leaders who sometimes care too much about power and too little about the general welfare.

# 5

# Poisoning the Well

During the depths of the Great Depression, a small businessman whose daughter had just taken the examination to qualify as a New York City schoolteacher received a phone call from the local Tammany Hall leader.

"We hear your daughter took the teaching test today, Mr. H.," the political boss said.

"That's true," Mr. H. answered.

"Conditions being what they are, everybody wants a nice, safe teaching job," Mr. H. was told. "Unless your daughter is very high on the list, she's not going to get an appointment. But just say the word, and we can arrange it."

"Why would you do this for me?" Mr. H. asked.

The Tammany leader was frank. "There are tight votes in your family," he said, "and you've got a lot of friends. One hand washes the other."

Times have changed. Tammany Hall has been fragmented and the power center in New York has shifted to the unions. Among the most powerful of these unions, with the muscle to humble the New York City Board of Education, is the 200,000-strong United Federation of Teachers, affiliated through its parents union, the American Federation of Teachers, with the AFL-CIO. Where Tammany worked its deals and compulsion behind the scenes or in the guise of political activity, the UFT operates openly in defiance of law, setting its own rules and imposing its will on the body politic in the name of "education." Starting out with the limited objective of improving wages and working conditions for New York's teachers, its avowed purpose today is to seize from the elected representatives of the people the direction of education—textbooks, curriculum, promotions, guidance, and how children's minds should be molded in their formative years. Implicit in its drive is the desire to determine the qualification for teaching, which, to the UFT, is simple possession of a union membership card.

The dominant posture of the UFT and its president, the

dour and dictatorial Albert Shanker—and the primary loyalty to the union that they exact from the membership—has raised serious questions of academic freedom. A corollary question plaguing parents and educators: "Can a school-teacher indebted to and controlled by the UFT retain his or her objectivity in the classroom?" The question was answered by the UFT itself in January 1970, when it distributed to its members in the high schools *The ABC's of the G-E Strike—A teaching Unit for Secondary School Teachers.* Prepared by Jeannette Di Lorenzo, a junior high school social studies teacher and the District 15 representative of the UFT, it was a crude, propagandistic, statistically bogus effort to indoctrinate captive students in the issues of the strike against General Electric that AFL-CIO unions were waging, and to enlist their support for the strikers.*

## LESSON 1

### The Economic Issues in the General Electric Strike

#### Aim
Why are the workers at General Electric on strike?

#### Content
1. G.E. is the largest corporation in America with 150 plants and 150,000 employees.
2. Profits of G.E. have risen 78½% since 1960.
3. Wages of G.E. employees have risen 25%.
4. Hourly wages of G.E. workers is $3.25 per hour; weekly wage average of $130; annual wage average is $6,780.
5. U. S. Labor Department statistics indicate $10,000 needed for moderate [*sic*] income for family of four.
6. G.E. annual salary of $6,780 resulted from the 1966 salary agreement which granted the workers a 12¾% increase over their previous salary. . . .
7. Labor Department statistics indicate the cost of living has risen 12.9%—wiping out the G.E. workers' raise of 12.75%.
8. G.E. workers want an increase of 35¢ an hour for the first year, 30¢ for the second year and 25¢ for the third year—a final average salary of $8,632. (Escalator clause to be included to cover rising cost of living.)
9. G.E. has offered 20¢ an hour increase for the first year; no increase spelled out for the second and third years; an option to negotiate additional increases in the second and third years.
10. G.E. maintains that it will not bargain for greater increases because it is holding the line on inflation. The unions

---

*The lesson plan was distributed by the AFT to locals around the country for use in the schools.

maintain that inflation is caused by rising prices and profits and not by wage increases.

### Procedure
Write the following statistics on the chalkboard:

1960–1969 Increases

1. G.E. Wages
   25%
2. G.E. Profits
   78½%

Ask pupils the following questions:
Which figure do you think, 25% or 78½%, contributes more heavily to the inflationary spiral? Why?

July–September 1969 . . .
2. Profit Increase over the Same Period 1968
   11%
   Price Increase on G.E. Products
   3.3% on electrical housewares
   8.5% on appliances

Ask pupils: Is it inflationary to raise prices if you have an 11% profit increase?
3. Wage increase Proposals
   G.E. Unions
       35¢ per hour—1969
       30¢ per hour—1970
       25¢ per hour—1971
   Annual Salary 1971=$8,632
   G.E. Corporation
       20¢ per hour—1969
       none [sic] —1970
       none [sic] —1971
   Annual Salary 1971 = $7,176*

### U.S. Labor Department
Moderate income for a family of 4
$10,000

Ask pupils: Do you think the unions' proposal for salary increases is reasonable? Do you think that it is unreasonable?

Lesson 2 was an even more flagrantly selective analysis of the strike and a broad-gauged attack on General Electric and on "Boulwarism" (after Lemuel Boulware, who headed GE's Employee Relations Department until 1960). The lesson plan completely distorted the nature of Boulwarism, as its summary shows:

### Summary
1. "Boulwarism" has been ruled an unfair labor practice by the courts.

---

*Note that wage increases to be negotiated in the future are given as "none" and that the cost-of-living increase is not included.

2. "Boulwarism" is an attempt to undermine the collective bargaining process.

3. G.E., in following the principles of "Boulwarism," is not bargaining in good faith with its employees.

4. "Boulwarism" tends to provoke strikes by its take-it-or-leave-it approach.

The summary of Lesson 4 speaks for itself:

### Summary

1. The AFL-CIO maintains that the legitimate demands of labor unions in America are not the cause of inflation.

2. Businesses and corporations which increase prices on products despite that their profits are already very high contribute to inflation.

3. The workers of America depend on their trade unions to win them a living wage and do not want to see their unions destroyed.

4. The unions in America will not permit the collective bargaining process to be destroyed. The government, the courts, and the public generally recognize the importance of collective bargaining in determining wages.

5. A consumer boycott was started against G.E. on November 28, 1969 to help the G.E. workers win their strike.

This was milder than the lesson itself, in which teachers were to say that "G.E.'s posture as an inflation fighter is questionable since G.E. was indicted by a federal grand jury in 1960 for conspiring with its competitors to fix prices and was found guilty of profiteering. In 1969 G.E. raised prices significantly." It did fit in with the suggested "Individual Pupil Activities," which included "explaining" the GE boycott to parents and friends, and interviewing "workers on picket lines to get their stories. Write an interview for the school newspaper or magazine."

Once upon a time, the teacher who wrote this lesson plan would have been drummed out of the ranks for prostituting her profession, and the teachers themselves would have risen up against a union that attempted to make them propagandists in the classroom. But though the UFT published the entire plan in its publication, the *United Teacher*, the only outcry came from a few columnists and writers who realized the direction in which American education was being dragged. The country had already been numbed by teachers strikes in which violence, tire slashing, intimidation of non-strikers, and obscenity in the collective-bargaining process had been practiced by those who, presumably, are to be models of deportment to the impressionable young. The major

59

concern among union activists was that the lesson plan was too overt where it should have done its work more subtly.*

To understand the American Federation of Teachers in its drive for "teacher power"—a mass union in which its bureaucrats would take over for school boards and state legislatures in the governance of education—it is necessary to understand Albert Shanker, now president of the 400,000-member organization, the white-headed boy of George Meany, and, given his skill at Machiavellian intrigue, possibly the next president of the AFL-CIO.

A former math teacher in New York schools, Shanker plunged into union work, first as an organizer and then as president of the UFT. By a series of crippling strikes depriving a million and a half New York children of their schooling for nine weeks, he was able to make the UFT the absolute arbiter of matters educational in New York and to reduce the Board of Education to impotence. He has increased salaries for teachers but has reduced the New York public schools, once the best in the nation, to an educational zero. The prestige of teaching, plus the dedication of teachers to their professsion, has followed the same downward curve. In the process, his ultimate victims have been schoolchildren everywhere—a consequence of his belief that teachers are no different from plumbers, with just about the same responsibilities to the public.

Have the teachers benefited by his ministrations? Have they achieved the "dignity" that he waves before the world as his great contribution? In mid-April 1974, "Bill Moyers Journal," a television program disseminated by the Public Broadcasting network, gave some answers. In the early minutes of the show, Moyers asked some relevant questions.

"Organized teachers in New York have come far since those days," he said. "Every triumph increases Albert Shanker's influence and power. But his victories mirror the predicaments of success. Do his teachers owe their first loyalty to the classroom, or to their local chapter? Are they trade unionists first and professionals second? Do increased teacher benefits spell better education . . . ? And what about Shanker himself? . . . Shrewd, sure, and single-minded in his rise so far, what happens if he becomes the nation's superteacher? What does he do with his power, and what will his power do to him?"

---

*Mortimer Smith, a respected educator who seeks a reform in what now passes for education, was constrained to write sadly in the *Bulletin* of the Council for Basic Education of unionists "who are devoted to education as indoctrination, who seek 'to give political tone or character' not only to 'general arrangements' but to the curriculum itself."

Fred Hechinger, the *New York Times* education editor: "To me, Al is a tragic figure rather than a heroic figure precisely because he has so much to contribute and does so little with it. . . . Many of the things that the schools need and that he could help give them would not, as he seems to think, in any way reduce his union's power. . . ."

Teachers: "I think now Mr. Shanker is more self-serving and power hungry. I don't think he's interested any more in the little teacher. Of course, we have gotten smaller classes, larger salaries. But in many ways we have been forgotten. . . . He has made our union into a—not a teachers' union, but just a labor union after big salaries."

Teacher: "I feel its divisive. I think it's absolutely wrong to turn it into a political organ."

Teacher: ". . . we've also been taught to be afraid of parents and students. And I think that's been part of the philosophy of the union leadership and—and I wish that they would be more open to allying with parents and getting together with them to fight for education."

Teacher: "I don't think there's a future in unionism when only Al Shanker decides. I don't think he's a bad man, but I think that, you know, power corrupts."

Victor Gotbaum, righthand man to Jerry Wurf, on an attempt by Shanker to raid an AFSCME local: "I would be less than honest if I stated to you that I didn't expect that kind of campaign [from Al], you know, calling us liars and goons. . . . Al's personal belief is, 'Don't get angry, get even.' Al has to get you. . . . He involves himself in overkill. . . . I regard Al as the single greatest tragedy of the American labor movement."

Shanker, responding to the criticism: "Any member who doesn't like what the union is doing, anyone who feels that it's dictatorial or discriminatory or that they don't have their voice . . . they can quit any day of the week."

That statement spoke volumes about the nature of Albert Shanker. The UFT and the AFT, it is true—and Shanker noted this—were very "democratic" about polling their members on such matters as the Vietnam war or their attitudes towards the President of the United States. But at the very time that he was telling Bill Moyers that a member could quit "any day of the week," Shanker and his union were working in tandem with the AFL-CIO for enactment of legislation that would impose compulsory unionism on all state and local government employees, either under the Clay-Williams bill or by amending the National Labor Relations Act to include government employees. This would mean that no teacher could resign from the union except by giving up his job. Even under the "maintenance of membership" contracts, which the AFT had in many jurisdictions, no member could resign during the life of the contracts.

The attitude of Shanker and the UFT toward discrimination can best be determined by their record in the great 1968 teachers strike, which established their power over the New York Board of Education and the public schools. At issue was an experiment in community control of the schools, in which parents and local school boards would become involved in the quality of education. The UFT strongly opposed this. It is, after all, easier to dominate one Board of Education, deriving its authority from a political city administration, than a congeries of local boards sustained by the nager of parents at teachers interested more in avoiding work than in educating children.

Despite this opposition, the Board of Education was able, after much debate with the union, to set up several "test" areas, particularly one in the Brownsville ghetto of Brooklyn. Whether community control is the answer is not the question. It may or may not be. But Shanker and the UFT set out to make the "test" end in failure. A number of UFT teachers in the Brownsville school district were assigned to sabotage it. The Brownsville school board fired them, and Shanker called out all of New York's teachers in a "protest" strike made uglier by its racial overtones. Eventually, Shanker won, by using his political muscle and by making a shambles of orderly life for New York parents, closing the schools from September 9 to November 19.*

Shanker has admitted that his drive to bring the country's three million teachers into Big Labor's camp has little to do with trade-union objectives since a nationwide strike would be counter-productive. He has frankly said that his goal is to amass the kind of power that leadership of the largest union in the country would give him. He could then put his stamp on the education of the young by the kind of indoctrination he is already injecting into the New York City schools. And he would have a political weapon before which even Presidents would tremble, financed by the kind of union treasury that compulsory unionism brings.

The AFT makes no bones about this. "The American Federation of Teachers is determined to control the public

---

*The New York Civil Liberties Union, in a report on the strike, stated that the UFT had used " 'due process' as a smokescreen to obscure its real goal, which is to discredit decentralization and sabotage community control." It should be noted that the UFT inspired fears of black control of the schools and black anti-Semitism to stir up racial tensions and win support for itself.

schools of the United States," says one of the union's top organizers. "And why not?" The quotation comes from R.J. Braun's *Teachers and Power*, a book which the AFT tried mightily to suppress. Writes Braun:

> It is useless to argue with this man about the ultimate desirability of a public school system which is genuinely public.... He is a warrior in a cause and he believes the cause to be just.... His job is to organize a local, prepare timid teachers for a strike, force angry teachers back to work, negotiate a contract. If he or his colleagues are heavy drinkers, it is probably because many a contract has been gained by winning a heavy drinking bout with the paid negotiator for the local school board.... If an AFT organized swears heavily, it is probably because many a school board has been intimidated into hard bargaining through the use of carefully chosen, adequately punctuated four-letter words. AFT organizers are not teachers, not theorists, not advocates of social betterment. They are soldiers.
> ... They are genuine fanatics, driven by the smell of battle, and often by a paranoid hatred of mayors, school-board members, injunction-granting judges, superintendents, representatives of community groups.... "I joined the union," one field organizer explained, "because there are about sixty school boards in this country I would really like to f——k. I was a state representative for the National Education Association, and those bastards wouldn't let me f——k the boards. Now I won't quit until I can f——k the NEA too."

To achieve its ends, the AFT has variously allied itself with any group that temporarily shares its hatred and can be of use in paralyzing a school board or bringing chaos to a community that resists it. In its war on San Francisco State College, the AFT made common cause with radical students, Black Panthers, crazies, hippies, and the homosexuals of the Gay Activist movement. In its battle to unionize the Newark (New Jersey) schools, the AFT developed working ties with Anthony Imperiale, the vigilante chief of antiblack, steel-helmeted hoodlums whose practice it was to go out on "jungle patrol" in the city's black ghetto. In New Orleans it gave tacit approval to an "anarchy committee" of teachers, which distributed cherry bombs to students, slashed tires, and firebombed a building—all in the name of collective bargaining and management-labor peace. It makes its strongest appeal to teachers on the most irresponsible of grounds that a strong union will prevent any assessment by school boards of their possible lack of competence; that there will be no gauge of performance in considering promotion, no accountability to determine how well or how badly the young are being educated.

To pursue its warfare, the AFT has needed money, and it got more than a million dollars from Walter Reuther, when he headed the AFL-CIO's Industrial Union Department. (When Reuther withdrew from the federation, Albert Shanker & Co., with typical gratitude, thanked him by remaining with George Meany.) That money was used first to analyze the techniques of disruption and then to put them on a production-line basis. The AFT discovered early in the game that winning a representation election did not guarantee an influx of new members. This had to be followed by a strike, no matter what the local conditions, which would politicalize the teachers. Won or lost, the strike would drive a wedge between teachers and school boards, and from that alienation would come the future, more violent and bitter strikes that would break the backs of boards and frighten the politicians. AFT officials have admitted that a lost strike can frequently be of more value than any contract, no matter how favorable to the union.

There is very little of a "local" nature in the mechanics of organization. The literature has all been prepared in Washington, with blank spaces for the pictures of local leaders and the insertion of purely local issues. Leaflets with endorsement of the AFT be national figures like Hubert Humphrey have been printed in the millions. (In one instance, a letter from Ralph Abernathy, then leader of the Southern Christian Leadership Conference, praising a Pittsburgh AFT local was doctored so that it was addressed to the Kansas City local, when the AFT was moving in on that city.) "Issue" fliers also are prepared in Washington, though they are purportedly the work of local teachers. Canned speechers are written for AFT leaders who visit the target community to rally the troops.

The AFT provides canteen service—coffee and doughnuts—for the teachers' common rooms in targeted schools, and there are afternoon get-togethers with liquor and music. At these get-togethers, the liquor table is flanked by an AFT representative who asks teachers to "just sign the card"— which some of the unwary do, not realizing that they are putting their signatures to checkoff authorizations. Once the representation election has been won (and it is always billed as the one way to maintain labor peace), strike committees of local teachers are set up, window dressing for the AFT representative who runs the operation. Standard contracts drawn up in Washington, making exorbitant demands, are delivered to the school board. And a battery of specialists— agit-prop men and public-relations experts—is flown in. Experts in testing the temper of the community wait for the psychological moment and then call the strike. Negotiations are controlled from Washington. Everything is systematized to the last detail. If the strike is won, the AFT has another city in its pocket. If it is lost, the AFT begins preparing for the next blow, the knockout punch, orchestrated with equal care. And the public is left with the impression that a hardy group of teachers, concerned over education, has had its spontaneous efforts defeated by reactionary authorities.

The cynicism that has characterized the AFT in its power drive, however, is best exemplified in a "Bill of Rights" it has widely disseminated, a document which may impress the uninformed but which makes the informed writhe. The first three articles pay lip service to "teachers' rights" that no one would think to abridge: freedom of religion, the right to "express themselves openly"—a right, incidentally, which is frequently denied at AFT meetings—the right to have "the same freedom in all things as other citizens."* The fourth article calls for the right of teachers "to live in places of their own choosing"—which few have ever questioned—and "to be free of restraints in their mode of living." To the AFT, that "right" includes having children out of wedlock and smoking marijuana with students.

Articles V states, *inter alia:* "No one shall be deprived of professional status, or the right to practice [teaching], or the practice thereof in any particular position, without due process of law." On the face of it, this means that any teacher has the "right" to be a principal or a supervisor or the chairman of a school department—which is nonsense. It also says that the AFT, which demands the "right" to fire any teacher who does not join the union, stands in violation of its own Bill of Rights.

Article VII states: "No teacher shall be deprived of employment or professional status but for *specific causes established by law having a clear relation to the competence or qualification to teach,* proved by the weight of the evidence" (emphasis added). But it is a rule of the AFT, inscribed in the collective-bargaining agreements it has been able to exact from municipalities, that a teacher *must* be summarily dismissed if he does not join the union or, in an agency-shop situation, pay dues and assessments to the union. Article IX indulges in the same hypocrisy: "After serving a reasonable

---

*From *Newsweek*, August 27, 1973: "Former UFT assistant treasurer Richard Parrish was expelled from the union's controlling caucus for campaigning against Shanker's control over the New York local. 'There's no right to dissent,' he complained bitterly. According to Herbert Hill, labor director of the NAACP, 'Shanker runs the UFT the way Stalin ran the Politburo.'"

probationary period a teacher shall be entitled to permanent tenure terminable only for just cause"—to which should have been added, "except at the pleasure of the union."

And Article XIII: "Since teachers must be free in order to teach freedom, the right to be members of organizations of their own choosing must be guaranteed"—except, of course, if a simple majority of other teachers vote for representation by the AFT, in which case that "right" suddenly becomes a compulsion and the "freedom" to do or not do is cast into oblivion. Article XIII further states: "[Teachers] are entitled to have the schools administered by superintendents, boards or committees which function in a democratic manner." To Albert Shanker, who as a young man shaped his philosophy in the Schachtmanite, or lowercase, communist movement, "democratic" is a figure of speech—preferably, like the Venus de Milo, armless.

If teaching is a profession, as the AFT's Bill of Rights repeatedly urges, then a teacher's function is to teach. To date, the unionization of education has debased teaching to the point where Johnny can no longer read or add, condemning the children of those with low income to perpetual penury. If teaching is a profession, then teachers must be part of the community, sharing in community purposes. In the past, dedicated teachers considered it part of their job to encourage bright students and help slow ones, but Shanker opposes this unless it is done at time-and-a-half. The AFT and other teacher unions claim for themselves the present prosperity of that profession although salaries were sharply rising long before the Albert Shankers had injected themselves into the picture.

What, then, has unionization accomplished? Among other things, it has brought to the surface a union demand that "seniority"—a pejorative term when applied to the Congress—be the rule in the filling of school supervisory posts, not ability but union time-serving. That, and hatred of school boards and other democratically elected officials.

# 6

# Teacher Unionism Pays
# —But Whom?

On Washington's lower Sixteenth Street—where real estate is high and the view pleasant—the passing tourist can remark a very large, very shiny structure. This is the headquarters of the National Education Association, an organization the uninformed may be led to believe has something to do with learning and teaching. A few years ago, the NEA building was half its size, but a growing bureaucracy and the need to use some of the money overflowing its coffers dictated expansion.

The National Education Association, which began years ago to bring teachers, supervisors, and school principals together in order to improve the quality of American education, has moved far beyond this laudable purpose. Today, the NEA is simply another labor union, and the nation's biggest in the field of elementary and high school education. The supervisors and principals have begun to drop out in large numbers, but the NEA can still boast of its 1.4 million members. With the passage of time, it has come to adopt the class-war doctrine of other teachers' unions, viewing school boards with the kind of animosity characteristic of the American Federation of Teachers, its principal rival.

The NEA has still to make use of the four-letter vocabulary of the AFT as a technique of collective bargaining. But its aims differ hardly one iota from those of Albert Shanker's disciples. It wants full control of the educational process, from top to bottom. Its 1972 president, Donald E. Morrison, said it succinctly and frankly when he announced that "our major power . . . is in political action. Teachers have power because they can elect; organized they can be a major power-broker."

Like the AFT, the NEA runs into problems stemming from a division between the legislative and the administrative functions in state and municipal government. In 1972, its affiliate, the Hawaii State Teacher's Association, was able to pummel the island's education authority into signing a collective-bargaining agreement. But the legislature would not agree to the contract, so ninety percent of Hawaii's nine thousand teachers, in the labor phrase, hit the bricks, leaving 181,000 students locked out of their schools. Along with its competitors, the NEA is responsible for the more than ten million student days lost through the 145 teacher strikes called in the 1972–73 school year. Like the AFT, the NEA wants not only exclusive bargaining agreements but the agency shop, which compels nonmembers to pay dues and assessments.

The desire to extract every last dollar from members and nonmembers alike, though not exactly praiseworthy, is understandable when the NEA's budgetary elephantiasis is considered. Though it likes to project itself as an organization of poor struggling teachers—little old ladies in tennis shoes whose only concern is their pupils—the NEA is big business. As of two years ago—and income has grown—the NEA, directly and through its affiliates, was taking in $200 million a year—on a par with the largest labor unions. The NEA's national office had a budget of $31.6 million. It owns expensive office buildings and runs at a profit a multi-million-dollar travel service. One of its affiliates owns an eight-passenger Beechcraft plane with a full-time pilot whose job description is buried away as "air transportation specialist."

The NEA's national president draws a $40,000-a-year salary, plus a $10,000 expense account; the president-elect, as he waits for a year to enter the green pastures, is paid $30,000. The salary of the executive secretary, an appointive position, is not announced, but it is no secret that it is in the neighborhood of $60,000. Staff salaries take up about $10 million of the NEA's national budget. Some $4 million is spent on "public relations and publications," and $1.4 million on lobbying on Capitol Hill, a sum the biggest corporations would not dare to match. Significantly, less than $2 million—roughly six percent of the NEA's national budget—is spent on educational activities. The improvement of teacher skills and research is not worth it to the NEA, and there is some question how the money budgeted for "education" is used. The rest of the NEA's annual income is spent by its affiliates—"locals" in trade-union parlance. Where that $170 million goes, the NEA is not anxious to disclose.

Is the NEA concerned with education and with the problems of teaching? Or is it interested mainly in dragooning every schoolteacher into further swelling its already swollen income? Speaking before a meeting of the Missouri NEA, national president Helen D. Wise told her audience, "You've Come a Long Way Baby," boasted of the half-million members NEA was about to pick up and of its tremendous success in electing everything from governors to congressmen,

68

boasted again that Senator Claiborne Pell of Rhode Island attributed his reelection to the NEA, and reiterated, "You and I belong to the most political of all professions." She said precious little about education—unless her talk of NEA's battle for women teachers whose miniskirts were a little too mini and for men teachers whose ponytails were a little too long for some school boards can be so interpreted. What NEA is about can best be assessed by observing the activities of its locals.

*Item.* An instruction sheet prepared by United Teachers of Los Angeles on how to deal with principals who want some kind of measurement of teacher achievement in educating their pupils. This has traditionally been standard in schools. The sheet is broken down into four categories, depending on how a principal reacts to union pressure. "The Deal," for handling "cooperative principals," called for teachers to make "a declaration that hierarchical accountability inhibits accountability to parents, and that therefore program development and evaluation will not be subject to the evaluation-for-retention process." Translated into English, this means that teachers should reject all attempts to have their work evaluated.

If the principal objects, then teachers are told to move to phase two, "Passive Resistance"—which to the NEA means telling the principal "to fill out the objectives, etc. on the Initial Planning Sheet; after all it's his responsibility by law." The third suggestion, headed "overkill," tells teachers to "Overcomply. . . . Sit down and list every textbook goal you ordinarily set. Then list every exam you intend to give throughout the year. Next, conference the principal to death showing him every single spelling, arithmetic, etc. test and discussing how this measures each student's progress. . . . Include piles of tests for filing with Final Evaluation Report."

Point four, however, is headed "War" and is frankly labeled a "battle plan." This includes a "no-confidence resolution" to be passed by the local and circulated to parents; a "Principal Performance Evaluation Form" undercutting the principal; "speeches before community groups" and "handouts to students and parents before and after school," all "stressing the damage being done to instruction" by "dehumanized bookkeeping of grades . . . phony accountability to hide real culprits"; "a letter and phone campaign" and "informational picketing by teachers and parents for humane and effective school programs." All of this, in the name of trade unionism because a principal had the temerity to ask whether Johnny was being taught to read and write.

*Item.* Tenure for teachers? Forget it, if you don't have a

union card and the NEA's blessing. Carol Applegate is a case in point. Mrs. Applegate taught in the Grand Blanc, Michigan, schools for twenty years, with one interruption when she resigned to raise a family. Like most schoolteachers, she thought she was protected by the state's Teacher Tenure Act. Under the law, she was removed from political pressure and could not be fired except for "reasonable and just cause"—such cause being a finding that she was of "immoral character," "dishonest while employed," or convicted of "a felony or any crime involving moral turpitude."

Mrs. Applegate's official rating as a teacher was of the highest, and her abilities were never questioned. But when the Grand Blanc Board of Education signed a collective-bargaining agreement with the Michigan Education Association, her days were numbered. To the union, Mrs. Applegate committed mortal sin by her refusal (a) to join NEA or (b) to knuckle under to agency-shop provisions that required her to pay dues to support activities of which she disapproved. She was fired forthwith at the behest of an organization presumably created to look after the rights of teachers.

Mrs. Applegate's reasons for refusing to join the union were ones which liberals in another time would have applauded: "I could not in all conscience stand before my classes and say, 'Think independently, make up your own minds,' when I was being denied the right to think independently and make up my own mind about membership in this organization. . . . My dismissal was entirely because I was unable to go along with the tactics of the union."

It seemed like an open-and-shut case when Mrs. Applegate's case came up before the five-member Michigan Teacher Tenure Commission. But the hand of the NEA reached into that presumably impartial body. Two commissioners were members of the Michigan Education Association, and they combined with the one nonteacher on the commission to vote three-to-two that Mrs. Applegate had been fired for "reasonable and just cause." That a conflict of interest existed clearly did not disturb the teachers who voted against the precious tenure that their profession had battled so long to attain. The union came first. They were not even troubled by the unambiguous statement in the state's Public Employment Relations Act that forbids discrimination "in regard to hire, terms or other conditions of employment in order to encourage or discourage membership in a labor organization." The NEA was above the law.

It took long and expensive litigation, and the intercession of the National Right to Work Legal Defense Foundation, to win reinstatement for Mrs. Applegate. Other teachers swallowed their principles and joined the union, unwilling or unable to put themselves and their families in the same terrible position or to endure the ordeal of a similar battle with Michigan authorities and a determined union.*

*Item.* Mrs. Applegate's case was not the only one to end up in court, however. Months before she was due to retire, and after thirty-one years of teaching, Mrs. Margaret Maki of Hancock, Michigan, was fired because she refused to join the NEA's Michigan Education Association or to pay the equivalent of dues to the union—demanded from her under the terms of an agency-shop contract signed by the local MEA and the Adams Township Board of Education.

Mrs. Maki, who called the demand for dues and/or membership "unadulterated slavery," could cite a new twist to her case. "It's ironic," she said, remarking on the fact that she had been a member of NEA for twenty-five years before she resigned in protest over its political activities, "that teacher union bosses have consistently *refused* to represent me in their dealing with the school board because I'm a nondegree teacher. They appeared before the school board to oppose a raise for me. Then they turned around and demand compulsory agency-shop fees on the ridiculous basis that since they're required to 'represent' me I should pay a 'fair share' of the costs involved. Some 'representation'!"

The NEA, through its Michigan affiliate, lost in the courts, but won its point in a union-dominated state legislature, which voted to circumvent the legal decision by enacting a compulsory agency shop statute.

Another affiliate, the St. Louis Education Association, working with the Teamsters union, demonstrated its much-vaunted "professionalism" by going on strike in defiance of the contract it had signed with the school board and in violation of a court order. The union's behavior during that strike was summed up by Superintendent Clyde C. Miller:

> At seventy-four schools Tuesday a normal instructional program was carried out peacefully and without incident inside. But the mob action outside by the illegal pickets has created such hazards to the safety of the teachers—and the children—

---

*The attitude of teachers' unions to the free-association provision of the First Amendment is matched by their contempt for free speech. In Madison, Wisconsin, where in 1972 the union had negotiated a compulsory-union-agency-shop agreement with School District No. 8, a teacher, Albert Holmquist, circulated a petition to the school board signed by a majority of the teachers, seeking a delay in the implementation of the contract. At a meeting of the school board, Holmquist was permitted to read his petition. The union thereupon filed unfair labor charges against the school board because Holmquist had been allowed to speak.

71

that these schools must be closed in addition to the ninety-two already shut down.

Incidents involving pickets Tuesday were so widespread and so numerous that it is literally impossible to list them all. Trucks carrying food to children were blocked. As teachers came to school they were taunted and threatened. While they were teaching the children, their cars were damaged. Convoys of roving pickets intimidated teachers as they left school. . . .*

This militancy took a new and far more serious form in July 1973, when the Michigan Education Association secretly circulated its *Final Recommendations on a Statewide Bargaining Strategy*. This document, later read into the record of the Michigan House of Representatives, called for statewide school strikes, even in districts with no grievances or with contracts the MEA considered adequate—the prelude to nationwide strikes to achieve local objectives and to create a "crisis" atmosphere. It was inspired in part by MEA recognition that it could no longer create panic among school boards simply by presenting a set of demands.

Said the MEA's Cabinet Task Force:

Local boards of education are becoming increasingly sophisticated and recalcitrant in their bargaining with local associations. They have begun to organize, hire bargaining specialists and coordinate their efforts under the banner of the Michigan School Boards Association. They no longer fear the strike as a bargaining weapon, and more inportantly, they no longer fear public reaction to it. . . .

Bargaining problems are compounded by economic pressures revolving around inflation, the wage-price freeze . . . local voter rejections of property taxes for schools, dwindling local revenues and the public image of teachers as "well paid for working such a short year."

Because of past association successes at the bargaining table, many teachers feel entirely too comfortable financially. Because this "fat cat" syndrome exists, militancy has waned.

The public . . . also see[s] teachers' salaries as being more than adequate, and tax increases are viewed as the inevitable result of teachers unions trying to make good teaching salaries even better. . . .

*Analysis of Alternative Bargaining Strategies*

a. *Settlement Between the Two Parties*
   Mutually acceptable compromises resulting in a settlement
   One side or the other "gives in" also resulting in a settlement
   Continuous bargaining with no settlement

---

*\*St. Louis Globe-Democrat*, quoted in an editorial, January 25, 1973.

b. *The Strike or Its Variations*
   Local, regional, state or national strikes
   "Work to the rule"
   Guerilla warfare
   Blue flu, "Professional Days", etc.
   Violence, sabotage, etc.
   Mass resignations, individual resignations, etc.
c. *Third Party Intervention*
   Mediation and factfinding
   Mutual agreement for binding arbitration on unresolved issues
   Legislation mandating binding arbitration. . . .

We also believe that any impasse resolution for public employees will fall into one of these catagories, no matter how great the temptation for unions to continually seek some mystical solution. . . .

*Some Basic Premises for a New Strategy*

Money, or lack of it, is not the sole cause of local bargaining frustration. Even now, many boards are, in fact, still able to squirrel away funds for contingencies. . . .
*The short-range solution to bargaining frustration and treadmilling is a burst of dramatic, visable, militant leadership. A new bargaining thrust and strategy is essential. We believe that thrust must come from the MEA. It cannot come from individual locals.*
*The long-range solution to our bargaining dilemma is legislative, not ever increasing escalation, i.e., a change in the bargaining law and/or statutory methods of resolving impasse. . . .*

*A Suggested Statewide Strategy (Short Range)*

The MEA immediately exposes, with all possible statewide fanfare, "the alarming and outrageous conspiracy by local boards of education designed to roll back hard won teacher contractual rights." . . .
Further, we:
   Denounce boards for banding together in secret and unholy coalitions under the banner of MASB. (We must be ready to handle the obvious fact that the MEA locals have done it since 1965.) . . .
   Because of these shocking attacks by conniving boards, the MEA states flatly that *local boards are precipitating an educational crisis next Fall.* We make *them* the culprits responsible for the crisis. . . .
   The time between now and the crisis next November is utilized to create a statewide atmosphere of grave urgency. . . .
   Local bargainers go to the table in each district and repeatedly accuse their board of being part of the MASB conspiracy.

If, after the appropriate crisis build-up, intervention by the Governor, etc., settlements are not secured in dramatic numbers, the MEA, on October 1, 1973, begins the coordination of tactical regional strikes designed to disrupt the educational process and keep the boards in a state of confusion while affording maximum security to our members on strike.

The MEA calls for *all* unsettled units in Wayne, Oakland and Macomb Counties to strike on October 1. We may want to consider other unsettled units going out on a regional basis. (October 1 is a Monday.) The strike(s) continues through the first of the following week. The MEA then announces that all striking teachers will return to work on Friday—they do. Bargaining continues, locally and through intermediaries, over the week-end (through Monday, October 8.) The MEA announces on Monday that there will be a continuation of the strike on Tuesday (9th) if outstanding issues are not resolved. The strike continues on Tuesday. The MEA announces teachers will go back next week while bargaining continues. They do. If no settlement, out again, etc. etc., until all units are under contract.

This plan to "disrupt the educational process and keep the boards in a state of confusion" would be implemented by a $64,000 campaign utilizing radio and television spots, with additional expenditures from the MEA locals. It is marked not only by a total disregard of the public's rights and of student welfare but by a cynical admission that the horrendous crimes of "crazy" school boards are no more than what the MEA had been doing all along. The arguments advanced against school boards, moreover, are clearly spurious and made to deceive the public. (In one instance, deleted from the above, the authors list a number of accusations to be made and end them by the clincher, "or whatever.") In short, that presumed *sine qua non* of collective bargaining, "good faith," is nonexistent.

But for the National Education Association, this lapse is of no consequence. The purpose of collective bargaining is to smash boards of education, to wrest from them their legal prerogatives, and to create a power base. In its public statements, the NEA speaks always of "friends of education" when what it means is "friends of the NEA." To reward those friends, the NEA needs money, which is why, in alliance with the American Federation of Teachers, it struck the Los Angeles schools when it was refused pay increases that would have cost the city $1.5 billion annually. This is why students majoring in education are called in by the deans and told that unless they join NEA they will not be permitted to engage in the student teaching, which is required for the degree. It is why NEA was responsible for 122 of the 145 strikes that shut down schools in the 1972–73 year. It is why, most chillingly, an NEA president felt no constraint about boasting that "we will not be satisfied until we are the most powerful lobby in Washington"—adding, "Within ten years, I think this organization will control the qualifications for entrance into the profession, and for the privilege of remaining in the profession."

Catherine Barrett, a later president, was equally unembarrassed. "We are the biggest potential striking force in this country and we are determined to control the direction of education." NEA, she asserted, would raise a political war chest of five million to ten million dollars for the 1976 presidential election. "Put this money with our people power and we would not only be competitive with any existing political force, but we would be the greatest political force." The price for NEA support of a presidential candidate will be a commitment that the federal government finance one-third of all education, at the trifling annual cost of $50 billion.

Helen Wise, who took over as president in 1974, told the *New York Times* that the NEA elected "141 of 184 congressional candidates" it supported, at a cost of $3 million. "Over the next several months," she said, the NEA would "pump time—millions and millions of dollars' worth of it—into the campaigns of candidates" who supported NEA objectives. "We must reorder congressional priorities by reordering Congress"—a statement whose import must have been intended. With an intimidated Congress and a manipulated President, the NEA would, indeed, be the most powerful force in the United States.

The emphasis in discussing teacher unionism has been on the public elementary and high schools, since strikes and collective bargaining in these institutions most closely affect the public and since the elementary and secondary public schools hold a near monopoly on education. But the less dramatic impact of unionism in the colleges and universities has a far greater impact on the nation. Objective studies show that the student turmoil of the late Sixties was stimulated and frequently led by radicalized faculty members. The great wrath of teacher unions was directed at administrators who took strong measures against student anarchy and violence— witness the propaganda assaults on S. I. Hayakawa during the teachers' strike at San Francisco State College. These assaults, parenthetically, were strained by a streak of vulgar antiintellectualism, which is increasingly the mark of collective bargaining.

A study* by Everett Carll Ladd, Jr. and Seymour Lipsett, prepared for the Carnegie Commission on Higher Education, notes:

If student activism and reactions to politicize academe explicitly proved to be the major developments affecting American campuses in the latter half of the 1960s, faculty trade unionism and formal collective bargaining are likely to constitute the most important new intramural issues in the 1970s.... As of spring 1973, 304 institutions were bargaining collectively in 205 bargaining units with representatives of their faculty. The most successful faculty bargaining agent, the National Education Association (NEA) represented professors and nonteaching professionals at 16 four-year colleges and universities and 92 two-year schools.... The American Federation of Teachers (AFT) had won rights to represent academics at ... 19 four-year and 41 two-year [institutions.]... And the traditional faculty professional association, the American Association of University Professors (AAUP), had plunged, albeit with more than a little reluctance, into the world of collective bargaining, serving as agent ... at 17 universities and four-year colleges, and at three community colleges. Over 90 percent of the bargaining units are in public institutions.

Competition for faculty support, particularly the younger instructors, by the NEA and the AFT forced the AAUP to give up its long-standing role as a professional association for trade-union status. As late as 1972, Sanford Kadish, the outgoing president of the AAUP, could argue: "I will simply point out that the strike proceeds by deliberately harming the educational mission." Collective bargaining, he added, "imperils the premise of shared authority" between faculty and administration, "encourages the polarization in interests," and "tends to remit issues which faculty should themselves determine to outside agencies such as ... union bureaucracies. In addition, since unions rest on continued support to their constituency, the process becomes susceptible to essentially political rather than essentially academic decision-making." That other faculty members at institutions of higher learning agreed with him became apparent when almost ten percent of the AAUP's membership resigned following its conversion to a bargaining collective.

Interestingly, while the unionism of higher education has advanced as a result of political pressure on college and university administrations, opposition to unionization has increased. In 1969, when the big push began, a Carnegie survey showed that fifty-nine percent of all academics favored

*Professors, Unions, and American Higher Education, published by the American Enterprise Institute, August 1973.

teacher unions. By 1972, this had changed. A second Carnegie survey in that year disclosed that only forty-three percent agreed that unionism on campus was "beneficial and should be extended." Forty-four percent disagreed and the remaining thirteen percent had mixed feelings. Significantly, in a 1972 representation election at Michigan State, a university whose milieu was one of the strongest prounion states in the country, sixty-four percent of the faculty voted for "no representation"—a reaction to the policies of NEA, AFT, and the other teacher unions.

The loss of support for these unions, moreover, came in a field that has led the country in its "liberalism." The reason for this is obvious. Confronted by a choice between left-wing ideology and their own best professional interests, faculties opted for their professions. The struggle to impose collective-bargaining norms and practices on education meant that academics, because of the polarization that results, were losing many prerogatives that they had fought for and attained over the years. Where a professor's salary increased as he attained academic status, the unions demanded equal pay for all those presumably doing equal work. Advancement, where the unions had their way, was by categories rather than by performance. A brilliant teacher and a mediocre one were to be rewarded and promoted solely according to seniority, and this the academics resented. Statistically, unionization advanced, but it was successful only where the politicians interfered or in schools of "low category"—the junior colleges whose instructors had little standing in the academic community and saw little chance to better themselves by their performance as teachers. They supported unions that hold that merit increases are "union-busting in disguise," an AFT phrase.

What faculties at institutions of higher learning discovered between 1969 and 1972 was that the NEA, the AFT, and—reluctantly—the AAUP wanted to punch out teachers with a cookie-cutter, thereby depriving good teachers of their "right" to inspire and educate students. The academic leveling demanded by the unions was stifling education. This vision did not appeal to the true academics. As Benjamin Aaron, director of the Institute of Labor and Industrial Relations at the University of California—and the chairman of a committee set up by the California legislature to advise it on collective bargaining for public employees—eloquently noted, such leveling would deprive academe of

> a quality of life in our colleges and universities in which eccentricity and nonconformity can still flourish; in which distinguished scholarship is still honored despite its lack of "relevance"—that mean little word; in which the main ties between

colleagues are their intellectual attainments; in which cost-benefit analysis is not the sole basis on which the value of every course or degree program is judged; and in which these institutions ... remain the guardians and transmitters of the world's cultural heritage.

For the teacher unions, this call for academic freedom, and for the removal of education from the political marketplace, is heresy and, worse than that, a call to the Bill of Rights.

# 7

# Strikes, Politics, and
# the Public Interest

When the Congress in its wisdom enacted the National Labor Relations Act and its various amendments, the authors of these statutes felt constrained to lay down what they conceived must be the policy of the United States, namely, that "a sound and stable industrial peace and the advancement of the general welfare, health, and safety of the Nation and the best interests of employers and employees can most satisfactorily be secured by the settlement of issues between employers and employees through the process of conference and collective bargaining." In this, the Congress was making obeisance to one of the most sacrosanct myths in the hagiography of labor-management relations.

A more accurate view of the impact of unionism and collective bargaining on the body politic was suggested by Professor Albert Rees of Princeton years later in his book, *The Economics of Trade Unionism:*

> If the union is viewed solely in terms of its effect on the economy, it must in my opinion be considered an obstacle to the optimum performance of our economic system. It alters the wage structure in a way that impedes the growth of employment in sectors of the economy where productivity and income are naturally high and that leaves too much labor in low-income sectors of the economy ... It benefits most those workers who would in any case be relatively well off, and while some of this gain may be at the expense of the owners of capital, most of it must be at the expense of consumers and the lower-paid workers....

If this is true in private enterprise where, according to the latest report of the Federal Mediation and Conciliation Service, "union organization in the private sector remains at about 20 percent, [whereas] in the public sector it exceeds 33⅓ percent,"* then what is the impact of public-employee

---

*Which deflates the grandiose claims of Jerry Wurf and other public-employee union leaders that they "represent" more than half of all public employees.

unions whose consumers are the entire population? Collective bargaining in the public sector not only has drastically reduced the productivity of government workers, but has not brought the "peace" proclaimed by the NLRA and the new bills before the Ninety-fourth Congress to make public-employee unionism mandatory. Collective bargaining in the public sector, moreover, has begun to create the kind of unemployment that scholars have noted as a result of similar practices in the private sector.**

The merits and demerits of collective bargaining as they benefit the union member lend themselves to interminable argument. But the effects of collective bargaining in the public sector can be determined statistically and beyond cavil. Whatever the Jerry Wurfs and Albert Shankers may argue about the social role of their unions, their claims that public-employee unions have brought peace and stability to government employment can be sustained only by setting truth on its ear. *Government Work Stoppages, 1960, 1969, and 1970*, a report issued by the Bureau of Labor Statistics of the United States Labor Department, nails down this point and also demolishes the contention of Big Labor that strikes and other disruptions of government were primarily the function of attempts to organize against the obstructionism of government management.

According to the BLS report, strike activity by government employees rose from thirty-six in 1960 to 411 in 1969 and 412 in 1970. The total number of workers involved rose from 28,600 in 1960 to 333,500 in 1970. The number of man-days idle because of strikes against government skyrocketed from 58,400 in 1960 to 2,023,200 in 1970. The key features of the government strike profile in the 1960–70 period, as analyzed by the BLS, were:

> Most of the increase in strike idleness in the government sector was attributable to work stoppages by local government employees. Man-days idle in this sector increased tenfold between 1960 and 1969 and then more than doubled between 1969 and 1970. . . .
> Even though total government employment rose by 650 percent over the 11-year period, the number of workers involved in strikes rose more. . . .
> Economic issues were responsible for [269 of all government work stoppages] in 1970. [There were only 59 organizational strikes.] . . .

---

**". . . any significant real financial benefit . . . that accrues through collective bargaining may well cause significant unemployment among union members" (Harry K. Wellington and Ralph K. Winter, Jr., *The Unions and the Cities*, a study written for the Brookings Institution).

Stoppages in public schools and libraries accounted for over one-half of the idleness and two-fifths of all workers involved in government strikes in 1970. . . .

Strikes conducted by unions and associations composed primarily of government employees rose from eleven in 1960 to 282 in 1969 and 291 in 1970. . . .

. . . Among the fifty states and the District of Columbia, Michigan [with the most prolabor statutes on its books] experiences the greatest number of strikes. . . .

By 1972, the percent of organizational strikes in government had fallen to five, the number of man-days lost in that category to 7.7 percent. Specific proof that collective bargaining brought an increase in strikes and other disruptions of government can be found in an unpublished analysis prepared by the Public Service Research Council, an organization devoted to the study of public-employee unionism. On a state-by-state basis, using available data beginning in 1958 when the Labor Department began compiling statistics in this field, the PSRC tabulated the number of strikes before and after enactment of collective-bargaining legislation.

Alabama: Years before legislation 9, strikes 5
      Years after legislation 4, strikes 18
Alaska: Years before legislation 10, strikes 3
      Years after legislation 3, strikes 6
California (only may represent members):
      Years before legislation 3, strikes 2
      Years after legislation 10, strikes 129
Delaware: Years before legislation 7, strikes 2
      Years after legislation 6, strikes 10
Florida: Years before legislation 2, strikes 0
      Years after legislation 11, strikes 41
Georgia (only firefighters):
      Years before legislation 13, strikes 23
      Years after legislation 1, strikes 9
Hawaii: Years before legislation 12, strikes 2
      Years after legislation 1, strikes 2
Idaho (firefighters and teachers):
      Years before legislation 12, strikes 2
      Years after legislation 1, strikes 1
Kansas: Years before legislation 12, strikes 6
      Years after legislation 1, strikes 2
Maryland (public school employees, Baltimore City and Allegheny County employees):
      Years before legislation 10, strikes 5
      Years after legislation 3, strikes 13
Massachusetts: Years before legislation 11, strikes 13
      Years after legislation 2, strikes 20

Michigan: Years before legislation 7, strikes 1
        Years after legislation 6, strikes 290*
Minnesota: Years before legislation 13, strikes 6
        Years after legislation 1, strikes 3
Missouri: Years before legislation 9, strikes 22
        Years after legislation 4, strikes 33
Montana: Years before legislation 11, strikes 3
        Years after legislation 2, strikes 3**
Nebraska (teachers only):
        Years before legislation 10, strikes 0
        Years after legislation 4, strikes 0
Nevada: Years before legislation 11, strikes 0
        Years after legislation 2, strikes 1
New Hampshire: Years before legislation 11, strikes 2
        Years after legislation 2, strikes 5
New Jersey: Years before legislation 10, strikes 31
        Years after legislation 3, strikes 62
New Mexico (state personnel under Personnel Board regulations):
        Years before legislation 13, strikes 5
        Years after legislation 1, strikes 3
New York: Years before legislation 9, strikes 37
        Years after legislation 4, strikes 111
North Dakota (teachers only):
        Years before legislation 11, strikes 2
        Years after legislation 2, strikes 1
Oklahoma (firemen, policemen, and teachers):
        Years before legislation 13, strikes 6
        Years after legislation 1, strikes 0
Oregon: Years before legislation 5, strikes 0
        Years after legislation 8, strikes 3
Pennsylvania: Years before legislation 10, strikes 23
        Years after legislation 3, strikes 141
Rhode Island: Years before legislation 13, strikes 25
        (Rhode Island enacted legislation in 1958)**
South Carolina: Years before legislation 14, strikes 3
        Years after legislation 3, strikes 3
South Dakota: Years before legislation 12, strikes 2
        Years after legislation 1, strikes 0
Vermont: Years before legislation 11, strikes 0
        Years after legislation 2, strikes 0

---

*Michigan's history is significant. The state's first law concerning collective bargaining opened few doors. In 1965, however the state passed a drastic amendment to the law governing collective bargaining in the public sector As a result though only 240 man-days had been lost through strikes in the *seven* years preceding 1965, 750,000 man-days were lost in the following *six* years.

**In those eleven years before legislation, Montana's three strikes involved a total of eighty workers. The two years after legislation saw three strikes involving some 1,700 workers.

**The greatest strike activity occurred after Rhode Island's statute received a major revamping, which brought on ten major strikes and 18,000 man-days idle.

Washington: Years before legislation 7, strikes 4
       Years after legislation 6, strikes 8
Wisconsin: Years before legislation 1, strikes 0
       Years after legislation 12, strikes 57**

In Michigan, a state with a history of aggressive unionism, the legislation that was to bring labor peace converted an average of 0.143 strikes a year to an average of 48.3 strikes a year. New York saw its 4.1-strikes-a-year average change to 27.75 strikes a year. The national average—the figure is deceptively low because it includes nonindustrial states, which have few strikes of any kind—swung from 0.76 before legislation to more than 8.2 strikes a year, an increase of roughly eleven times.

Logic would have dictated this result, since handing a pugnacious man a gun does not increase his affability. The question then is why state legislatures, one after another, meekly enacted laws that were foreseeably disruptive of governmental civility and ran directly counter to the interests of the voters who had put them in office. One argument accepted by legislators and governors, and now being thrust at the federal government, was that since rape was inevitable, the public and its elected representatives had best relax and enjoy it. Historians and philosophers have always told us that nothing is inevitable in life but death and the belief that some things are inevitable—but no one expects the sense of history to pervade the thinking of politicians.

Another argument, with some surface gloss, was that public employees were being deprived of "rights" enjoyed by those in the private sector and that therefore public employees were being treated as "second-class citizens"—a line peddled assiduously by Jerry Wurf and his union brothers. This will be taken up at greater length in a succeeding chapter. At this point, however, it is sufficient to note that the courts have repeatedly stated that collective bargaining is not a "right" guaranteed by the Constitution, and that in certain instances it is violative of the Bill of Rights. A three-judge federal district court, in *Atkins* v. *City of Charlotte*, stated: "There is nothing in the United States Constitution which entitles one to have a contract with another who does not want it." And in a 1974 litigation against a state statute prohibiting collective bargaining in the public sector, another three-judge court declared:

While the First Amendment may protect the right of plaintiffs to associate and advocate, not all of their associational activi-

---

** States not listed have no collective-bargaining laws for public employees.

ties have the protection of that amendment. The State is not required to provide plaintiffs with a special forum in order to advocate their views. It is under no duty to provide a "guarantee that a speech will persuade or that advocacy will be effective."

The arguments that prevailed in the state legislatures were neither law nor logic. They were, very simply, politics and money, two forms of power that are very comprehensible even to politicians. When Walter Reuther put the AFL-CIO's Industrial Union Department and a million dollars behind Albert Shanker's drive to organize New York teachers, this was something that could be understood at all administrative levels, from the school board to the governor of the state. Unions, moreover, are political instruments funded by billions of dollars in income from the dues that collective bargaining and compulsory membership exact annually. As political instruments, unions must spend and spend and elect and elect in order to augment the size of their treasuries and the scope of their power.

Though there were no labor unions of any consequence in his day, James Madison was aware of the problem they pose when he wrote of the Constitution's "tendency to break and control the violence of faction," which he defined as any "number of citizens ... united and actuated by some common impulse of passion, or of interest, adverse to the rights of other citizens or ... the community." To this a special report, "The Role of Politics in Local Labor Relations," published by the UCLA *Law Review* added: "Public employee groups are now 'factions' in American society. ... They have become an organized force capable of achieving their own particular aims through the political process, aims that may not parallel and in fact are often adverse to those of the average citizen."

Through the political process, which includes lobbying, public-employee unions have, as a city official noted despairingly, "something which gives them two blows at the bargaining table" to a municipal negotiator's one. Even the get-out-the-vote drives of unions, which win them plaudits for their "devotion" to the electoral process, tilt in their favor since local elections usually command a small turnout of voters. But long before collective bargaining was instituted in many jurisdictions, unions were scoring advances through lobbying in city councils and state legislatures, which determined wages and conditions of employment for public employees. In fact, one of the arguments advanced by those seeking collective-bargaining statutes was that it would eliminate what had come to be a pernicious practice. Public-employee unions, however, simply added the bargaining table to the lobbying approach, maintaining the clout of one and the evil of the other.

Lobbying can be practiced at the local or the state level. In Los Angeles, the Fire and Police Protective League, unable to negotiate the kind of contract it wanted, was able to put sufficient pressure on the city council to win a $20-million pay increase. In New York City, when the mayor refused to negotiate a contract provision allowing policemen to moonlight, the state legislature reversed him. In Syracuse, New York, firemen who had not been able to get a forty-hour week at the bargaining table were able to extract that concession from a pliant and politically sensitive legislature. In Hartford, Connecticut, firemen refused to bargain with the nonelective city manager, as required by state law, because they had more influence with the city council.

In New York City, the Patrolmen's Benevolent Association went directly over the heads of elected officials in its battle to amend the city charter. At issue was a campaign promise of Mayor Lindsay to set up a civilian review board, which would investigate citizen complaints of police misconduct. Every major political figure in the state supported the creation of such a board, but the police union spent $500,000, sent out its members to collect 45,000 signatures for a referendum—and won. In Washington, D.C., in two successive years, teachers in the AFT local organized school children to demonstrate in favor of causes dear to the union.

The effect of union political activity is best demonstrated by the about-face of Mayor Lindsay in New York in his relations with public-employee unions. Having fought them for illegally going on strike but aware of the degree to which they contributed to Governor Rockefeller's election victories, Lindsay decided to join them. When he ran for reelection, he had the support of the Uniformed Sanitation Men and of AFSCME, both of which had potent political machines and which gave him their endorsement. The *New York Times* summed up the change that Big Labor pressure had induced in Lindsay when it editorialized: "In addition to giving [AFSCME] exclusive representation rights for municipal employees, Mayor Lindsay has been sympathetic with [the union's] efforts to gain an agency shop provision through negotiations and enabling legislation through the legislature." The Transit Workers Union was less subtle when it contributed $10,000 to Lindsay's campaign and, on the day after his reelection, presented a set of exorbitant demands to the City Transit Authority.

Public-employee unions are not shy about the uses of political power. Several years ago, AFSCME's newspaper, the *Public Employee,* announced the formation of a Department of Political Action and boasted that "the separate, beefed-up political action department ... is expected to bring AFSCME more effective political clout by more directly involving the union in specific election campaigns." Even more blunt was the Los Angeles Federation of Labor, which, on behalf of a striking Sacramento firefighters' local, voted censure of the mayor because he had supported a Sacramento City Council resolution requesting aid from California's forestry firefighting personnel. In a letter to the mayor, the federation stated its position clearly:

> This resolution was given searching consideration by our executive board, particularly as to the question of responsibility held by a representative of the labor movement elected to public office and what the labor movement has the right to expect from office holders put into office through its efforts.
>
> I don't suppose anybody can say that a labor-endorsed candidate—even one who earns his living directly within the labor movement—should be expected to act as a rubber stamp, mindlessly acceding to every demand placed upon him. However, it must be held that any responsible liberal—particularly one with ties to labor and especially one whose bread comes directly from labor—can never be wholly indifferent to the obligations inherent in his relationship to organized labor.
>
> This means, as we see it, that a person in your position ... should not arrogate to himself a stance of being above the battle. ...

It was this kind of reasoning that caused the *New York Times* to condemn roundly the Patrolmen's Benevolent Association when, in 1970, it endorsed a number of candidates for political office. The *Times* argued that this endorsement put the candidates in the position of being obligated to the PBA and created a clear conflict of interest, though less of a one than contributing directly to campaign treasuries. Such contributions are a matter of fact and record—and when public-employee union lobbyists approach members of state legislatures or city councils, the question of contributions hangs over the room like a Damoclean sword. But, as the UCLA special report noted, public-employee unions do not always wait for election day to flex their muscles:

> One final tactic that is available to public employee organizations deserves mention—the recall petition. A recall petition began in the city of Thornton, Colorado, after the city council voted against recognizing a union representing a number of city employees. Those named in the petition were the councilmen who had voted against recognizing the union, although the coun-

cilmen claimed that the city charter and various state statutes precluded them from recognizing any unions. This is perhaps the ultimate weapon.... By judicious use of the recall petition, organizations can retaliate against officials who defy the organizations' mandates even when there is no election in sight.

Is it any wonder then that the Economic Development Council of New York, after a six-month study, warned in 1973 that public-employee unions in that city had gotten to be so strong that city officials were finding it easier "to accede to union demands than to oppose them and face the danger of work stoppages, adverse political feedback from the indignant citizenry, and electoral retaliation by public employees and their supporters." The report further warned that public-employee unions were determining operational policies of public agencies and that they were influencing "such basic political issues as the allocation of public resources among alternative purposes, and the content and implementation of public programs."

The effect of the political weapon may be overestimated. There have been cases, though not many on state and local levels, in which union-sponsored candidates have lost. But politics goes hand in hand with money, particularly at a time when running for office is increasing geometrically in cost. It is here that public-sector unions—with their growing success in imposing on government an exclusive bargaining privilege, compulsory membership, and the agency shop—strike directly at the public interest. As membership grows, so does the union's bank account, and the use of union general funds and union facilities can mean the difference between victory and defeat to a candidate. Big Labor's successes in the electoral field, through the lavish use of union funds and facilities, were the subject of a report by Alexander Barkan, political commissar of the AFL-CIO and a power in the Democratic Party's inner councils, to the Executive Council of the AFL-CIO when it met at Bal Harbour, Florida, in October 1973.

The political programs of the trade union movement in 1972 achieved their primary goal: to retain a progressive Congress.... The results bear out the effectiveness of labor's political role in 1972.... Overall, COPE [the AFL-CIO's political arm] endorsed a total of 408 candidates for the U.S. House, U.S. Senate and governor. Of these 244 won their contests, a percentage just shy of 60. In the House races, 362 endorsements were made; 217 were winners. In the Senate, endorsements were made in 29 contests; 16 won. There were 11 winners among the 17 gubernatorial endorsements....

The overall percentage of union members registered nationally set a new high of between 75 and 80 percent, reaching the

90 percent range in five states and in the 80s in nine states, compared to a 65 percent registration in 1970. . . .

Besides manpower and money to conduct an effective political educational campaign, COPE assisted state and local central labor bodies by providing other tools needed to reach and motivate members.

Hundreds of thousands of leaflets and flyers, special radio announcements in support of labor-backed candidates, a million copies of voting records in various marginal races. . . . Layouts and photographs of the candidates were prepared for use by unions as special inserts in their official journals. . . . The hundreds of thousands of letters and other literature generated under this program were paid for, signed and distributed to their members by local unions. . . .

The AFL-CIO averred that it had spent about $2 million on these political campaigns. But this did not include the salaries of union officials who devoted full time to their political chores, the cost of data banks, of telephone canvassing, of printing and transportation, of a thousand-and-one costly items that candidates not enriched by the beneficence of the AFL-CIO could not afford. In the 1968 campaign, Big Labor spent an estimated $60 million to $100 million. Most of this was buried behind the facade of "local" committees, which do not have to report their expenditures, or represented direct out-of-pocket expenditures by unions for services to candidates. This, however, is not to minimize the overt cash flow.

Total contributions from Democratic and Republican party committees to Senate and House candidates in 1968 came to $3,329,302. Labor committees alone contributed $2,318,080 in those races. Of the $6.6 million contributed by all sources, thirty-five percent came from Big Labor. How union-endorsed candidates for the Senate fared can be seen from the following:*

---

*These figures come from *Financing the 1968 Election* by Herbert E. Alexander of the Citizens' Research Foundation. In describing how Labor National-Level Committees spent an admitted $7.1 million, Alexander makes some interesting observations:

"Labor's floor set-up at the Democratic Convention included walkie-talkies and mobile telephones under the direction of COPE's chief, Alexander Barkan. In addition, 221 union officials or members were delegates in 44 of the state delegations.

"Each year, COPE transfers approximately one-half of its funds to its state affiliates. While the usual reason given for these transfers is that the states can then decide to which candidates the money will be given, it is also true that the recipients of these funds will then not appear in the Federal reports which COPE files in Washington. In 1968, COPE reported transfers of $710,000 to state COPEs for redistribution to candidates. Other AFL-CIO unions distributed 55 million pieces of literature (local and state unions distributed an additional 60 million pieces), and COPE made and distributed 250,000 bumper stickers and 250,000 buttons."

| Candidates | Total Contributions | Union Contributions |
|---|---|---|
| John Gilligan (Ohio) | $204,594 | $180,344 |
| Birch Bayh (Ind.) | 108,045 | 79,645 |
| Gaylord Nelson (Wis.) | 105,439 | 61,250 |
| Joseph Clark (Pa.) | 74,899 | 47,299 |

What Big Labor spends in electing candidates of its choice and persuasion to state legislatures and city councils has never been estimated. The sum is great because local unions are aware that these bodies are easier to manipulate and more amenable to lobbying. The inquiring mind need look no further for an explanation of the willingness of the states to bow to union demands for compulsory collective bargaining and compulsory unionism.

# 8

# Studies in Collective
# Misery

"Government, long hostile to other monopolies, suddenly sponsored and promoted widespread labor monopolies, which democracy cannot endure, cannot control without destroying, and perhaps cannot destroy without destroying itself." These words by Henry C. Simon are the epigraph to the chapter on labor unions in 1974 Nobel economist F. A. Hayek's germinal book, *The Constitution of Liberty*. They are appropriate in a chapter on the experiences of widely different communities in coping with the onslaught of public-employee unions.

*Exhibit A.* A plaintive statement of their case by the Franklin County, Pennsylvania, commissioners in the course of collective bargaining with a public-employee union.

In order to avoid any confusion regarding the current labor dispute between the County of Franklin and AFSCME—AFL-CIO, the following explanation is respectfully submitted to the taxpayers of Franklin.

1. Are employees in Franklin County forced to work long and excessive hours for low wages?
The answer is emphatically no. Some employes within the county work only 20 hours per week. Many employes work 37½ hours per week. Within the courts, some employes work only during those periods when court is in session.
When confronted with a similar situation concerning a variation in hours of work the commissioners of Allegheny as well as several other counties insisted in union negotiations that all employes work a standard 40-hour week so as to equalize the situation. No such demand has been made by the Franklin County Commissioners.
Turning to the wages that Franklin County employes presently receive, a few illustrations serve to dramatically illustrate that as a group they are not underpaid. Aside from the smaller counties, certainly no one would expect Franklin County to compete with large counties such as Westmoreland and Delaware. Yet the extraordinary fact is that Franklin County is quite competitive. For example, a survey of clerical

and stenographic job classifications in these counties indicates the following average annual salaries:

| | Delaware | Westmoreland | Franklin |
|---|---|---|---|
| Clerical | $5,661 | $5,544 | $6,000 |
| Stenographic | 7,150 | 6,954 | 6,800 |

2. How did Franklin County get into its present bargaining dilemma?

In the opinion of some individuals, the present dilemma, in large part, has been caused by past generosity. Last year, the county provided among other things:

(1) A wage increase that on the average exceeded five per cent of the employes' salary.

(2) Modification of the vacation policy.

(3) Modification of the holiday schedule.

From the preceding, the simple conclusion that the end of the road must be reached is obvious. The country simply cannot continue to grant increases of the size and type that it has done in the past. In this regard the board of commissioners feels an obligation to the taxpayers.

3. Has the union been reasonable with regard to its demands?

The written proposal prepared by the union and offered to the county among other things demanded:

(1) A one year contract.

(2) (A) Average wage increase for probation officers of $2,147 plus a longevity increase of three per cent for those with five years or more of service amounting to approximately $112 plus a cost of living increase based upon the most recently published index. On the basis of the most recently published index, this would amount to an increase of approximately $570.45. Therefore, the total wage increase for probation officers would approximate $2,829 which the union is demanding be applied retroactively to Jan. 1, 1973. The union is also demanding an additional $700 raise be applied retroactively to Jan. 1, 1972.

(B) Average wage increase for clerical and stenographic personnel would amount to $2,000 plus a longevity increase of three per cent for those with five years or more of service amounting to approximately $210 plus a cost of living adjustment amounting to $360. Therefore, the total wage increase for these personnel would amount to $2,570. The union is demanding that this raise be applied retroactively to Jan. 1, 1972.

(3) The county shall provide eating facilities at all work locations.

(4) Seventeen paid holidays. In the event an employee is required to work on a holiday, he shall receive 2½ times his normal rate of pay for all holiday hours worked.

(5) Eighteen days' sick leave per year, accumulative to 200 days.

(6) Unlimited leave or absence without pay for any employe who is elected or appointed to a union office.

91

(7) Four personal leave days a year, accumulating to 10. The reason for taking these days does not have to be divulged

(8) Vacation schedule as follows:

| Years of Service | Number of Days |
|---|---|
| Less than five years | Three weeks |
| Five years but less than 10 | Four weeks |
| 10 years or more | Six weeks |

Any employe who is requested to work during his vacation shall receive four times his normal rate of pay for all vacation hours worked. Further, employes may accumulate unlimited vacation days.

(9) Overtime rate of 1½ times normal rate of pay for all hours worked over 7½ in one day or 37½ in one week as well all work performed on sixth day. All work performed on seventh day shall be compensable at double time.

(10) The county shall pay 100 percent of hospitalization for employe and dependents. The hospitalization plan shall include dental care, optical care and prevailing fee.

(11) A fully paid $10,000 life insurance plan with $2,250 paid up policy at time of retirement.

(12) Reimbursement for authorized travel at 16 cents per mile; $20 per day for meals and $25 for lodging in any given 24 hour period when overnight travel is required.

(13) County shall pay for the personal auto insurance of employes who are required to use their car for county business.

(14) County to supply uniforms and all protective devices where appropriate. In addition, county shall provide a uniform allowance of $200 per year for care of uniforms.

4. What would the above union demands cost the taxpayer in 1973–74?

After carefully evaluating and reviewing the union demands and the overall cost implications for the entire county, the commissioners estimate that the costs for just the salary, hospitalization and life insurance increases would approximate $698,800. Add to this amount a fixed payroll cost of eight per cent or for 55,904 increased Social Security, retirement, etc., the total cost would amount to $754,704.

If the commissioners were to agree to these demands, they would have to increase taxes by five mills.

Should the taxpayers of Franklin County assume such an increased burden?

The county commissioners think not.

*Exhibit B.* It is difficult to work up any sympathy for New York City's municipal government. Not only have the elected representatives bowed to the *force majeure* of unions in the one hundred or so bargaining units, but they have gone out of their way to deliver the city to union dominance. New York's Administrative Code goes far beyond a recognition of the political "realities" of that beleaguered city; it declares it to be "the policy of the city to favor and encourage" the very practices that are bringing it low. And, in setting up "impartial" arbitration machinery for the labor disputes in which it is perpetually entangled, it gives public-employee unions representation on arbitration boards—as well as the right to pass on those who are appointed to these boards as representatives of the public.*

Up until now, the increased power of locally operating public sector unions has generally manifested itself in the "economic" area. As a case in point, unions representing New York City's public employees have registered extensive economic gains for their memberships during the past decade and a half. Wages and salaries have risen out of all proportion to similar gains achieved by local private sector workers. Fringe benefits, such as pensions and retirement payments, have increased substantially, while public employees' obligations to assume part of the burden of the costs involved have been virtually eliminated.

Moreover, some New York City public employees are now eligible for benefits from no less than three retirement systems: (1) the public employer's retirement plan, (2) social security payments, and (3) disbursements from annuity funds, financed by City contributions, but administered by public employee unions.

Additional benefits obtained for public employees by public employees' unions include hospital insurance and direct payments by the City to the unions to purchase items ranging from eyeglasses and dental insurance to group life insurance programs and partial scholarships for children of union members attending institutions of higher learning.

To the extent that the costs of these generous employee benefits are now underwritten by the public employer, dues collected from public employees' unions are freed for other purposes. According to one estimate, in 1969, dues paid to unions by New York City employees totalled more than $10 million annually. This did not include payments by employees of the Board of Education, the Board of Higher Education, the Transit Authority, and various other non-municipal agencies operating within the City. Thus, a more realistic estimate (or "guesstimate") of total union income derived from members' dues payments might exceed $15 million per year.

Research and public information programs to influence public opinion as to the "proper" relationships which ought to apply in public sector labor relations, and intensive lobbying with legislative bodies to influence the content and application of public sector collective bargaining legislation, are but some of the uses to which the "freed" union funds may be devoted. Thus, the ev-

---

*What follows is condensed from the final section of a 137-page report by the Economic Development Council, which gives the full story of New York's public-employee unionism and which leans over backward to make a case for Big Labor.

idences of increased union power will increasingly become manifest in the "political" as well as the "economic" spheres.

As indicated in this report, public sector unions have attempted to extend the scope of collective bargaining to virtually every issue related to their members' working conditions, job descriptions, and job performance. These efforts have been largely successful and collective bargaining now covers items formerly considered to be legitimate management prerogatives. . . .

With unions now increasingly involved in determining a wide range of operational policies for public agencies, they are inevitably coming to exert a powerful influence on the outcome of such basic political issues as the allocation of public resources among alternative purposes, and the content and implementation of public programs.

To the extent that current trends in the content of public sector collective bargaining agreements increase operating costs for New York City's public programs, the City's capacity to provide minimally acceptable public services while avoiding imposition of economically deleterious tax burdens becomes increasingly questionable.

The City could be confronted with a set of policy alternatives, all unpleasant and some completely unacceptable. For example, it could choose to decrease the number of public employees, while simultaneously seeking to increase their productivity. Should personnel reductions adversely affect the quality of vital public services, such as education and protection of life and property, however, this could induce persons and institutions who can conveniently leave the City to do just that. This, in turn, would trigger an over-all economic downward spiral with a contracting tax base, declining public revenues, and diminishing investment in the productive enterprises which provide employment and the housing stock which furnishes shelter for the City's population.

At the same time, if the City chose to maintain the existing quantity and quality of public services, and to finance the added costs through additional taxes this, also, could persuade increasing numbers of productive business enterprises and tax-paying middle-class residents to take themselves elsewhere.

One important, albeit as yet unanswered, question relates to the City's ability to develop both intelligent, long-range strategies, and effective short-run tactics, to deal with union claims. At present, New York City, as the public employer, bargains with a number of public employees' unions, which have staff facilities capable of developing the strongest possible case for ever-increasing employee benefits. Because of limited financial resources and possibly other reasons, staff facilities available to the City's bargaining representatives have been less effective in working up supporting date to challenge union proposals. . . .

In New York City, the 400,000 locally employed public personnel, together with their families, friends, and sympathizers, constitute a political force that elected officials find extremely difficult to oppose. Moreover, the general citizenry usually has a greater short-range interest in avoiding the inconveniences resulting from interruptions in public services than a long-range concern for the harmful consequences of acceding to unreasonable union demands.

Unions are very much aware of their relatively strong power position vis-a-vis public employers. They can, and often do, engage in delaying tactics during both the initial direct negotiations phase of collective bargaining, and subsequently, if and when the legally prescribed impasse procedures are brought into play. If the City, as the public employer, refuses to accede to union demands, it is inevitably faced with the threat of a strike—if not with the real thing, itself. This has happened repeatedly, in spite of statutory prohibitions against strikes, work stoppages, inducements to strike, mass absences, or similar actions taken by public workers, to interrupt public services.

All things considered, a situation has developed in this City where the public employer inevitably finds it easier to accede to union demands than to oppose them and face the dangers of work stoppages, adverse political "feed-backs" from the indignant general citizenry, and electoral retaliation by public employees and their supporters. This has resulted in a policy of piecemeal, bit-by-bit concessions to continuously increasing union demands, with no discernible instances of successful attempts to reverse the course. . . .

The basic imbalance in the local political structure will inevitably result in formal procedures being implemented (or not implemented), interpreted (or misinterpreted) in ways unlikely to halt the progressive encroachment by the unions' demands on management's prerogatives and the public's interests. Any conceivable procedural pattern will by itself, in practice constitute little more than a paper barrier set up to resist the very tangible thrust of union power. Given these conditions, the results are not difficult to predict.

There is only one way to change this unsatisfactory situation. The general public must be made aware of the extremely harmful consequences which inevitably result from the labor relations policies which New York City officials have pursued in recent years. It will not be easy to carry out this type of basic public education program in a major metropolitan center, such as New York City, where special interests are many, strongly supported, lavishly financed, and assiduously defended, while the pubic interest is diffuse, ofttimes mute, and almost always unorganized. . . .

However, whatever the difficulties involved, there is no other way to bring about significant improvements in a public sector collective bargaining system, less than satisfactory in its present characteristics, and potentially disastrous in its long-range implications.

The City Administration is currently attempting to respond to its high labor costs by demanding from employees and middle management fundamental improvements in productivity. In effect, it is asking that employees, who have won substantial gains in pay and fringe benefits, now respond by providing greater production. . . .

There is an obvious risk in attempting to increase productivity through bargaining, however. Union leaders and their memberships are not likely to surrender hard-won gains without some "quid pro quo." If productivity becomes a matter of bargaining rather than a matter of management control and direction, each step toward increased productivity will cost something. In some cases, where management decision has already been bargained away, getting back control may require agreement between the City and the unions.

*Exhibit C.* The sick and the dying, from Victor Riesel's column.

. . . striking hospital workers linked themselves in human chains to block deliveries of foods to the deathly sick and blood plasma to those in emergency surgery.

There were fights. Police were injured. Arrests made. Snarling pickets howled lasciviously and earthily at nurses, supervisors, doctors and technicians entering hospitals to minister to the sick. These are the same physicians and semi-professionals who ofttimes go without food for eight and ten hours in emergencies to succor the injured, the poor and the clinic patients from the city's Dostoyevskian inner darkness of poverty.

No one really knows who did what. But there was sand in gas tanks. Auto tires on cars near the stricken 48 hospitals were slashed. Friends of mine in several hospitals were threatened if they reported for duty——though the hospitals had thousands of sick and injured and helpless.

*Exhibit D.* An Associated Press story by Timothy Harper from Hortonville, Wisconsin, which suffered one of the longest teachers' strikes in history.

Along Hortonville's mile-long Main Street, from the gravel pit to the animal hospital, the big issues are dimmed by small outrages.

Those who have participated in the bitter confrontation remember specific incidents, not great philosophies. At McHugh's Tap and Parker's Hardware Store they talk not of the right of teachers to strike for better pay but of the good hunting dog hanged by its own chain from a porch railing. . . .

"Those striking teachers did it," they agree.

Long after the stirring rhetoric is forgotten . . . the people of Hortonville remember merchandise missing from their store shelves, slashes in their truck tires, paint splashed on their homes, and the teachers who called them "dumb farmers." . . .

This didn't sit well with Hortonville's 1,500 residents, who are outnumbered by the 1,900 students at the sprawling one-story red-brick district school on the edge of town. . . .

In January, when the teachers staged a "mini-strike," refused overtime and counseled students to make trouble for substitutes in case there was a strike, parents became irate.

"This one teacher told me I could do anything I wanted if they went on strike and we had a substitute," said Rich Greisbach, 18, a high school senior. "He said that anything that happened while he was on strike didn't matter because he was coming back." ...

Rallying to the strident protests of the Wisconsin Education Association, 500 teachers and public employees from across the state came to Hortonville to join the picket lines. ...

More than 200 law officers from surrounding communities followed them to back up Hortonville's lone policeman. Seventy-five arrests were made on charges of obstructing police as demonstrators tried to block streets, sidewalks and school doorways. ...

Many of the replacement teachers, even those offered contracts for next year, say they don't want to stay in Hortonville.

"I don't think I'd want to live in a town that's been torn apart like this one," [a teacher] said. "Everyone here has been touched by it, and it's something you can't walk away from but you'll remember it all your life."

"We may never get over this," said [village president Paul] Steinert, shaking his head sadly and slowly at the village he has presided over for a decade.

That is the only point everyone agrees upon.

Labor peace? The public welfare? Orderly government? Prosperity for all? *Quod erat demonstrandum.*

# 9

# Public-Employee Unions
## vs. the People

It is frequently said by proponents of compulsion in government-labor relations that the closed shop and mandated collective bargaining are necessary to protect government employees from their rapacious employer. To sustain this conclusion, these proponents have had to strike out at the merit system under civil service or to indulge in casuistic arguments over nonexistent differences between the "merit system" and the "merit principle." Civil service commissions, it is asserted, are merely arms of government, representing the employer rather than the employee—although those who have had dealings with bureaucracy at the federal, state, or local level may argue that these commissions afford too much protection to inefficiency and arrogance. A "no layoff" policy in the United States Postal Service, dictated by the postal unions, has led directly to a drastic decline in its ability to deliver the mail expeditiously and well, not to mention a growing deficit.

It is further stated that compulsory collective bargaining is necessary to make wages, fringe benefits, and working conditions in the government establishment "comparable" to those in the private sector. That this is sheer poppycock is widely known in Washington, D.C., where it is impossible to hire a private secretary at less that a starting salary of $9,000 a year because she can do better in government. This may be a local and subjective circumstance. But the broad picture was clearly drawn by the *Washington Monthly,* a publication of distinctly liberal orientation:

> From 1960 to 1970, the annual cost of salaries (excluding benefits which now raise the cost of each employee an additional 35 percent) for Federal workers grew from $13.2 billion to $30.5 billion. Including state and local employees, the total cost of public employment rose from $39.6 billion to $106.8 billion during the same period. Between 1961 and 1971 the average earnings of all public employees rose more than 80 percent while the average for workers in private industry increased by only 53 percent. . . .

98

Federal employees are among the highest-paid workers in the country. One-third of all Federal workers on GS scale are paid more than $15,000 and receive supplemental benefits equal to one-third of their salaries. Officially, Federal white-collar employees are supposed to be paid salaries "comparable" to what they would earn in private industry. But in practice, many Federal employees, especially those in the middle grades and those just below the highest paid "supergrades," are paid significantly more than they would get on the open market. . . . And the Federal government has become so top-heavy that, for example, 52 percent of the employees of the Department of Transportation are GS-12s or above. The starting salary for a GS-12 is $18,463.*

With more than sixteen million Americans on the public payroll, or roughly one in six of those employed, it can hardly be said that this substantial segment of the labor force is the victim of wage discrimination. But the issues of public-sector unionism and the all-inclusive compulsory collective bargaining, which Big Labor is attempting to thrust down the throat of government, go far beyond wages. What wages are paid in the public sector are, after all, the province of Congress and the fifty state legislatures, which have so lavishly rewarded their charges. At the heart of the matter, however, is the vital question of constitutional democracy in these United States. Can government as we have practiced it in this country survive the imposition of a new branch, superior in power to the three established by the Founding Fathers? Are the rights and duties of a sovereign people, entrusted to their elected representatives, to be surrenderd to a Big Labor oligarchy responsible only to itself? If these questions sound hortatory, consider these words of Professor Clyde Summers, an outspoken defender of compulsory unionism and therefore nowhere suspect of an "antilabor" bias:

> Unions, in bargaining, are not private organizations but are governmental organizations garbed with the cloak of legal authority . . . The union is, in short, the employee's economic government. The union's power is the power to govern.

Professor Summers' words, embarrassingly frank in the view of those who advocate even greater union power, were descriptive of the situation in the private sector where labor leaders not only determine wages and working conditions but, under powers arrogated to them by the NLRB, also control means and methods of production and even the right of an employer to subcontract or to go out of business. When ap-

---

*"Government Unions: The New Bullies on the Block," *Washington Monthly*, December 1974.

plied to the public sector, via the instrumentality of compulsory unionism and collective bargaining, union power creates a situation in which a small minority within the body politic assumes independent government control over the vast majority—the people—control which gives its special interests the color of law. In the private sector, compulsory unionism has deprived industry of its right to due process and property, wage earners of their freedom of association. In the public sector, it would also deprive the people of the sovereignty guaranteed to them under the Constitution.

All of this is grandly brushed aside by academic and Big Labor proponents of compulsory collective bargaining in the public sector. Their counterargument is not based on fact or logic or the national experience. Instead, the country is told, Big Labor is "bound" to have its way; therefore, Congress must speed it on. With nothing more than his abounding grace to sustain him, Professor Joel Seidman can write that public employees "are unlikely to be satisfied with bargaining rights inferior to those accorded employees in the private sector." Like others who carry his banner, he ignores completely the essential differences between the public and the private sectors—differences which are both political and economic.

In their most basic form, those differences can be easily observed. Industry is the servant of the marketplace. If, by acceding to the demands of the United Auto Workers, the Ford Motor Company has to price its automobiles beyond the range of consumer tolerance, it goes out of business. The union, when it has exhausted its rhetoric, eventually must consider the correlation of wages, prices, and profits. In any labor-management dispute, of course, the cards are stacked against industry by the various federal labor statutes as they are interpreted by the NLRB. A corporation is a voluntary association, whereas compulsory unionism gives the union its conscript troops.

But this is a matter for concern for those who are impressed into the service of Big Labor. Without the compulsory unionism aspect, labor-management would be a perfectly legitimate contest in a free society. The consumer may sometimes be the proverbial innocent bystander, and he may suffer to a degree. But in most instances, his interests are only minimally affected. If the UAW strikes Ford, he can buy a Chevrolet. If pickets bar his entry into the A & P, he can always shop at the neighborhood Safeway. In the United States, he is struck down only when strike action shuts off his telephone or his electric power. In that case, there are no alternative services to which he can turn.

But government, by its very nature, is a monopoly. There

are no competing post offices, police departments, public school systems, or sanitation units for the citizen to turn to. The people are victimized directly and immediately when Big Labor sets out to "shut down" states and municipalities. The strike is not against federal, state, or local government but against the people, (1) because they are deprived of essential services for which they have already paid, and (2) because government is their agent—in a real sense, their property, which under the Constitution cannot be taken from them without due process.

Professor Seidman is, despite his strong emotional and professional ties to organized labor, aware of this, even as he is aware that there is neither historical nor moral justification for his statement that "union-management relationships are likely to be most satisfactory where the law establishes exclusive bargaining rights for the majority union. . . ." Satisfactory for whom? Samuel Gompers, whose dedication to trade unionism cannot be gainsaid, saw it differently; he asserted that American workers "adhere to voluntary institutions in preference to compulsory systems which are held to be *not only impractical but a menace to their rights, welfare, and liberty*" (emphasis added). Mr. Justice Brandeis, whose humanitarianism is enshrined in our child-labor laws, was far more specific:

> It is not true that the success of labor unions necessarily means a perfect monopoly. The union, in order to maintain and preserve for its members industrial liberty, must be strong and stable. It need not include every member of the trade. Indeed, it is desirable for both the employer and the union that it should not. Absolute power leads to excesses and to weakness. Neither our character nor our intelligence can long bear the strain of unrestricted power.

"A nucleus of unorganized labor," said Brandeis, "will check oppression by the union as the union checks oppression by the employer." The wisdom of his words has since been amply demonstrated in right-to-work states, where the unions have been more responsive to the rights and prerogatives of their members precisely because the tyranny that Brandeis deplored and that we see in compulsory-union states can only be counterproductive for the Big Labor hierarchy. Proponents of compulsory unionism in the public sector have evaded the weakness of their argument by stating that the "public" wants collective bargaining by public-employee unions, and that it is in response to public pressure that state legislatures have enacted this practice into statute.

How far this is from the truth can be quickly ascertained

by studying the results of an in-depth poll taken by Opinion Research Corporation of Princeton, New Jersey, whose reputation for accuracy and objectivity is unmatched in the field. ORC asked its large and scientifically selected sampling these questions:*

Should your state legislature pass a law which would allow agreements requiring employees to join or pay dues to a union in order to work for the state, county, and municipal governments?

|  | Percentages | | |
|---|---|---|---|
|  | Yes | No | No Opinion |
| Total U.S. public | 10 | 78 | 12 |
| Union members | 18 | 74 | 8 |
| Union families | 16 | 75 | 9 |
| Republican | 10 | 78 | 12 |
| Democrat | 11 | 78 | 11 |
| Independent | 9 | 83 | 8 |

Should the U.S. Congress pass a law which would allow agreements requiring employees to join or pay dues to a union in order to work for the Federal government?

|  | Percentages | | |
|---|---|---|---|
|  | Yes | No | No Opinion |
| Total U.S. public | 11 | 79 | 10 |
| Union members | 19 | 71 | 10 |
| Union families | 17 | 74 | 9 |
| Republican | 11 | 78 | 11 |
| Democrat | 13 | 77 | 10 |
| Independent | 9 | 84 | 7 |

Which of these arrangements do you favor for Federal, state, and local government employees?
1. A person can work for the government whether or not he belongs to a union
2. A person can go to work for the government if he doesn't belong to a union, but has to join after he is hired to hold his job
3. A person can get a job with the government only if he already belongs to a union
4. No opinion

|  | Percentages | | | |
|---|---|---|---|---|
|  | 1. | 2. | 3. | 4. |
| Total U.S. public | 83 | 10 | 1 | 6 |
| Union members | 77 | 17 | 2 | 4 |
| Union families | 77 | 16 | 2 | 5 |
| Republican | 85 | 7 | 2 | 6 |
| Democrat | 81 | 11 | 2 | 6 |
| Independent | 87 | 9 | 0 | 4 |

*See Appendix I for the complete results.

This preponderance of opinion against compulsory union-ism and compulsory collective bargaining in the public sector notwithstanding—a preponderance known long before it was reduced to statistical terms—"authorities" in labor law with few exceptions have accepted and propagated that perverse metonym that a microscopic part of the body politic, union officials, represent the whole of the American people. Yet the ORC poll discloses that union compulsion is rejected by the public as a whole, by union members and their families, and by those who are affiliated with one or another of the major political parties to almost the same degree.

Those who profess expertise, either as scholars or as pro-fessionals in the field of labor-management relations, shy away from the inevitable question. If only a scattering of Americans support legislation that introduces compulsion into public-sector unionism, why has one state legislature after an-other enacted statutes that impose it on government and em-ployee? Legislators may not always be as responsive to the popular will as some may wish, but they do not go out of their way to antagonize their constituencies without good rea-son. It does not require Pope's "microscopic eye" to detect the answer.

That answer can be found in part in the definition of "con-stituency." Once upon a time, when an elected official spoke of his "constituents," he was refering to all of the voters in his electoral subdivision—with an anxious eye turned to the majority that had elected him. Big Labor, with its unsur-passed power of purse and organization, and with its privileged access to an increasingly unionized media, has changed this. Elections cost money. And though candidates sometimes win without union support and financing, that mountain gets harder to climb with each passing election. Once upon a time, business could throw its financial weight on the side of sym-pathetic candidates. But the selective and punitive use of the Corrupt Practices Act, invoked almost exclusively against the business community, is drying up that well. Big Labor knows that the hand of friendship must be kept well and continu-ously greased. With compulsory unionism in the public sector coming up before the Ninety-fourth Congress, unions in both the private and public sector saw to it that every Democratic member of the House Education and Labor Committee, which must pass on such legislation, was greased well in ad-vance.

The tally:

| | |
|---|---|
| Michael Blouin of Iowa | $36,900.00 |
| Paul Simon of Illinois | 34,400.00 |

| | |
|---|---|
| John Dent of Pennsylvania | 29,275.00 |
| Robert Cornell of Wisconsin | 29,175.00 |
| Frank Thompson of New Jersey | 26,300.00 |
| Ron Mottl of Ohio | 23,830.00 |
| Lloyd Meeds of Washington | 22,550.00 |
| William Clay of Missouri | 18,850.00 |
| John Brademas of Indiana | 18,700.00 |
| Ted Risenhoover of Oklahoma | 18,600.00 |
| William Lehman of Florida | 18,550.00 |
| Leo Zeferetti of New York | 15,062.00 |
| James O'Hara of Michigan | 14,300.00 |
| Phillip Burton of California | 13,050.00 |
| Dominick Daniels of New Jersey | 12,550.00 |
| George Miller of California | 12,000.00 |
| Tim Hall of Illinois | 11,150.00 |
| William Ford of Michigan | 10,650.00 |
| Mario Biaggi of New York | 7,400.00 |
| Joseph Gaydos of Pennsylvania | 6,450.00 |
| Ike Andrews of North Carolina | 6,250.00 |
| Edward Beard of Rhode Island | 5,350.00 |
| Patsy Mink of Hawaii | 3,560.00 |
| Shirley Chisholm of New York | 2,125.00 |
| Carl Perkins of Kentucky | 500.00* |

As has been elsewhere demonstrated, money is but the tip of the iceberg of union contributions to campaigns. And, legislatively speaking, Big Labor has strong and well-organized lobbies that roam the halls of Congress, the corridors of state legislatures, and the waterholes neighbor to city halls. It is at these places that many national and state/local legislators meet the only "constituents" that count to them. A lobbyist for a big corporation can be politely—and sometimes rudely—turned away. But when the NEA or AFSCME or the other public-section unions rattle the millions in their political pockets or refer to the number of people they can assign to canvassing, legislative majorities pay close attention.

Those in Congress and elsewhere whose political future depends on Big Labor's cash and goodwill have attempted to cloak their drive for a federal law to compel unionism in the public sector in a popular demand for "fairness" to public employees and to the unions that would inherit their freedom of action. They have offered casuistic justification for the nature of the legislation proposed in Washington or the vari-

---

*Perkins was a shoo-in and spent $4,287.50 on his reelection campaign. A scattering of Republicans received sums ranging from zero to $2,300.00, with the exception of Peter Peyser of New York, who received $21,555. For a full tabulation of labor contributions as compared to total contributions, see Appendix II.

ous state capitals—legislation that ignores and subverts the rights of minorities and majorities both. By intermediate steps, they have leap-frogged from the constitutionally legitimate right of public employees to join unions of their choice, which few today would deny them, to a closed or agency shop. In this they have forgotten the Gompers warning that "no lasting gain has ever come from compulsion." In the long run, Big Labor will either have to retreat or declare a union dictatorship over the country. Until that time, it is compelled to struggle with the oxymoronic slogan "free compulsory unionism."

With an overflowing heart, Professor Seidman has written: "Since an exclusive bargaining agent has the duty to represent fairly all employees in the unit, it is not unreasonable to permit the [collective-bargaining] unit to require some payment toward the expense of operating a union from all who receive its services." This avowal of what might be regarded as a laborist eminent domain over the public employee's work product also delivers to public-sector unions the right to tax, which is held exclusively by government. The payment of dues by nonunion members in an agency-shop situation is taxation pure and simple, with the funds collected being employed for purposes and activities frequently repugnant to those who have refused to join the union. The American colonies went to war over this.

What "fairness" to Wurf, Shanker & Co. consists of is one question; why it should be imposed by law is another. Public-sector collective bargaining not only casts aside the rights of nonunion public employees. It imposes strains on government that are transmitted to the taxpayer, who clearly has no call on fairness. Collective bargaining has driven up tax rates, dislocated orderly government budgeting, subjected municipalities and their citizens to unconscionable strains, brought loss of employment to those least capable of sustaining shutdowns, and introduced jungle law in cities subjected to illegal strikes. It has deprived young people of adequate education and sent them into the streets for long periods of time. What price, then, the "fairness" that translates into power concentrations and the subversion of law.

# 10

# Popular Sovereignty vs. Big Labor Feudalism

That the majority of Americans opposes compulsory unionism and mandated collective bargaining in the public sector is, in a narrow sense, a political consideration. That they are ignored by the nation's majority party represents the drift towards the tragic condition now afflicting England.* It also reflects the decline and possible end of the popular sovereignty upon which the American Republic was founded. Ironically, the piecemeal maceration of that sovereignty is vociferously celebrated by elements that cloak their activities in the demagogic cry, "Power to the People."

In recent years, the word *sovereignty* has become unfashionable because it is misunderstood; but as Sylvester Petro notes in a brilliant essay, "the reality which it has grown to identify over the centuries remains as vital to the existence of decent, well-ordered society as ever." Petro continues:

> The need for undiluted government power, if people are to be free and secure in their daily activities, does not magically disappear merely because some writers, especially self-styled pluralists, choose to put quotation marks around the word "sovereignty." Neither is analysis improved by replacing it with the hopelessly vague but more fashionable expression, "the normal American political process." A collection of people lacking a government endowed with supreme——*sovereign*——power within its appointed sphere of action, is not a pluralist nation, is not a nation at all, not an ordered society, but a simple aggregate of human beings living in a condition probably best

---

*See Anthony Lejeune's "London Letter" in the January 31, 1975, *National Review:* "[Prime Minister] Wilson's government was, in fact, virtually helpless, tied hand and foot by its subordination to the unions . . . Its only weapon was the vaunted 'social contract,' under which the unions were supposed to restrain their demands in return for socialist policies from the government. The socialist policies were delivered all right, in plenty; but, of course, the unions continued exactly as before. . . ."

described as anarchic, although it might well also be called feudalistic.*

To some, sovereignty has a monarchical penumbra, yet it is the very core of the American system. Deriving from the *Declaration of Independence* and the Constitution, American sovereignty resides in the people who exercise it through their elected representatives. Neither the executive nor the legislative branch can assign its sovereign powers as carefully spelled out in the Constitution—a document which, having limited those powers, specifically states in Article 10 of the Bill of Rights that "The powers not delegated to the United States by the Constitution, nor prohibited by it to the States, are reserved to the States respectively, or to the people." The authors of that Constitution drew much of their political and intellectual sustenance from John Locke. In his *Second Treatise of Government*, he spoke directly to the point:

> There is one way whereby ... a government may be dissolved, and that is when he who has the supreme executive power neglects and abandons that charge....
> Whensoever ... the legislature shall transgress this fundamental rule of society, and either by ambition, fear, folly, or corruption ... put into the hands of another, an absolute power over the lives, liberties, and estates of the people, by this breach of trust they forfeit the power the people had put in their hands for quite contrary ends....
> [Those who dilute the authority of the established government are] highly guilty of the greatest crime I think a man is capable of.... And he who does it is justly to be esteemed the common enemy and pest of mankind, and is to be treated accordingly.

Woodrow Wilson, whose writings on government and the Congress in his academic days remain classics in political science, approached the point somewhat differently, but to the same end. "The business of government," he wrote, "is to see that no other organization is as strong as itself; to see that no group of men, no matter what their private business is, may come into competition with the authority of society." Wilson and Locke might have been writing today. Equally contemporary is a decision of the Supreme Court in 1793: "Let a *State* be considered as subordinate to the people; but let everything else be subordinate to the *State*. The *latter* part of this position is equally necessary with the former" *(Chisholm* v. *Georgia.)* And two state supreme courts have

---

*"Sovereignty and Compulsory Public-Sector Bargaining," Sylvester Petro, *Wake Forest Law Review* (March 1974).

spelled out these strictures with particular reference to collective bargaining.

In *City of Springfield* v. *Clouse* (1947), the Missouri Supreme Court ruled:

> Under our form of government, public office or employment never has been and cannot become a matter of bargaining and contract. . . . This is true because the whole matter of qualifications, tenure, compensation and working conditions for any public service involves the exercise of legislative powers. Except to the extent that all the people have settled these matters by writing them into the Constitution, they must be determined by their chosen representatives who constitute the legislative body. It is a familiar principle of constitutional law that the legislature cannot delegate its legislative powers and any attempted delegation thereof is void. . . . If such powers cannot be delegated, they surely cannot be bargained or contracted away, and certainly not by any administrative or executive officers who cannot have any legislative powers.

The Connecticut Supreme Court in 1951 (*Norwalk Teachers Association* v. *Board of Education*), in a decision that tacitly gave the legislature the power to prohibit both unionization and collective bargaining in the public sector, said:

> Under our system, the government is established and run for all of the people. They can delegate it to a government which they create and operate by law. They can give to that government the power and authority to perform certain duties and furnish certain services. The government so created and enpowered must employ people to carry on its task. These people . . . occupy a status entirely different from those who carry on a private enterprise. They serve the public welfare and not a private purpose. . . .

The function of a union is not the public welfare but the special interest, ideally, of its members. In practice that special interest is usually identifiable with the leadership and the union hierarchy. This is implicit in George Meany's attitude that *l'état, c'est moi,* his repeated assertion that violation of the law by unions is morally justifiable, and the role he and his associates have played in partisan politics. It is, as well, implicit in the attitude of AFSCME, AFT, NEA, TWU, and other public-employee unions that municipalities must despoil essential services in order to satisfy their demands. That the union interest frequently runs counter to the needs and the rights of governmental units, of the public, or of nonunion employees is frankly acknowledged by the leadership, although it attempts to confound fact and reason by a pretense that Big Labor *is* the people.

108

To achieve its ends, Big Labor must first organize, by whatever means are necessary, in order to confront city, state, or federal government at the bargaining table or the picket line. It makes no bones of the fact that in this confrontation, it is setting itself up as a co-equal force with government. Unless government bows to all of its demands, it threatens to impose its will on the people and their elected representatives. Collective bargaining, as union literature quickly discloses, is deemed a form of warfare against "the bosses." If collective bargaining fails to get for the union what it has demanded, the strike follows. But to strike against the government is by definition a form of insurrection. In his Farewell Address, George Washington said it loud and clear: "The very idea of the right and power of the people to establish government presupposes the duty of every individual to obey the established government." This the collective-bargaining process patently negates.

To facilitate the organizing process, the union must instill a spirit of militancy and hostility into the public employees it hopes to bring into the ranks. But civil servants tend to be complacent. Whatever complaints they may have, they are grudgingly aware that they receive good-to-better pay, that their fringe benefits and pension rights are far superior to those of their counterparts in the private sector, that they have longer vacations, and that except under extreme circumstances they will never be fired. This complacency must be transmuted into active hostility by manufacturing grievances where none exists or by exaggerating those that do. The public employee must be led to believe that the union will get him the promotions that he has not been able to earn under the merit system, that the union will protect him from putatively rapacious supervisors and liberate him from the "work ethic." Any sense of duty that he may have towards his job and the public is deliberately eradicated.

To this must be added the social pressures that union organizers so skillfully employ. The nonunion public employee is subjected to ridicule, intimidation, and worse. If he insists on the right to abstain from membership granted by presidential order and its state analogues, he is accused of being a "fink," a "free-loader," and an "easy rider"—and often subjected to violence once the inevitable strike has been called. In short, compulsion and coercion are the order of the day. At the same time, massive public-relations campaigns are mounted to convince the public that only official obduracy and heartlessness are preventing a "peaceful" solution of the dispute via the collective bargaining that is a "right" of workers in the private sector.

Public-employee unions first seek recognition, the camel's nose under the tent, and the privileges that go with that recognition. Then they demand exclusive representation and bargaining "rights," thereby depriving public employees of a choice between competing unions or the right to bargain for themselves. The next step is the demand for the compulsory membership of all employees or an agency shop, which exacts dues and other assessments from those who do not subscribe to the union's political program or who disapprove of the union's tactics. Recently, some unions have been asking for the equivalent of the hiring hall—a procedure whereby the state or municipality must hire only through the union. At some point after recognition has been granted, the union begins to prepare for a strike, on the theory that this is the only way it can "politicize" its members and command their absolute loyalty.

That from the very first step this process is an assault on the sovereignty of government—which means the viability of government as well—is brushed aside by Big Labor and its apologists who invoke the "private-sector analogy," an argument that, as Professor Petro points out, simply professes that two wrongs make a right.

Another factor in the equation strikes hard at the private-sector analogy. Industry cannot force the consumer to pay prices for goods or services that have been forced up as a result of collective bargaining. It cannot coerce anyone to work for it. But government *does* force every consumer to work for it via the instrumentality of taxation, which every year devours a larger share of the taxpayer's income. The wages and fringe benefits that public-sector collective bargaining, as a starter, exacts from government must come from the consumer's pocket. The union is therefore assuming the coercive powers of government when as a result of collective bargaining it increases the tax rate. As Professor Petro says:

> Governmental sovereignty and public-sector collective bargaining are contradictory, as well in practice as in logic. The contradiction is so corrosive, indeed, as to dissolve into meaninglessness. Sovereignty *means* the supreme and unchallengeable power of compulsion. How can a genuine sovereign be *forced* by a private person or agency to do something and remain sovereign? . . .
> There is no doubt that governments which do not draft their civil servants subject themselves in a material degree to the economic laws ruling the private sector. Governments are constantly competing with private employers for employees. . . .
> There is, however, nothing incompatible with sovereignty in such practice. . . . On the contrary, sovereignty is critically impaired when, after volunteering for government service, civil or

military, the volunteers, either themselves as individuals or through representatives, challenge the rules, orders, and commands of the government; when . . . they insist upon an effective voice in formulating those rules, orders, and commands. If a platoon leader says, "Take that hill!" and those under his command are authorized to refuse to do so, sovereignty is nonexistent. But it is nonexistent also if they are authorized to compel a delay in the execution of the command pending further discussion.*

The question of sovereignty and of the government's right and power to carry out the people's business as their elected representatives see fit—given the constraints and restraints that getting reelected impose—is not an academic one. Public-employee unions are not merely demanding the power to determine wages and working conditions. As the record shows, they are neck-deep in setting public policy on every aspect of management—promotions, qualifications, seniority, curriculum, educational content. Jerry Wurf has not been shy about insisting on a "power relationship where public officials and policymakers respect you as equals and deal with you"—the private-sector analogy with a vengeance when one recalls Walter Reuther's contention that unions should sit with management to determine what will be produced, how it will be produced, how materials should be allocated, etc., etc., etc. The merit system itself, which has been the greatest protector of public employees from reprisal by extragovernmental meddlers, was attacked by Wurf in 1969, when he was feeling his oats and his muscle, in a proclamation that public-sector union laws "must make it unmistakably clear that where there is a conflict between the desires of the parties, as evidenced by the collective-bargaining agreement, and merit system rules and regulations, that the contract shall prevail"—an assertion in favor of a new spoils system.

Can public-sector collective bargaining function without destroying the fabric of viable government? The answer is self-evident. Once a governmental unit has signed a collective-bargaining agreement, it has surrendered its right to the

---

*The military analogy is an excellent one. A soldier is not compelled to obey an illegal command, but he cannot decide that he is tired of fighting and needs a vacation or that he will not wear the uniform because he does not like its cut. Similarly, a police officer would have the right to disobey an order to shoot every third man in suppressing a violent demonstration and a tax collector to refuse to bash in the head of everyone deemed delinquent. However, the police officer cannot decide what laws he would like to enforce or a tax collector determine what tax rate he believes just—just as a teacher cannot conclude that the teaching of reading and writing is irrelevant, the NEA notwithstanding.

labor and loyalty of its employees. If the union calls a strike then the employee must submit to the strike call. Under the terms of the contract, government has relinquished to the union the employee's primary loyalty. If the employee defies the union, then he is subject to union discipline and endangering his future employment. The strike is, as more than one court has ruled, "rebellion," yet Victor Gotbaum, one of AFSCME's makers and shakers, has candidly said that "you can't have collective bargaining and take away the right to strike." In the bargaining process itself, negotiators on both sides are usurping the legislative function of setting public policy on wages, conditions of employment, qualifications for employment, and any other matters taken up in the contract. In short, by the very process of collective bargaining in public sector, the union asserts and imposes its sovereignty over government and the *res publica*.

This, of course, is most evident when the union resorts to the strike as the instrumentality of that sovereignty. For that reason, apologists and strategists for public-sector unionism have cast about for a substitute that will not so obviously offend the public or expose the rawness of public-sector union power. Increasingly, the public has become aware that unions are indeed what they have been called, "professional strike agencies," whether or not they call a strike or disguise it under such terms as "blue flu" and "job action." The public, too, has become aware that it was not an idle boast when Jerry Wurf said that his union "always" wins its strikes.

The substitute proposed, somewhat like the Jamesian "equivalent of war," is binding arbitration. Two sovereign powers, government and Big Labor, finding that they cannot agree, do not take to the trenches but submit their dispute to an "impartial" arbitrator. In fact, of course, the arbitrator is seldom impartial. He owes his employment to the unions and officials who have sought him out, and it is his job to placate both of them, with no thought to the people who must pay the bill. If the union has demanded an increase of X percent and management, with a pistol to its head, has offered ¼ X percent, then the "impartial" arbitrator can make a statesmanlike compromise of ½ X percent, with no thought that the state or municipality cannot afford the ¼ X percent in the first place. The arbitrator is also influenced by the developing relationship between administrators and union negotiators in which one hand washes the other, an arrangement of considerable coziness but one leaving the public sucking wind.

Compulsory arbitration is subversive as well of the commonweal as of the principle of governmental sovereignty. It takes the legislative process one step further away from those

112

who alone can legitimately exercise it. Arbitrators are accountable and responsible to no one, least of all to the popular sovereign—the people. And they become, in effect, "more powerful in the disposition of community resources, gain greater control of the taxing process, than the citizens and their elected representatives possess."*

One of the arbitrators in a dispute between the city of Marquette, Wisconsin, and its policemen's union asked afterward:

> Who elected the arbitration panel of which I am a part? To whom is this panel responsible or responsive? What pressures can the citizens of the City of Marquette bring to bear on the panel? How do they express their satisfaction or dissatisfaction with the panel's decision? . . .
> With no reflection on their integrity intended, it is simple that the two panel members who endorse the majority decisions are not citizens of the City of Marquette nor even of Marquette County. And yet their decision, which has very far-reaching implications, and will ultimately, no doubt, result in increased taxes for the people of the City of Marquette, is final and binding upon those people, their government and its employees.*

The public so far has not been inspired to battle for its own sovereignty. It sees its cities slipping into impotence and bankruptcy, but it perceives no connection between what the unions are doing to municipal government and what is happening in the city schools. Tycoon and taxi driver feel that they are not involved, that what they read in the newspapers—when the newspapers tell them anything—is just a fight between city hall bosses and Big Labor bosses. They do not realize that the direct taxes they pay—and the far greater indirect taxation to those union treasuries that purchase public officials—are a result of the permissiveness that comes of an elected officialdom that must go to the unions for campaign contributions or perish. They are not yet aware that the combination of political action and public-sector collective bargaining is creating, in the words of a former assistant general counsel of the UAW,

> a mutual back-scratching mechanism, whereby public-employee representatives and politicians each reinforce the other's interest and domain, with the individual public employee and the individual citizen left to look on, while his employment condition

*National League of Cities et al. v. Hon. Peter J. Brennan and State of California v. Hon. Peter J. Brennan. Brief of the Public Service Research Council as amicus curiae.
*Quoted in Joan Zeldon McAvoy, "Binding Arbitration of Contract Terms: A New Approach to the Resolution of Dispute in the Public Sector," Columbia Law Review 72 (November 1972): 1192.

and the tax rate and public policies generally are being decided by entrenched and mutually supportive government officials and collective-bargaining representatives over whom the public has diminishing control.**

Rome fell because of its bread and circuses, but at least the populace got the bread and enjoyed the circuses. Today, both the bread and the fun are going to Big Labor while the wheels of government turn even more erratically and the cost of government sabotages the productivity that makes survival in a technological society possible. It took hundreds of tragic years for mankind to lift itself from the brutishness of feudalism. With Big Labor feudalism knocking at the door, and the fate of the individual hanging on the whim and ambition of the labor lords, it has taken less than two decades to reopen a chapter of history once thought permanently closed.

---

**Kurt L. Hanslowe, "The Emerging Law of Labor Relations in Public Employment" (Ithaca, N.Y.: New York School of Industrial and Labor Relations, Cornell University, 1967).

# 11

# Above the Law? Perhaps!

"In many liberal minds," a maverick C. Wright Mills has written, "there seems to be an undercurrent that whispers: 'I will not criticize the unions and their leaders. There I draw the line.' This . . . keeps them leftward and socially pure." Advocates of unbridled union power maintained their social standing by remaining silent when British Labourite Barbara Wootton, in a burst of frankness, said: "It is in fact the business of a union to be antisocial." To act otherwise would constitute a "just grievance" for union members.

The unions, however, are not really to be blamed for antisocial or illegal behavior. They are merely responding to the unconscionable privilege that bemused lawmakers have thrust upon them—and simultaneously documenting Lord Acton's axiom that power corrupts in direct ratio to its extent. That scholar of freedom, F. A. Hayek, contemplating Big Labor's privileged sanctuary in his already classic book, *The Constitution of Liberty*, was simply stating historical fact when he wrote:

> The acquisition of privilege by the unions has nowhere been as spectacular as in Britain, where the Trade Dispute Act of 1960 conferred "upon a trade union a freedom from civil liability for the commission of even the most heinous wrong by the union or its servant, and in short confer[red] upon every trade union a privilege and protection not possessed by any other person or body of persons, whether corporate or incorporate."* Similar friendly legislation helped the unions in the United States, where first the Clayton Act of 1914 exempted them

---

*A. V. Dicey, *Law and Opinion*. Hayek also quotes J. A. Schumpeter: ". . . in exempting trade union funds from liability in action for damages for *torts*—which practically amounted to enacting that trade unions could do no wrong—this measure in fact resigned to the trade unions part of the authority of the state . . ."—an argument sustained by the lord chief justice of Northern Ireland, who held that it "put trade unions in the same privileged position which the Crown enjoyed until [1947] in respect to wrongful acts committed on its behalf."

from anit-monopoly provisions of the Sherman Act; the Norris–La Guardia Act of 1932 "went a long way to establish practically complete immunity of labor unions to torts";** and finally, the Supreme Court in a crucial decision sustained "the claim of a union to the right to deny participation in the economic world to an employer."† More or less the same situation had gradually come to exist in most European countries by the 1920s, "less through explicit legislative permission than by the tacit toleration by authorities and courts."‡ Everywhere the legalization of unions was interpreted as a legalization of their main purpose and as recognition of their right to do whatever seemed necessary to achieve this purpose—namely, monopoly. More and more they came to be treated not as a group which was pursuing a legitimate selfish aim and which, like every other interest, must be kept in check by competing interests possessed of equal rights, but as a group whose aim—the exhaustive and comprehensive organization of all labor—must be supported for the good of the public.

The privilege in law and practice granted to unions in the private sector has allowed them to assume a dominant position in the political life of nations. In the United States, where their membership is less than a tenth of the population, they have been able to impose their will on Congress and on state legislatures and to subvert the orderly process of law by intimidating both the Justice Department and the Presidents who presumably set law-enforcement policy. And their hold on the liberal mind has created a climate of opinion that affects the thinking of the Olympians on the Supreme Court. Repeatedly, that august body—ever obsessed by the rights of criminals—has dodged any meaningful confrontation with the constitutional issues raised by federal labor legislation.

In the public sector, however, what was intolerable in union privilege becomes impossible if representative government is to survive in these United States. Yet it is precisely in this area that some of the courts have comported themselves as if the Constitution had been printed in disappearing ink— the most extreme case being a recent ruling that when the Constitution and a public-sector union contract are in conflict, the contract must prevail!

Yet even in a society whose freedoms are being so perilously compromised by the doctrine that "the king can do no wrong"—the king in this instance being George Meany and his satraps—there are still means and instrumentalities that have slowed the onrush to power of Big Labor. A series of

---

** Roscoe Pound, *Legal Immunities of Trade Unions.*
† Mr. Justice Jackson, dissenting in *Hunt* v. *Crumboch.*
‡ Ludwig von Mises, *Die Gemeinwirtschaft.*

suits filed by union members against the glaring abuses of Big Labor, and by non-members who have resisted being forcibly impressed into the involuntary servitude of compulsory unionism, have begun to bring legal victories to the individual—much to the shock of "King George" Meany and his ministers.*

That many of those suits have been won against the increasingly prosperous and aggressive public-sector unions in spite of the political pressures they can exert is a hopeful sign. As in all legal contests with Big Labor, the plaintiffs have faced considerable odds. Archibald Cox, solicitor general of the United States under John F. Kennedy and more recently the Watergate special prosecutor—and the holder of unassailable liberal credentials—has enumerated a few of the odds against litigants who challenge the privileges of the unions:

> The cost is likely to be heavy, and [the plaintiffs] have little money with which to post bonds, pay lawyers' fees, and print voluminous records. Time is always on the side of the [union] defendants.... Individual workers who sue union officers run enormous risks, for there are many ways, legal as well as illegal, by which entrenched officials can "take care" of recalcitrant members.

The risk of suit against public-sector unions is, of course, increased since state and local governments are often included among the defendants. Having surrendered some of their rights to the unions, these governmental units all too often enter into an unholy alliance with them for dubious and narrow political purposes, as Kurt Hanslowe, the former UAW assistant general counsel, underscored.

In a sane world, it would have been assumed that the American Civil Liberties Union would have offered its prestige and funds to carry employee suits through the courts. But the ACLU, tugged as it is between its golden rhetoric on civil rights and its need for financial and other support from Big Labor and the Liberal Establishment, has followed a schizoid course. When driven to the wall of principle, it may file an *amicus curiae* brief deploring compulsory unionism with one hand while it pats Big Labor with the other. Had government employees waited for the ACLU to act in their behalf, they would still be cooling their heels in some anteroom.

Most of the suits would not have been filed, nor the victo-

---

*It can be noted here that the impressment of American sailors by the British Navy led to the War of 1812—with a cautionary word that the war ended in a stand-off, with a burnt-out White House.

ries won, had it not been for the financial help and moral support of the National Right to Work Legal Defense Foundation, whose charter—much to the chagrin of Big Labor—is identical in almost every respect to that of the defense fund set up by the National Association for the Advancement of Colored People. Because of this help, lawyers skilled in labor law could be retained and the high cost of litigation met. As a result of these legal challenges, the privileged sanctuary of Big Labor was for the first time breached. Simultaneously, union efforts to remove what few restraints remain on unlimited power have in some cases been rebuffed.

One such effort, a suit whose purpose was to have the Hatch Act declared unconstitutional, was brought by one of the postal unions. In its adverse ruling, the Supreme Court held that its decision "would no more than confirm the judgment of history, a judgment made by this country over the last century that it is in the best interest of the counry, indeed essential, that federal service should depend on meritorious performance rather than political service." Another suit, filed by a teachers' union to test the constitutionality of a North Carolina statute prohibiting state governmental units to enter into collective-bargaining agreements, also led to defeat for public-sector unions.

The most important cases litigated by the National Right to Work Legal Defense Foundation are suits such as *Ball* v. *City of Detroit and the American Federation of State, County and Municipal Employees*. In a complaint the implications of which go far beyond the rights of Detroit public employees, sixty-five city employees urged that the compulsory agency shop—a prime aim of Jerry Wurf's AFSCME and other public-sector unions—is illegal. Though the suit is still being fought in the Michigan courts, a restraining order against the city and the union prevented the collection of coerced fees from some 1500 non-union members for almost five years. Among the charges made by the plaintiffs was that the fees exacted from non-members would be used for political purposes which they found repugnant. Proof of this was not hard to come by, since Wurf had admitted the practice in a sworn deposition.

But *Ball* v. *City of Detroit* and other such suits served a greater purpose than bringing relief to individual public employees. They focused a light on the murky world of compulsory unionism and alerted city and state employees in other jurisdictions to their peril. For example, AFSCME lost a series of representation elections to the Minnesota State Capital Employees Union, which opposed the agency shop and "an involuntary 'un-fair-share' fee." Ironically, in one state government unit, AFSCME received fifty votes less than its claimed membership total. What made the difference in these elections was the public statement by MSCEU that "union membership and union support must be voluntary."

In Trenton, New Jersey, AFSCME had signed a collective-bargaining agreement with the city—the "first in the state," the union boasted—imposing a compulsory agency shop on public employees. It would have been ratified by the Trenton City Council but for a telegram from the National Right to Work Committee; the contract was referred to city attorney Victor Walcoff, who declared that it violated New Jersey's right-to-work law.

All of this has served to educate both the public and their elected representatives. The extent of concern over compulsory unionism in the public sector even carried over to the normally cautious governors. At the National Governors' Conference, which met in February 1975, a resolution opposing bills pending in Congress mandating compulsory unionism at the state, county, and local levels was unanimously approved on the limited but important ground that these bills constituted interference and were "not properly the subject of federal legislation." The governors had not yet read the results of the Opinion Research poll showing the overwhelming opposition of their constituents to compulsory public-employee-unionism laws, but they could see the cutting edge of the knife.

The battle, however, will be a long and a bitter one. With unlimited power almost in their grasp, and with it hegemony over all of Big Labor, the sachems of public-employee unionism will not give up easily. They have demonstrated in the past their ability to ride heedlessly over the public and over the nation's basic laws, and they are certain they can do it again. If they succeed, then these United States will succumb to a government of, by, and for a Big Labor oligarchy.

Sylvester Petro, in his incisive essay on sovereignty and public unionism, concludes with these words:

> We have been dealing, I believe, with the most serious issues that can confront a people who wish to live in a civilized social order, one in which life has a chance to be reasonably prosperous, reasonably happy, reasonably secure. These ends, mankind has learned through the bitterest experience over the centuries, are unachievable in the absence of government endowed with those attributes to which we have given the name "sovereign." I have tried to demonstrate that compulsory public-sector bargaining laws are incompatible with governmental sovereignty and that they constitute a fatal threat to popular sovereignty as well. They can make no contribution to the peace and produc-

tivity of society. They point in the direction of anarchy, and of all the dread consequences of anarchy and disorder.

To this must be appended the epigraph to Petro's essay, the grim words of Oswald Spengler in *The Decline of the West*:

In the period of the Contending States, torrents of blood had reddened the pavements of all world-cities, so that the great truths of Democracy might be turned into actualities, and for the winning of rights without which life seemed not worth living. Now these rights are won, but the grandchildren cannot be moved, even by punishment, to make use of them.

Those rights having been secured in the Constitution, will they survive the present attack on them? It is to this question that the preceding pages have been addressed.

# Appendix I

## Compulsory Unionism in the Public Sector

### Detailed Findings of the Opinion Research Corporation, Princeton, New Jersey "Caravan Survey," January 1975

### FOREWORD

This report presents the findings of a personal interview research survey conducted among 2,038 men and women, 18 years of age or over, living in private households in the continental United States.

Interviewing for this Caravan Survey was completed during the period January 10 through February 3, 1975, by members of the Opinion Research Corporation national interviewing staff. All interviews were conducted in the homes of respondents.

The most advanced probability sampling techniques were used in the design and execution of the sample plan; therefore, the results may be projected to the total U.S. population of men and women 18 years of age or over.

Only one interview was taken per household, regardless of the number of people 18 years of age or over in the household. Weights were introduced into the tabulations to ensure proper representation in the sample.

The Technical Appendix at the end of the report describes in detail the sampling methods and other procedures employed in the survey. Also described are characteristics of the sample and sampling tolerances of survey results.

As required by the Code of Ethics of the American Association for Public Opinion Research, we will maintain the anonymity of our respondents. No information can be released that in any way will reveal the identity of a respondent. Also, our authorization is required for any publication of the research findings or their implications.

Caravan Surveys, a division of Opinion Research Corporation, is a syndicated, share-cost data collection vehicle. Caravan reports, such as this one, are presented in tabular form. Interpretive analysis is provided by Caravan only if specifically contracted for by the client.

The tables read across. Except for the first two columns, all figures in the body of the tables are percentages. The unweighted number of interviews appears in the column headed "UNWTD" and the weighted numbers—tabulation units resulting from the weighting process—appear in the column headed "WTD."

Throughout the tables, an asterisk (*) signifies any value less than one-half percent.

The weighted numbers for sex and region of country may not add to the total because they are subject to the limitation of the computer to round weighted numbers. In all demographic groups—other than sex and region—the unweighted numbers may not add to the total number of respondents because they are dependent upon a respondent's answer and, therefore, do not include the "Not Reporteds."

The following definitions are provided for some of the sidebreaks by which the data are analyzed. Other sidebreaks are self-explanatory.

*Occupation* refers to the occupation of the chief wage earner in the household.

*City Size* is based on interviewer observation of the respondent's location in terms of area, and the age and type of dwelling. This sidebreak does not add to the total number of interviews, as some respondents simply do not qualify within a definition. For example, a suburban garden apartment does not fit the description "single family dwelling."

For those categories that are not self-explanatory, the following definitions are provided:

> Old Suburb—single family dwelling in a small town or suburb built prior to World War II
>
> New Suburb—single family dwelling built since World World II
>
> City 1 Family—single family dwelling within a metropolitan area
>
> City Multifamily—multiple family dwelling, which would include a duplex, double house, residential house with more than one family living in it, etc., within a metropolitan area

*Geographic Regions* include:

> Northeast: Maine, New Hampshire, Vermont, Massachusetts, Rhode Island, Connecticut, New York, New Jersey, Pennsylvania

| | North Central: | Ohio, Indiana, Illinois, Michigan, Wisconsin, Minnesota, Iowa, Missouri, North Dakota, South Dakota, Nebraska, Kansas |
| --- | --- | --- |
| | South: | Delaware, Maryland, District of Columbia, Virginia, West Virginia, North Carolina, South Carolina, Georgia, Florida, Kentucky, Tennessee, Alabama, Mississippi, Arkansas, Louisiana, Oklahoma, Texas |
| | West: | Montana, Idaho, Wyoming, Colorado, New Mexico, Arizona, Utah, Nevada, Washington, Oregon, California |

*Income* is total family income in 1974, before taxes.

## DETAILED FINDINGS

QUESTION N1        71026        JANUARY 1975

Should the U.S. Congress pass a law which would allow agreements requiring employees to join or pay dues to a union in order to work for the Federal Government

| | Number of Interviews | | | | No |
| --- | --- | --- | --- | --- | --- |
| | Unwtd | Wtd | Yes | No | Opinion |
| Total U.S. Public | 2038 | 6707 | 11 | 79 | 10 |
| Men | 1031 | 3233 | 12 | 80 | 8 |
| Women | 1007 | 3475 | 9 | 78 | 13 |
| 18–29 Years of Age | 522 | 1918 | 14 | 77 | 9 |
| 30–39 | 421 | 1145 | 12 | 78 | 10 |
| 40–49 | 328 | 1117 | 8 | 84 | 8 |
| 50–59 | 311 | 1041 | 9 | 84 | 7 |
| 60 Years or Over | 456 | 1487 | 10 | 74 | 16 |
| Less than High School Complete | 666 | 2395 | 13 | 72 | 15 |
| High School Complete | 712 | 2502 | 11 | 81 | 8 |
| Some College | 648 | 1776 | 8 | 86 | 6 |
| Professional | 270 | 772 | 9 | 85 | 6 |
| Managerial | 242 | 696 | 8 | 85 | 7 |
| Clerical, Sales | 207 | 677 | 9 | 86 | 5 |
| Craftsman, Foreman | 378 | 1288 | 12 | 80 | 8 |
| Other Manual, Service | 473 | 1731 | 14 | 75 | 11 |
| Farmer, Farm Laborer | 42 | 181 | 6 | 86 | 8 |
| Rural | 297 | 940 | 11 | 80 | 9 |
| Old Suburb 1 Family | 362 | 1286 | 8 | 80 | 12 |
| New Suburb 1 Family | 260 | 731 | 6 | 86 | 8 |
| City 1 Family | 619 | 1976 | 14 | 77 | 9 |
| City Multifamily | 122 | 425 | 13 | 78 | 9 |
| City Apartment | 200 | 804 | 16 | 67 | 17 |

| | | | Yes | No | No Opinion |
|---|---|---|---|---|---|
| Northeast | 537 | 1552 | 14 | 74 | 12 |
| North Central | 583 | 1900 | 11 | 78 | 11 |
| South | 630 | 2136 | 9 | 82 | 9 |
| West | 288 | 1120 | 9 | 82 | 9 |
| Under $5,000 Family Income | 349 | 1653 | 14 | 69 | 17 |
| $5,000–$6,999 | 229 | 705 | 15 | 75 | 10 |
| $7,000–$9,999 | 346 | 943 | 12 | 78 | 10 |
| $10,000–$14,999 | 464 | 1420 | 10 | 82 | 8 |
| $15,000 or Over | 595 | 1831 | 7 | 87 | 6 |
| No Children in Household | 1003 | 3525 | 10 | 78 | 12 |
| With Children Under 18 | 1035 | 3182 | 12 | 80 | 8 |
| With Teenagers 12–17 | 507 | 1622 | 12 | 82 | 6 |
| White | 1803 | 5874 | 9 | 81 | 10 |
| Nonwhite | 226 | 810 | 23 | 65 | 12 |
| Own Home | 1388 | 4292 | 9 | 82 | 9 |
| Rent Home | 630 | 2361 | 14 | 74 | 12 |
| Total U.S. Public | 2038 | 6707 | 11 | 79 | 10 |
| Union Members | 296 | 941 | 19 | 71 | 10 |
| Union Families | 581 | 1933 | 17 | 74 | 9 |
| Nonunion Families | 1439 | 4710 | 8 | 81 | 11 |
| Republican | 368 | 1174 | 11 | 78 | 11 |
| Democrat | 882 | 3009 | 13 | 77 | 10 |
| Independent | 603 | 1850 | 9 | 84 | 7 |

QUESTION N2      71026      JANUARY 1975

Should the U.S. Congress pass a law which would allow agreements requiring employees to join or pay dues to a union to order to work for State, County, and Municipal Governments

| | Number of Interviews | | | | No |
|---|---|---|---|---|---|
| | Unwtd | Wtd | Yes | No | Opinion |
| Total U.S. Public | 2038 | 6707 | 10 | 79 | 11 |
| Men | 1031 | 3233 | 11 | 81 | 8 |
| Women | 1007 | 3475 | 8 | 78 | 14 |
| 18–29 Years of Age | 522 | 1918 | 11 | 79 | 10 |
| 30–39 | 421 | 1145 | 10 | 81 | 9 |
| 40–49 | 328 | 1117 | 8 | 81 | 11 |
| 50–59 | 311 | 1041 | 9 | 82 | 9 |
| 60 Years or Over | 456 | 1487 | 8 | 76 | 16 |
| Less than High School Complete | 666 | 2395 | 10 | 73 | 17 |
| High School Complete | 712 | 2502 | 11 | 80 | 9 |
| Some College | 648 | 1776 | 7 | 87 | 6 |
| Professional | 270 | 772 | 11 | 83 | 6 |
| Managerial | 242 | 696 | 5 | 87 | 8 |

| | Unwtd | Wtd | Yes | No | No Opinion |
|---|---|---|---|---|---|
| Clerical, Sales | 207 | 677 | 6 | 89 | 5 |
| Craftsman, Foreman | 378 | 1288 | 11 | 80 | 9 |
| Other Manual, Service | 473 | 1731 | 11 | 78 | 11 |
| Farmer, Farm Laborer | 42 | 181 | 7 | 74 | 19 |
| Rural | 297 | 940 | 8 | 79 | 13 |
| Old Suburb 1 Family | 362 | 1286 | 7 | 81 | 12 |
| New Suburb 1 Family | 260 | 731 | 5 | 86 | 9 |
| City 1 Family | 619 | 1976 | 12 | 79 | 9 |
| City Multifamily | 122 | 425 | 13 | 77 | 10 |
| City Apartment | 200 | 804 | 12 | 71 | 17 |
| Northeast | 537 | 1552 | 12 | 77 | 11 |
| North Central | 583 | 1900 | 12 | 77 | 11 |
| South | 630 | 2136 | 6 | 82 | 12 |
| West | 288 | 1120 | 9 | 82 | 9 |
| Under $5,000 Family Income | 349 | 1653 | 10 | 71 | 19 |
| $5,000–$6,999 | 229 | 705 | 11 | 79 | 10 |
| $7,000–$9,999 | 346 | 943 | 11 | 79 | 10 |
| $10,000–$14,999 | 464 | 1420 | 11 | 81 | 8 |
| $15,000 or Over | 595 | 1831 | 7 | 86 | 7 |
| No Children in Household | 1003 | 3525 | 10 | 77 | 13 |
| With Children Under 18 | 1035 | 3182 | 9 | 81 | 10 |
| With Teenagers 12–17 | 507 | 1622 | 9 | 82 | 9 |
| White | 1803 | 5874 | 9 | 81 | 10 |
| Nonwhite | 226 | 810 | 13 | 69 | 18 |
| Own Home | 1388 | 4292 | 9 | 81 | 10 |
| Rent Home | 630 | 2361 | 11 | 76 | 13 |
| Total U.S. Public | 2038 | 6707 | 10 | 79 | 11 |
| Union Members | 296 | 941 | 19 | 73 | 8 |
| Union Families | 581 | 1933 | 16 | 75 | 9 |
| Nonunion Families | 1439 | 4710 | 7 | 81 | 12 |
| Republican | 368 | 1174 | 10 | 78 | 12 |
| Democrat | 882 | 3009 | 10 | 79 | 11 |
| Independent | 603 | 1850 | 9 | 84 | 7 |

QUESTION N3    71026    JANUARY 1975

Should your State Legislature pass a law which would allow agreements requiring employees to join or pay dues to a union in order to work for the State, County, and Municipal Governments

| | Number of Interviews | | | | No |
|---|---|---|---|---|---|
| | Unwtd | Wtd | Yes | No | Opinion |
| Total U.S. Public | 2038 | 6707 | 10 | 78 | 12 |
| Men | 1031 | 3233 | 12 | 80 | 8 |
| Women | 1007 | 3475 | 8 | 77 | 15 |

| | | | | | |
|---|---:|---:|---:|---:|---:|
| 18–29 Years of Age | 522 | 1918 | 12 | 78 | 10 |
| 30–39 | 421 | 1145 | 10 | 80 | 10 |
| 40–49 | 328 | 1117 | 9 | 81 | 10 |
| 50–59 | 311 | 1041 | 11 | 80 | 9 |
| 60 Years or Over | 456 | 1487 | 8 | 75 | 17 |
| | | | | | |
| Less than High School Complete | 666 | 2395 | 10 | 73 | 17 |
| High School Complete | 712 | 2502 | 11 | 79 | 10 |
| Some College | 648 | 1776 | 8 | 85 | 7 |
| | | | | | |
| Professional | 270 | 772 | 10 | 83 | 7 |
| Managerial | 242 | 696 | 5 | 85 | 10 |
| Clerical, Sales | 207 | 677 | 7 | 88 | 5 |
| Craftsman, Foreman | 378 | 1288 | 10 | 80 | 10 |
| Other Manual Service | 473 | 1731 | 14 | 75 | 11 |
| Farmer, Farm Laborer | 42 | 181 | 7 | 72 | 21 |
| | | | | | |
| Rural | 297 | 940 | 10 | 78 | 12 |
| Old Suburb 1 Family | 362 | 1286 | 7 | 81 | 12 |
| New Suburb 1 Family | 260 | 731 | 6 | 85 | 9 |
| City 1 Family | 619 | 1976 | 12 | 77 | 11 |
| City Multifamily | 122 | 425 | 16 | 74 | 10 |
| City Apartment | 200 | 804 | 15 | 69 | 16 |
| | | | | | |
| Northeast | 537 | 1522 | 14 | 74 | 12 |
| North Central | 583 | 1900 | 12 | 78 | 10 |
| South | 630 | 2136 | 7 | 81 | 12 |
| West | 288 | 1120 | 9 | 80 | 11 |
| | | | | | |
| Under $5,000 Family Income | 349 | 1653 | 12 | 70 | 18 |
| $5,000–$6,999 | 229 | 705 | 14 | 75 | 11 |
| $7,000–$9,999 | 346 | 943 | 10 | 80 | 10 |
| $10,000–$14,999 | 464 | 1420 | 10 | 80 | 10 |
| $15,000 or Over | 595 | 1831 | 7 | 86 | 7 |
| | | | | | |
| No Children in Household | 1003 | 3525 | 11 | 76 | 13 |
| With Children Under 18 | 1035 | 3182 | 10 | 80 | 10 |
| With Teenagers 12–17 | 507 | 1622 | 10 | 81 | 9 |
| | | | | | |
| White | 1803 | 5874 | 9 | 80 | 11 |
| Nonwhite | 226 | 810 | 19 | 63 | 18 |
| Own Home | 1388 | 4292 | 9 | 81 | 10 |
| Rent Home | 630 | 2361 | 13 | 74 | 13 |
| | | | | | |
| Total U.S. Public | 2038 | 6707 | 10 | 78 | 12 |
| | | | | | |
| Union Members | 296 | 941 | 18 | 74 | 8 |
| Union Families | 581 | 1933 | 16 | 75 | 9 |
| Nonunion Families | 1439 | 4710 | 8 | 80 | 12 |
| | | | | | |
| Republican | 368 | 1174 | 10 | 78 | 12 |
| Democrat | 882 | 3009 | 11 | 78 | 11 |
| Independent | 603 | 1850 | 9 | 83 | 8 |

Which of these arrangements do you favor for Federal, State, and Local Government Employees

1. A person can work for the Government whether or not he belongs to a union
2. A person can go to work for the Government if he doesn't already belong to a union, but has to join after he is hired to hold his job
3. A person can get a job with the Government only if he already belongs to a union
4. No opinion

| | Number of Interviews | | | | | |
| | Unwtd | Wtd | 1 | 2 | 3 | 4 |
|---|---|---|---|---|---|---|
| Total U.S. Public | 2038 | 6707 | 83 | 10 | 1 | 6 |
| Men | 1031 | 3233 | 83 | 11 | 2 | 4 |
| Women | 1007 | 3475 | 82 | 9 | 1 | 8 |
| | | | | | | |
| 18–29 Years of Age | 522 | 1918 | 82 | 11 | 1 | 6 |
| 30–39 | 421 | 1145 | 84 | 11 | 1 | 4 |
| 40–49 | 328 | 1117 | 84 | 9 | 1 | 6 |
| 50–59 | 311 | 1041 | 86 | 8 | 2 | 4 |
| 60 Years or Over | 456 | 1487 | 80 | 8 | 2 | 10 |
| | | | | | | |
| Less than High School Complete | 666 | 2395 | 77 | 11 | 2 | 10 |
| High School Complete | 712 | 2502 | 84 | 10 | 1 | 5 |
| Some College | 648 | 1776 | 89 | 8 | * | 3 |
| | | | | | | |
| Professional | 270 | 772 | 90 | 7 | * | 3 |
| Managerial | 242 | 696 | 90 | 7 | 0 | 3 |
| Clerical, Sales | 207 | 677 | 87 | 7 | 1 | 5 |
| Craftsman, Foreman | 378 | 1288 | 83 | 11 | * | 6 |
| Other Manual, Service | 473 | 1731 | 81 | 12 | 2 | 5 |
| Farmer, Farm Laborer | 42 | 181 | 76 | 2 | 4 | 18 |
| | | | | | | |
| Rural | 297 | 940 | 81 | 10 | 3 | 6 |
| Old Suburb 1 Family | 362 | 1286 | 82 | 8 | 2 | 8 |
| New Suburb 1 Family | 260 | 731 | 87 | 8 | * | 5 |
| City 1 Family | 619 | 1976 | 85 | 10 | 1 | 4 |
| City Multifamily | 122 | 425 | 71 | 20 | 0 | 9 |
| City Apartment | 200 | 804 | 78 | 10 | 3 | 9 |
| | | | | | | |
| Northeast | 537 | 1552 | 78 | 13 | 2 | 7 |
| North Central | 583 | 1900 | 79 | 12 | 1 | 8 |
| South | 630 | 2136 | 88 | 5 | 2 | 5 |
| West | 288 | 1120 | 87 | 7 | * | 6 |
| | | | | | | |
| Under $5,000 Family Income | 349 | 1653 | 76 | 11 | 3 | 10 |
| $5,000–$6,999 | 229 | 705 | 80 | 12 | * | 8 |
| $7,000–$9,999 | 346 | 943 | 80 | 11 | 1 | 8 |
| $10,000–$14,999 | 464 | 1420 | 86 | 9 | 2 | 3 |
| $15,000 or Over | 595 | 1831 | 89 | 7 | * | 4 |

| | | | | | | |
|---|---|---|---|---|---|---|
| No Children in Household | 1003 | 3525 | 82 | 8 | 2 | 8 |
| With Children Under 18 | 1035 | 3182 | 84 | 10 | 1 | 5 |
| With Teenagers 12–17 | 507 | 1622 | 86 | 10 | 1 | 3 |
| White | 1803 | 5874 | 85 | 8 | 1 | 6 |
| Nonwhite | 226 | 810 | 70 | 21 | 1 | 8 |
| Own Home | 1388 | 4292 | 85 | 9 | 1 | 5 |
| Rent Home | 630 | 2361 | 79 | 11 | 2 | 8 |
| Total U.S. Public | 2038 | 6707 | 83 | 10 | 1 | 6 |
| Union Members | 296 | 941 | 77 | 17 | 2 | 4 |
| Union Families | 581 | 1933 | 77 | 16 | 2 | 5 |
| Nonunion Families | 1439 | 4710 | 85 | 7 | 1 | 7 |
| Republican | 368 | 1174 | 85 | 7 | 2 | 6 |
| Democrat | 882 | 3009 | 81 | 11 | 2 | 6 |
| Independent | 603 | 1850 | 87 | 9 | * | 4 |

# Technical Appendix

*Opinion Research Corporation's Master Sample*

Opinion Research Corporation's master sample is based on a new probability sample design, prepared in consultation with J. Stevens Stock of Marketmath, Inc., and modified and updated by ORC.

The essential characteristic of probability sampling is that, for each person in the population under study, the probability that he will be included in the sample can be specified. This means that the degree of reliability of any finding from a study based on a probability sample can be estimated mathematically.

This new sample design is a major improvement over standard areal probability designs now in common use. These areal methods depend upon the use of maps showing geographic segments for which rough population estimates can be made. These maps are often out of date and otherwise inaccurate, and population estimates are frequently unreliable for small geographic areas, particularly as time passes from one census to another. The new sampling method eliminates these important problems of traditional probability sampling by using current address directories as the basis for a system of defining interviewing starting points—a system which, of course, includes in the sample those households which are not in the directory as well. The new method is both statistically and administratively as efficient as possible, providing the most reliable data for any given expenditure.

The ORC master sample consists of 360 counties in the

contiguous United States. This master sample of 360 counties comprises, in fact, six subsamples of 60 counties each. Each of these subsamples is itself a national probability sample. Depending on the needs of any particular study, the master sample can be used as a whole, or any combination of the six subsamples can be used.

To construct the sample, the counties within each state were arranged in order of descending population size; and all the states were grouped in geographical order from Maine to California. Sixty counties were then chosen by statistical procedures that insure representative geographical distribution. This process was repeated to obtain the six subsamples that make up the master sample of 360 counties.

The next step in the sampling design was to select an area from each of the 360 counties in the master sample. Again, a probability sampling method was used to select, within each county, a minor civil division (MCD) as defined by the Bureau of the Census. A minor civil division may be a town, township, city, or part of a city. The probability that any particular minor civil division was selected in a county was proportional to the population of that minor civil division.

Thus, the larger a minor civil division, the greater the likelihood that it be selected. The minor civil division, then, is the primary sampling unit.

Once the MCD has been selected, the next step is the determination of those households where interviewing is to take place. Under the ORC National Probability Sample procedure, any current listing of household locations, even if incomplete, constitutes the first stage of the sampling plan. From this list of households one or more addresses are chosen at random. Each of these addresses defines the place that the interviewer begins following the interviewing site selection process. The interviews in a cluster or "neighborhood" do not begin at the household selected from the list, but at the adjacent household, which may or may not be on the original list. Thus, the list does not define the universe of households in an MCD, but rather a list of households adjacent to possible starting points. Depending on the number of households contacted from each starting point, the number of starting points chosen, and the criteria for being included on the original list, every household in the MCD has a known, or knowable, probability of being included in the ORC sample.

Because they are the most up-to-date and the most complete listing of addresses available, telephone books are the sources of locations next to interviewing starting points when general public surveys are being done.

The specific persons to be interviewed are selected as follows:

(1) A certain number of starting points are selected from the telephone books covering the minor civil divisions, or communities, selected. The starting points are chosen in a manner that each household, within the minor civil division, listed in the phone book has an equal chance of being selected.

(2) Each starting point selected determines a group of households, called a "cluster," in which interviews are conducted. This cluster of households includes households both with and without listed telephones. The first household in which an interview is conducted is the household immediately to the left of the household selected from the telephone book as the starting point. Thus, the first household can be one either with or without a telephone.

(3) The interviewer conducts an interview in the first household and then works through the group of households following a prescribed rule. The interviewer continues working through the cluster until interviews have been completed in a preassigned number of households.

(4) A respondent-selection procedure determines for the interviewer which person to interview in any given household. Every eligible respondent in the household has the same chance to be interviewed as any other eligible respondent. The interviewer is not allowed to make any substitutions.

Once all interviews have been completed, weighting procedures are employed to insure that the sample properly represents the population from which it was drawn.

This sampling procedure is rigorous in concept and practice and allows for the exact determination of the statistical precision of any finding.

*Sample Characteristics, January 1975 Caravan*

The data in the table below compare the characteristics of the weighted[1] Caravan sample with those of the total population, 18 years of age or over. The table shows that the distribution of the total sample parallels very closely that of the precision of any finding.

---

[1]Weights were introduced into the tabulations to ensure proper representation of the interviews in the sample.

| | Total | | Men | | Women | |
|---|---|---|---|---|---|---|
| | Popu-lation[2] | Caravan Sample | Popu-lation[2] | Caravan Sample | Popu-lation[2] | Caravan Sample |
| *Age* | | | | | | |
| 18 – 29 years of age | 29% | 29% | 30% | 30% | 28% | 27% |
| 30 – 39 | 17 | 17 | 17 | 17 | 17 | 17 |
| 40 – 49 | 16 | 16 | 17 | 17 | 16 | 16 |
| 50 – 59 | 16 | 16 | 16 | 16 | 15 | 15 |
| 60 years or over | 22 | 22 | 20 | 20 | 24 | 25 |
| | | | | | | |
| *Race* | | | | | | |
| White | 89% | 88% | 89% | 88% | 88% | 88% |
| Nonwhite | 11 | 12 | 11 | 12 | 12 | 12 |
| | | | | | | |
| *Geographic Region* | | | | | | |
| Northeast | 23% | 23% | 23% | 23% | 24% | 24% |
| North Central | 27 | 28 | 28 | 29 | 27 | 27 |
| South | 31 | 32 | 31 | 31 | 32 | 33 |
| West | 19 | 17 | 18 | 17 | 17 | 16 |

### Reliability of Survey Percentages

Results of any sample are subject to sampling variation. The magnitude of the variation is measurable and is affected by the number of interviews and the level of the percentages expressing the results.

The table below shows the possible sample variation that applies to percentage results reported from the Opinion Research Corporation sample. The chances are 95 to 100 that a Caravan survey result does not vary, plus or minus, by more than the indicated number of percentage points from the result that would be obtained if interviews had been conducted with all persons in the universe represented by the sample.

### Approximate Sampling Tolerances Applicable to Percentages at or Near These Levels

| Size of Sample on Which Caravan Survey Result Is Based | 10% or 90% | 30% or 70% | 50% |
|---|---|---|---|
| 2,000 interviews | 2% | 3% | 3% |
| 1,000 interviews | 2% | 4% | 4% |
| 500 interviews | 3% | 5% | 5% |
| 250 interviews | 5% | 7% | 8% |
| 100 interviews | 7% | 11% | 12% |

[2]Source: Latest data from the U.S. Bureau of the Census, regular and interim reports.

## Sampling Tolerances When Comparing Two Samples

Tolerances are also involved in the comparison of results from different parts of any one Opinion Research Corporation sample and in the comparison of results between two different ORC samples. A difference, in other words, must be of at least a certain size to be considered statistically significant. The table below is a guide to the sampling tolerances applicable to such comparisons.

| Sizes of Samples Compared | Differences Required for Significance at or Near These Percentage Levels[1] | | |
|---|---|---|---|
| | 10% or 90% | 30% or 70% | 50% |
| 2,000 and 2,000 | 2% | 4% | 4% |
| 2,000 and 1,000 | 3% | 4% | 5% |
| 1,000 and 1,000 | 3% | 5% | 6% |
| 1,000 and 500 | 4% | 6% | 7% |
| 500 and 500 | 5% | 7% | 8% |
| 500 and 200 | 6% | 9% | 10% |
| 200 and 200 | 7% | 11% | 12% |
| 200 and 100 | 9% | 14% | 15% |
| 100 and 100 | 10% | 16% | 17% |

[1]Based on 95 chances in 100.

### Quality Control Measures

Quality control measures are applied to every phase of the Caravan survey.

Specialists in many fields are available for consultation with the Caravan survey director in the development of the questionnaire.

Interviewers are hired and trained, in person, to staff the probability sample, and their work is regularly checked for accuracy and validity.

Questionnaires are prepared for data processing by experienced coders, under the supervision of the survey director.

The processing of data is subject to rigorous internal checks designed to detect both machine and human error.

# Appendix II

## Union Campaign Contributions to Members of the Committee on Education and Labor, U.S. House of Representatives, 94th Congress

SOURCE: Clerk of the House

| | | |
|---|---|---|
| *Michael Blouin (D-Iowa) | $36,900 | 4 |
| *Paul Simon (D-Ill.) | $34,400 | 4 |
| John Dent (D-Pa.) | $29,275 | 2,3,4 |
| *Robert Cornell (D-Wis.) | $29,175 | 4 |
| Frank Thompson (D-N.J.) | $26,300 | 2,3,4 |
| *Ron Mottl (D-Ohio) | $23,830 | 4 |
| Lloyd Meeds (D-Wash.) | $22,550 | 2,4 |
| Peter Peyser (R-N.Y.) | $21,555 | 4 |
| William Clay (D-Mo.) | $18,850 | 2,3,4 |
| John Brademas (D-Ind.) | $18,700 | 2,4 |
| *Ted Risenhoover (D-Ok.) | $18,600 | 4 |
| William Lehman (D-Fla.) | $18,550 | 4 |
| *Leo Zeferetti (D-N.Y.) | $15,062 | 4 |
| James O'Hara (D-Mich.) | $14,300 | 2,4 |
| Phillip Burton (D-Cal.) | $13,050 | 2,4 |
| Dominick Daniels (D-N.J.) | $12,550 | 2,3,4 |
| *George Miller (D-Cal.) | $12,000 | 4 |
| *Tim Hall (D-Ill.) | $11,150 | 1,4 |
| William Ford (D-Mich.) | $10,650 | 2,3,4 |
| Mario Biaggi (D-N.Y.) | $ 7,400 | 2,3,4 |
| Joseph Gaydos (D-Pa.) | $ 6,450 | 2,4 |
| Ike Andrews (D-N.C.) | $ 6,250 | |
| *Edward Beard (D-R.I.) | $ 5,350 | 1,4 |
| Patsy Mink (D-Hawaii) | $ 3,560 | 2 |
| Ronald Sarasin (R-Conn.) | $ 2,350 | |
| Shirley Chisholm (D-N.Y.) | $ 2,125 | 2,3,4 |
| Al Quie (R-Minn.) | $ 2,000 | |
| Alphonzo Bell (R-Cal.) | $ 1,900 | |
| Marvin Esch (R-Mich.) | $ 1,900 | |

---

*First-term congressman elected in 1974.
[1]Public statements indicate support of compulsory unionism in public sector.
[2]Voted in 1970 against the Right-to-Work provision in the Postal Reorganization Act.
[3]Has sponsored legislation which would compel federal, U.S. postal service, or state, county and local government employees to support unions in order to work for their own government.
[4]Received ten percent or more of total campaign contributions from union sources.

133

| | | |
|---|---|---|
| Augustus Hawkins (D-Cal.) ............... | $ 1,400 | 2 |
| John Ashbrook (R-Ohio) ................ | $ 500 | |
| *Bill Goodling (R-Pa.) .................... | $ 500 | |
| Carl Perkins (D-Ky.) .................... | $ 500 | 2,3,4 |
| John Buchanan (R-Ala.) ................ | None | |
| John Erlenborn (R-Ill.) ................ | None | |
| Edwin Eshleman (R-Pa.) ............... | None | |
| *James Jeffords (R-Vt.) ................. | None | |
| *Larry Pressler (R-S.D.) ............... | None | |
| *Virginia Smith (R-Neb.) ............... | None | |
| Total ................................... | $428,032 | |

# Appendix III

## Public Attitudes Toward Right-to-Work Laws

### 1974 Opinion Research Corporation "Caravan Survey" Summary of Findings

**Question:** Do you think there is or is not too much power concentrated in the hands of labor leaders of the big unions in this country?

|  | Total U.S. Public | Union Members | Union Households | Men | Women |
|---|---|---|---|---|---|
| Yes, There Is | 70% | 60% | 61% | 71% | 70% |
| No, Is Not | 19% | 34% | 31% | 21% | 16% |
| No Opinion | 11% | 6% | 8% | 8% | 14% |

**Question:** In some places in order to hold a job you have to belong to the union and pay dues. Do you think union officials should be permitted to use this dues money to campaign for political candidates, or should this be forbidden?

| | | | | | |
|---|---|---|---|---|---|
| Should Be Permitted | 12% | 17% | 15% | 14% | 10% |
| Should Be Forbidden | 79% | 78% | 79% | 79% | 79% |
| No Opinion | 9% | 5% | 6% | 7% | 11% |

**Question:** Which of these arrrangements do you favor for workers in industry: 1) A man can hold a job whether or not he belongs to a union; 2) A man can get a job if he doesn't already belong, but has to join after he is hired; 3) A man can get a job if he already belongs to a union; 4) No Opinion.

| | | | | | |
|---|---|---|---|---|---|
| 1. | 68% | 43% | 49% | 67% | 69% |
| 2. | 24% | 48% | 42% | 26% | 22% |
| 3. | 3% | 6% | 6% | 4% | 3% |
| 4. | 5% | 3% | 3% | 3% | 6% |

**Question:** Some states have passed Right-to-Work laws which provide that a worker cannot be discharged from his job for either joining or not joining a union. If you were asked to vote on such a law, would you vote for against it?

| | | | | | |
|---|---|---|---|---|---|
| Would Vote For | 69% | 60% | 61% | 68% | 70% |
| Would Vote Against | 20% | 31% | 30% | 23% | 18% |
| No Opinion | 11% | 9% | 9% | 9% | 12% |

**Question:** The Right-to-Work laws we have been talking about are permitted under Section 14(b) of the Taft-Hartley Act. If Congress keeps Section 14(b) of the Taft-Hartley Act it means that states can continue to have Right-to-Work laws if they want. If Congress repeals Section 14(b) of the Taft-Hartley Act, it means that states cannot have Right-to-Work laws. Which do you think the Congress should do?

| | | | | | |
|---|---|---|---|---|---|
| Keep Section 14(b) | 74% | 69% | 74% | 73% | 75% |
| Repeal Section 14(b) | 11% | 21% | 15% | 14% | 8% |
| No Opinion | 15% | 10% | 11% | 13% | 17% |

# Appendix IV

U.S. Senate Colloquy on Compulsory Public-Sector Bargaining Legislation; March 6, 1975; Senators James L. Buckley (New York), Carl T. Curtis (Nebraska), Paul J. Fannin (Arizona), Jake Garn (Utah), Clifford P. Hansen (Wyoming), Jesse A. Helms (North Carolina), James A. McClure (Idaho), Strom Thurmond (South Carolina)

Governmental Sovereignty or Compulsory Public Sector Bargaining

Mr. GARN. Mr. President, in a letter to L. C. Steward, president of the National Federation of Federal Employees, President Franklin Roosevelt said:

> ... militant tactics have no place in the functions of any organization of government employees. ... A strike of public employees manifests nothing less than an intent on their part to obstruct the operation of government until their demands are satisfied. Such action, looking toward the paralysis of government by those who have sworn to support it, is unthinkable and intolerable.

For 200 years Americans have recognized and fought for the representative, ordered, and sovereign government that President Roosevelt stood for in his statement. Yet forces are mounting which threaten this Government and the elements which support it. I refer to the drive to carry compulsory bargaining even deeper into the public sector. The battle cry has reached Capitol Hill, and as all of us in Congress know, a serious legislative drive will soon be underway to enact compulsory bargaining laws—laws that any objective analysis will show to be violently incompatible with a sovereign, responsible government.

The key ingredients we will doubtless see in forthcoming public sector collective bargaining legislation are:

First. Federal imposition of compulsory public sector bargaining on all governments—in other words, the law would force a sovereign government to negotiate as an equal with a private organization—in this case, a labor union.

Second. Monopoly bargaining privileges—that is, individual public employees would be compelled to accept unwanted

137

union officials as their "exclusive representatives" in dealing with their own government employer.

Third. Compulsory membership where all public employees, including those who do not want the alleged "services" of the union, will have to join or pay money to the union—or lose their right to work for their own government.

It is my purpose and that of several of my colleagues to take a careful look today at a wide range of legislative proposals covering public employees. We contend that these proposals, if enacted, will severely damage the public interest. Our quality of life will be diminished through the wanton disregard of the individual rights of millions of Americans. And, the free spirit of democracy will be crushed by those who seek to compromise it.

What has led us to the point where we can actually seriously discuss the transfer of any of the sovereign functions and powers of government to a private, independent organization not subject to public control and rarely subject to public scrutiny?

The answer can be found in the enormous growth of employment in Federal, State, and local governments. The Bureau of Labor Statistics estimates that public employment has grown faster than any other sector of the economy. There are now some 14 million government workers—three million Federal employees and 11 million State, county, and municipal employees—and their number is growing by leaps and bounds. Public employment unions, having discovered that government unionism holds the most lucrative potential of all, are the fastest growing and best organized labor unions in the country. From 1951 to 1972, government work forces grew by 151 percent, payrolls by 596 percent, union membership by 130 percent, and strikes by public employees by 1,000 per cent. And, I might add that one need not be a Philadelphia lawyer to realize the cost of these strikes to the taxpayer both in terms of higher taxes and in terms of disruption to the community.

Therefore, it is hardly unexpected that Americans have begun to take a closer look and active interest in labor relations of State, local, and Federal Governments. And, as a result, several States and legislatures have passed legislation governing labor relations of public employees. What have we reaped from this activity? Where has it left us and where will it take us?

Legislators have usually been persuaded to adopt the "orderly process" of collective bargaining from the private sector. The enactment of such laws are usually justified in the name of peace and tranquility. Union supporters assure the public employee/employer conjugal bliss and reduced "industrial strife." Yet the facts support the contrary.

Virtually every "solution" has created more unionization problems than have been solved. Conflicts, unrest and illegal strikes continue to mount. Moreover, the concessions employees are not able to get at the bargaining table they frequently try to get from the legislatures. The solutions, for the most part, often do nothing more than merely add to the power and privileges of union organizers.

The prohibition of public employees from striking is based on a sound premise which recognizes their unique position and potential ability to paralyze the community by a strike action. However, the record shows that officials of public employee unions openly flout laws which stand as obstacles to their quest to take over control of public services—openly flout them and then brag about their illegal actions. Seldom has this resulted in any significant legal penalty, however, because of fear on the part of public officials that strong punishment will be met with even more intensive retaliation. In New York City a few years ago, officials of public employee unions convincingly proved that they can put a major U.S. metropolis out of business whenever they choose to do so. What happened in New York City has also happened in recent years in Philadelphia, Baltimore, Albuquerque and dozens of other major cities.

Further, the majority of economists recognize the power of labor unions to force up wages and costs year after year without corresponding advances in productivity. This monopoly element, as we have recently seen first hand, is a prime cause of inflation.

Moreover, it is widespread knowledge that many candidates and elected officials have depended on contributions from labor organizations. Many newly elected Members of Congress are indebted to organized labor for their financial backing that helped them win elections. All unions including public employee unions are out for political control. Yet, the implications of political power in the hands of the public sector are far more threatening than for other unions.

And of course there is the fundamental question of whether employees should be forced to relinquish their bargaining rights to unions which they do not want.

Contrary to the evidence, a wide range of proposals will be presented for our consideration based on the hypothesis that compulsory collective bargaining for government employees "safeguards the public interest and contributes to the effective conduct of public business." Despite the profound differences between the public and private sectors, there are those who

139

approve extension to the public sector of the same kind of compulsory collective bargaining legislation which has been operative in the private sector for some 40 years.

When the Federal Government sanction was given to exclusive union representation and compulsory unionism in private employment for private industry in 1935—through the National Labor Relations Act—it thereby extended a private organization—a union—the power of government.

But several public employee legislative proposals would go far beyond NLRA. Bills suggested by the American Federation of State, County, and Municipal Employees and the National Education Association would force a wide aggregation of union powers and special privilege on every government unit in the country outside of the Federal Government. Among a long list of special privileges these proposals would: grant monopoly status to a union without secret ballot elections, authorize strikes of public employees, permit union officials to engage in coercive acts, authorize and approve full compulsory union membership and obligate every State, political subdivision, town, city, county, borough, district, school board, board of regents, public or quasipublic corporation or any other entity which is tax supported to abide by its provisions and to obey the decisions of a national public employment relations commission.

Today's discussion will look into all aspects of these various legislative proposals as well as the development of a new spoils system through public employee political action, the rights of State and municipal governments and their employees, compulsory arbitration and the role of individual freedom in an orderly society.

This discussion will also define the distinctions between the public sector and the private sector. The public and the private sectors are as different as night and day. And, a fundamental problem lies in the fact that private sector models are being applied to the public sector where they are not appropriate. By definition collective bargaining suggests a parity of powers which is essential to the bargaining process. In the public sector this party is nonexistent. Management in the private sector is granted a greater degree of economic leverage than its counterpart in the public sector. Because of market restraints, it is possible for an employee of private industry to negotiate himself out of a job. However, because government supplies essential services for the public, it is not possible for him to "lock out" the employees or go out of business.

The most fundamental question we will address in this dialog is whether government sovereignty can survive in the wake of compulsory public-sector bargaining. Noted law professor Dr. Sylvester Petro states:

> There is an absolute and ineradicable incompatibility between government sovereignty and compulsory public-sector bargaining, an incompatibility which must necessarily weaken if not ultimately destroy effective governing power and the integrity of government vis-a-vis the general citizenry, since the necessary consequence of according public-employee unions exclusive bargaining status is to encourage among government employees a tendency to repose their loyalties primarily in the units which they have been induced to believe are their protagonists.

Obviously, what we need asked and answered is whether the government—by its nature a monopoly and the protector of all citizens' rights and liberties, has the authority legally or morally, to transfer any of its functions to a private, independent organization. When public officials acting under authority granted to them by other public officials, give union organizers the right to say who will perform public service and how those services will be performed, do not we have a situation in which the authority of government has been divested from the public?

Unwelcome as it may be in many quarters, and unrealistic as it may seem in others, the proper labor relations policy for any government might well be one which rejects collective bargaining in every form.

Last September, the U.S. District Court for the Middle District of North Carolina held constitutional a State law which declared contracts between government and unions in that State to be void. In its decision the Court said:

> . . . to the extent that public employees gain power through recognition and collective bargaining, other interest groups with a right to a voice in the running of the government may be left out of vital political decisions. Thus, the granting of collective bargaining rights to public employees involves important matters fundamental to our democratic form of government. The setting of goals and making policy decisions are rights inuring to each citizen. All citizens have the right to associate in groups to advocate their special interests to the government. It is something entirely different to grant any one interest group special status and access to the decision-making process.

It is our hope that the discussion today will generate a serious national dialog about compulsory public-sector bargaining laws and governmental sovereignty. I would like to suggest that the American people and their representatives take a hard look at the validity of legislation that sanctions compulsory unionism. I, for one, intend to introduce legislation to

141

protect this country against universal adoption of compulsory public sector bargaining laws, and I urge my colleagues to support it.

I want to make it clear that I am not opposed to voluntary unionism, or the right of individual public employees to organize and join unions if they so desire. But I am a great believer in the right of free people to decide whether they wish to do that or not. I am also a great believer in the right of the States to decide whether they shall have compulsory unionism or not.

I am not proposing or intending to propose national right-to-work laws. There are only 19 States that do so, and that is their right, to make such decisions on their own. They should not be mandated by the Senate or by Congress in efforts to impose their will on all the local governments of this country. As a former mayor, I could not tolerate that intrusion into my ability as the chief administrative officer of a city to make such decisions, and be held accountable to the citizens of my city for those decisions.

The ACTING PRESIDENT pro tempore. The Senator's 15 minutes have expired.

Mr. GARN. I ask unanimous consent that Elizabeth Yee be accorded the privileges of the floor during the remainder of the discussion on this subject.

The ACTING PRESIDENT pro tempore. Without objection, it is so ordered.

Under the previous order, the Senator from South Carolina is recognized for not to exceed 15 minutes.

Mr. THURMOND. Mr. President, my colleagues here today will address the question of whether the Federal Government should impose upon the States and their political subdivisions a system of compulsory public sector collective bargaining. More broadly, we will be considering whether it is in fact in the public interest and is sound public policy for any government to be compelled to recognize and bargain with unions.

I believe that in consideration of this issue, we may pay careful attention to the question of the effect that such a system of compulsory bargaining would have on the sovereignty of government.

In this area, I would like you to consider what sovereignty consists of, whether it can exist where government is forced to submit itself and its decisionmaking processes to the negotiating table. I hope that at the conclusion of these remarks, it will be crystal clear that governmental sovereignty is absolutely essential and that it is so diametrically opposed to any system of compulsory public sector collective bargaining that it would not only be a grave error for us to legislate such a system for the States and their political subdivisions, but an equally grave error for this body to approve any system whereby the agencies of the executive branch of the Government of the United States would be compelled to bargain with unions representing its employees.

I wish to say at the outset that I do not believe that this position reflects on my part or on the part of my colleagues any antiworker sentiment whatsoever. We are faced with a very difficult question of public policy, and I believe the interest of the entire public, including all the employees of Government at all levels in America, is best served by systems of redress of grievances and terms of employment under which elected representatives hold and retain complete and ultimate control of the decisionmaking process. Employees of Government, like all employees, have the right of association in unions to present their position on these matters. However, because of the uniquely different character of Government employment, it is clear that collective bargaining is a system completely inappropriate to determining the terms and conditions of employment.

However, the question is sovereignty and the different nature of government which makes compulsory collective bargaining completely out of the question.

First of all, Government is a monopoly. There is not, and there cannot be, any competition with Government in its activities. There are those who will argue that Government is engaged in many activities in direct competition with the private sector. However, rather than being an argument against the concept of monopoly in Government, this should be considered an argument against these activities of Government, and we should reserve that discussion for another day. I do not think anyone will seriously question the necessity of a governmental monopoly on national defense, law enforcement, judicial proceedings, taxation, the coinage of money, or a long list of functions which belong entirely to the people through their elected representatives.

Second, in Government, as opposed to the private sector, there is no profit motive. I regard the profit motive as one of the single most important forces in giving America its tremendous productive capacity. It is at the very heart of our system of competitive free enterprise, a system which has produced a higher standard of living and more goods and services at lower prices than any other economic system, but we must submit that the profit motive is absent from considerations of Government employer-employee relations. In short, if we or any other body of elected officials pay our em-

143

ployees less money, not 1 cent of that money goes into our pockets. Our commission, as is that of every other elected public body, is to provide necessary services to the people in the best and most efficient manner possible. To provide those services, we must employ people, and the better people we employ, the better service we can provide. Thus it is in our interest and in the public interest to employ and keep in our employment the very best employees. In order to do this, we must keep ever mindful that the total compensation of our employees and their working conditions must be comparable with those in the private sector.

Now we come to the last and most crucial difference between public and private employment. That is the very nature of Government itself. The ruling principle of action in the private sector is free contract. That is, every action that takes place between free individuals in a free society is done by mutual agreement. This is true in employment, in purchase, in all of our obligations. However, the ruling principle of action in Government is force. Government is government only because it and it alone has the power to rule by compulsion. This is the way it must be because only through compulsion can Government insure the ordered, peaceful society upon which all other segments of society depend for their existence.

This is the crux of the question, can any government exist as government once it has lost its sovereignty? Furthermore, can any government retain sovereignty when it must submit important decisions of public policy to collective-bargaining negotiations with unions?

The answers to these questions are simple and clear, because of the very nature of unions and collective bargaining.

A collective-bargaining relationship—any and every collective bargaining relationship—depends on establishing an adversary relationship between employer and employee. Unions, in order to win and hold the loyalty of their members, must demand more than the employer is willing to offer. If a union were to accept only what the employer offered, it would serve no useful purpose for its members and soon it would have no members. So unions by virtue of their very nature and to preserve their existence must make demands. The only instrument that unions have at their disposal to support their demands is the withdrawal of the services of their members—the strike. The strike is, even when it is peaceful, the use of force. It cannot be defined or construed any other way. No government can call itself sovereign if it permits the use of force to enforce demands against it. We can see from this that there can be no true collective bargaining without strikes and there can be no true government with strikes.

This is the essential question we must face. Are we to have sovereign government, or are we to have public sector collective bargaining? We cannot have both. I am confident that the vast majority of American people will agree with this position.

For us, my colleagues, the question is equally simple. We must decide whether we as the elected representatives of the people are going to continue to run our Government, or whether we are going to turn it over to a relative handful of professional union organizers.

I am firmly convinced that we must do everything in our power to resist any attempts to institute a system of compulsory public sector collective bargaining at any level of Government. I do not doubt for a moment that the future of our system of government depends on it.

The ACTING PRESIDENT pro tempore. Under the previous order, the Senator from Arizona is recognized for not to exceed 15 minutes.

### UNIONIZATION OF FEDERAL, STATE, COUNTY, AND MUNICIPAL EMPLOYEES

Mr. FANNIN. Mr. President, I commend my colleagues, the Senator from South Carolina, and the very able and distinguished Senator from Utah; the Senator from South Carolina, who served with distinction as Governor, and who has great knowledge in the field which he is discussing, and who has worked with the employees both at the State and the local levels. I am very pleased to follow him in discussing this subject, so important to all the people of America, and my colleague from Utah, the former mayor of Salt Lake City, that great city that stands as a symbol of good government in this country of ours, and who performed admirably as its mayor, and who is now a U.S. Senator. We are proud that we have him with us, with his knowledge of the affairs of municipalities that has proven to be very helpful to us, having had recent experience in these particular fields, because we are in a period of changing times, some better and some otherwise. However, we know that there are different issues that face our municipalities today than, perhaps, when some of us served in our particular States several years ago.

Mr. President, Congress is now confronted by demands from union spokesmen to sanction the forced unionization of the 14½ million individuals employed by the States, local jurisdictions, and the Federal Government. These incredible demands were dramatized last November 6 by the first meeting of the AFL-CIO's new Public Employees Department. That meeting was featured by an address by the labor federation's president, George Meany, who said:

> Certainly, it's against the law to strike the civil service, but it's AFL-CIO policy to ignore those laws.

Now, just imagine that.

Mr. President, I was appalled by the irresponsibility of that statement.

Mr. Meany advised our 14½ million civil servants to "quit working for the guy who's kicking you around." Is that not a fine way to address these people?

> You stop the job. You shut it down. You take the consequences, and you fight. And if the guy happens to be the mayor of a city or the governor of a state, it doesn't make a damn bit of difference.

That is the end of the quote, that particular quote. I think that is a shameful quote.

It was reassuring to note that Mr. Meany was censured on the editorial page of the *New York Times*. That newspaper is influential. I do not always agree with it, but it observed in its edition of November 10:

> The accent Mr. Meany chose to put on militant action to bring Governors and Mayors to heel—with or without a law—raised new doubts that the general welfare would benefit from a Federal mandate to strengthen civil service unions.

On November 11 the *New York Daily News* editorialized as follows:

> The 94th Congress must screw up its courage and take a firm stand against such reckless labor adventuring. Government workers are entitled to representation and bargaining. But strikes against the public should be taboo—period. And that goes also for compulsory union membership. We simply cannot afford these callous, indefensible threats to the health, safety and economy of the nation. Nor should civil service workers be compelled to pay tribute to unions to hold jobs won on merit.

Mr. President, I think that illustrates exactly what we are discussing today.

These people are proud public servants. They want to hold their jobs on the basis of their merit, their work, they want to go forward, they want to earn a right to go forward.

Mr. President, today public employees in 34 of the 50 States are shielded from compulsory unionism by constitutional provisions, laws and executive orders.

Those States are Alabama, Arizona, Arkansas, California, Connecticut, Delaware, Florida, Illinois, Iowa, Kansas, Louisiana, Maine, Maryland, Mississippi, Missouri, Nebraska, Nevada, New Hampshire, New Jersey, New Mexico, New York, North Carolina, North Dakota, Ohio, Oklahoma, Pennsylvania, Rhode Island, South Carolina, South Dakota, Texas, Utah, Vermont, Virginia, and Wyoming.

Mr. President, the people of these States have afforded their friends and neighbors that work for their government this protection that is so vital to their State and the future of their particular communities, and certainly vital to this great Nation of ours.

Obviously, the safeguards now enjoyed by civil servants in those States would be eliminated by a new Federal law authorizing the forced unionization of citizens employed by the States and their political subdivisions.

Mr. President, the erection of barriers against involuntary union membership in the public sector was strongly recommended by the Advisory Commission on Intergovernmental Relations. In March 1970, that distinguished bipartisan body published its recommendations dealing with employer-employee relations in the public sector.

Mr. President, it is advantageous for us to recall that this Commission was created by the Congress in 1959. Its members represent the general public and the legislative and executive branches of Federal, State, and local governments. The Commission oversees the operation of our federal system with its division of powers, and it submits carefully studied recommendations relating to improvement of the system.

In their 1970 report members of the Advisory Commission on Intergovernmental Relations declared:

> While recognition of the right to membership is fundamental, of equal importance is the principle that no public employee should be required or coerced into joining an organization as a condition of employment ... the right to refrain is just as basic and precious as the right to join, and the Commission supports this position.

> Some authorities contend that State legislation should not include language that gives employees the option of not joining an employee organization. They point out that the States should not mandate the "choice" provision since it would preclude employer and employee representatives from negotiating union and closed shop agreements. The preferable approach, according to this argument, is for the State laws to remain silent on this matter, thereby providing a greater degree of flexibility for public agencies and employee organizations to arrive at agreements tailored to fit their own special circumstances.

> The Commission believes these contentions ignore the fact

that in the public service the right to join an employee organization must be accompanied by the right not to join. When the right to join becomes a duty, obviously freedom of choice becomes merely a catchword.

The union shop and the closed shop may or may not be appropriate for various crafts and trade portions of private industry. But given the size of many governmental jurisdictions and agencies, the diversity of employee skills, and the intense competition between and among public employee organizations, this arrangement is wholly unsuitable in the public service.

A similar view of impropriety of compulsory unionism in the Federal service was expressed 13 years ago by then-Secretary of Labor Arthur Goldberg. He spoke out in defense of prohibition against the union shop and the closed shop in Executive Order 10988, issued by the late President John F. Kennedy to authorize collective bargaining in the Federal service.

Addressing members of the American Federation of Government Employees, Secretary Goldberg said:

> I know you will agree with me that the union shop-closed shop are inappropriate to the Federal government. And because of this, there is a larger responsibility for enlightenment on the part of the government union. In your own organization you have to win acceptance by your own conduct, your own action, your own wisdom, your own responsibility, and your own achievements ... so you have an opportunity to bring into your organization people who come in because they want to come in and who will participate, therefore, in the full activity of your organization.

Now, Mr. President, that was Secretary Goldberg addressing this Government employees' organization, so this is not a partisan issue, this is an issue of righteousness, this is an issue of freedom.

Significantly, the ban on forced unionism in the Federal service has been maintained by President Kennedy's three successors. A similar prohibition was incorporated by the Congress in the Postal Reorganization Act of 1970.

Mr. President, if we permit ourselves to be stampeded on the issue of authorizing involuntary unionism in the public sector, exposing 14½ million public employees to union coercion, then the American people will recognize clearly that the Congress merits their contempt.

Mr. President, we should listen to the voice of the American people. We should take the actions by the people that are close to the scene of activity, to understand what is happening. They are the ones that have made the decisions as to what to be done in their particular States, particular localities.

Mr. President, I think it would be highly irresponsible for us to take an action that is contrary to their best interest.

I yield the floor, Mr. President.

The ACTING PRESIDENT pro tempore. Under the previous order, the Senator from Idaho is recognized for not to exceed 15 minutes.

Mr. McCLURE. Mr. President, I ask unanimous consent that the time allotted to the Senator from Idaho under the special order be allotted to the Senator from Utah (Mr. GARN).

The ACTING PRESIDENT pro tempore. Without objection, it is so ordered.

Mr. GARN. Mr. President, I wish to amplify my previous remarks with some specific examples of the effect of laws passed by Congress that are not nearly as severe as the matter we are condemning today, that being mandatory collective bargaining and binding arbitration, and the effect these laws have had on the cities and States of this country. I refer specifically to the imposition of the Fair Labor Standards Act upon municipal and State and county governments of this country last year, despite the position of the National League of Cities Board of Directors representing 15,000 cities across this country, despite the fact that the Governor's Conference took a similar position in opposition to the Congress of the United States imposing the Fair Labor Standards Act and the provisions of it on local government, despite the fact that we testified opposed to it—Mayor Tom Bradley of Los Angeles and I, he being a Democrat, I being a Republican—despite the fact that the National League of Cities Board of Directors representing 15,000 cities, both liberals and conservatives, Republicans and Democrats, came back and testified before House and Senate committees in opposition, so that a very united bipartisan, nonpartisan effort opposed this, nevertheless it was imposed upon the cities of this country at a tremendous cost to the taxpayers of this country. I use my own city as an example.

It will require us to pay time and a half to firemen for sleeping. There will be no additional firemen, no better quality of fire service, and just in my relatively small city a cost of $3 million a year to the local taxpayers for nothing. There is an additional half million dollars because of rules that are involved with telling us how to run our personnel management system.

I will put in a specific example here. Most people know that in Salt Lake City you have very distinct seasons. You have hard winters and warm summers. So our park department employees would work a lot of overtime on the parks and golf courses during the summer and build up overtime, I might add this was on a voluntary basis. They enjoyed taking that compensatory time off in the middle of the winter when they were not needed. They would take 5 or 6 weeks off at a time and enjoy the long periods. The snow removal crews would do the opposite and would take their time off during the summer. So it enabled us to balance our work force. The employees loved it. As I said, it was voluntary and 85 percent of the employees chose to work in that manner. It saved the taxpayers some money.

Now, because Congress, due to the influence of the national labor organizations, has decided to ignore all of the mayors and Governors of this country, because I do not suppose we have as much political power, they changed those rules and said that you cannot grant compensatory time off unless you grant it during the week in which the overtime was incurred, or the following week, or you have to pay it in cash in time and a half.

That is an imposition of another half million dollars of cost on Salt Lake City government.

Congress in their great wisdom passed revenue sharing. Salt Lake City received $4 million in revenue sharing. Because of the imposition of the Fair Labor Standards Act, Congress has taken $3.5 million of it away. But more importantly, it has taken away the right of an elected mayor and a city council to make decisions in their own community, in their own sovereign community, and be held accountable to the voters of that community for their actions. So the Congress giveth and they taketh away. We have a net of a half million dollars left.

Well, we were ignored. We were not listened to by the Congress. A small group of labor leaders obviously had more effect on the outcome of this imposition of the Fair Labor Standards Act than the representatives of all of the cities in this country. So we decided to take it to court. We did, and we have received an injunction, a restraining order, from the imposition of this law. We are going to find out whether the Congress of the United States has the constitutional right to impose their will on the locally elected officials to this country.

The Governors Conference is supporting the National League of Cities and the U.S. Conference of Mayors in this effort.

I wish to add that I hope the American people will wake up to what is being done, to demonstrate the arrogance of some people in the labor movement to impose their will, despite the feelings of the elected representatives of this country.

I wish to report to the Senate a meeting held this week with the Congressional Cities Conference Workshop on Collective Bargaining held March 3, 1975, 2 p.m. to 4:30 p.m., at the International Ballroom East, Washington Hilton Hotel, Washington, D.C.

I refer to a memorandum addressed to me from Commissioner Jennings Phillips, Jr., of Salt Lake City, Utah.

This concerns the Congressional Workshop on Collective Bargaining held during the League of Cities Conference at the Washington Hilton Hotel.

Present were: Robert LaFortune, mayor, Tulsa, presiding; Robert Moss, General Counsel, House Subcommittee on Labor of the House Committee on Education and Labor; and George P. Sape, Associate Counsel, Senate Committee on Labor and Public Welfare, representing Donald Elisburg.

I want the arrogance of this statement to be carefully noted in the RECORD:

> In the introductory remarks, both Mr. Moss and Mr. Sape advised those present that regardless of what the Supreme Court's decision was on the suit brought by the League of Cities contesting the right of Congress to interfere with the employment practices of the cities and counties of this country, it was their opinion that Congress would move ahead to impose such regulations on the cities and counties.
>
> After questions by those present, Mr. Moss and Mr. Sape stated Congress could very well make collective bargaining and the right to strike a condition of getting a federal grant.

That is really something, when employees of the Senate and the House of Representatives of the United States are telling mayors of this country that even if we win a suit in the Supreme Court of the United States declaring the very act of the Congress to be unconstitutional, that Congress will go ahead and stuff it down our throats anyway.

Mr. Moss and Mr. Sape were extremely arrogant and in essence said that we could do nothing to stop it and had just as well sit back, relax, and enjoy it.

I submit that it is time the American people awakened to what is being imposed upon them. If they want to have Government close to the people, if they want their local mayor and city council, county commissioners, Governors, and legislators able to be anything but local stooges for the Federal Government, then we cannot tolerate further extension of the power of the Federal Government into the internal affairs of local and State government. We cannot tolerate a bill that

151

imposes mandatory collective bargaining and binding arbitration on the cities and counties of this country.

We need to work to repeal the imposition of the Fair Labor Standards Act which interferes with the sovereign right of a mayor or a Governor to administer the affairs of his own city or State.

I yield back the remainder of my time.

The ACTING PRESIDENT pro tempore. Under the previous order, the Senator from Wyoming is recognized for not to exceed 15 minutes.

Mr. HANSEN. Mr. President, I have consistently supported efforts to require private sector unions to conduct a secret ballot vote among their members before calling a strike. I have also supported efforts to require that each new offer from management be voted on by the membership. I believe that these measures are necessary to instill the greatest amount of democracy into union affairs. Under this system, a strike could not be called unless a majority of members desired it, and union leaders would not be allowed to reject management offers without first consulting the membership. This would go a long way toward placing control of their own affairs back in the hands of the workers instead of a few union leaders.

Mr. President, in the public sector we are faced with increasing union demands for a federally mandated system of compulsory collective bargaining. A major concern has to be the question of strikes.

The undesirability of public sector strikes and the reasons for this are obvious to all of us. One needs only to look at the havoc wrought by these strikes—such as those in San Francisco and Baltimore—to realize their danger.

In Baltimore—police, prison guards, and sanitation workers on strike at the same time. The result: Garbage piled on the streets; individuals attempting to take their own garbage to the dumps harassed and physically threatened by strikers, in one instance fired upon—an uprising of inmates at the city prison subdued only with the assistance of nonrebellious inmates—looting and arson erupt within hours after the police walk off the job, resulting in millions of dollars of property damage and at least one death. And the national president of the union threatens Governor Mandel that Baltimore City would burn to the ground unless their demands were met.

In San Francisco—the city crippled by a massive strike of its employees. Public transportation shut down—schools experiencing 25 percent attendance and on a half-day schedule—San Francisco General Hospital operating on an emergency-only basis, all but 150 critically ill patients moved

152

to other locations—over 100 million gallons of raw sewage a day being pumped into the bay. After the settlement, a local labor leader tells the strikers:

> I want to compliment you on the way you mounted your picket lines—the way you kept this city in turmoil until our demands were met.

One would think that something really terrific had been accomplished, without ever giving a thought to the havoc and the pain and suffering that resulted from this illegal strike.

The scene has been repeated across the country: a firemen's strike in Albuquerque that resulted in residents attempting to put out fires with garden hoses; a prolonged teacher strike in Wisconsin that led to deep divisions and outbreaks of violence within the community; a recent bus strike in Washington that, as reported in the *Washington Post,* most adversely affected low-income individuals that relied on the buses to get to jobs far from their homes; a recent case in New York City where the leadership of the firefighter's union called a strike after the membership had voted against it.

As a rule, have we been able to prevent these work stoppages? Experience shows that we have not. Learned opinion holds that under a system of compulsory public sector collective bargaining these strikes are, in fact, unavoidable.

Experts in the field of labor relations have reached this conclusion. Theodore H. Kheel, the well-known arbitrator, has said that "collective bargaining and strikes are like Siamese twins." Robert Hillman, former labor commissioner for the city of Baltimore, at a conference on public sector labor relations held this past December at the University of Maryland said, "collective bargaining means strikes." He further characterized as "hypocritical" those who believe strikes can be prevented through the enactment of legislation which obligates government to bargain with unions.

Labor leaders have echoed this and, as their actions demonstrate, have shown a total lack of regard for the law and society by engaging in illegal strikes. George Meany, speaking at the founding convention of the AFL-CIO's new Public Employee Department, said:

> If you just quit working for the guy who's kicking you around. And if that guy happens to be the mayor of the city or the Governor of a State, it doesn't make a damn bit of difference.

Actual experience with public sector collective bargaining further verifies this. The State of Michigan, for example, enacted public sector bargaining legislation in 1965. In the 7 years prior to this, they had experienced one strike. In the 3 years that immediately followed, there were 103 illegal strikes. In fact, a statistical compilation of all States shows an average of 1.92 strikes per State per year before the enactment of compulsory collective-bargaining legislation and 6.58 strikes per State per year thereafter.

Let me repeat those figures: The average statistical compilation of all States prior to the enactment of this legistation was 1.92, and after the enactment of compulsory collective-bargaining legislation, that figure rose to 6.58 per State per year thereafter.

Legislated strike bans have proven ineffectual, as have penalties for illegal strikes. The vast majority of public sector strikes have been and continue to be illegal. The penalties against both the union and the individuals striking have rarely been enforced, even in those States where the law has been written so as to make these penalties automatic and mandatory. Prime among the reasons for this has been the tendency to include in the "negotiated" settlement of a strike a clause granting amnesty to the strikers and their union.

The simple fact is that collective bargaining and strikes are inseparable. Public sector unions are going to strike when and where they feel like it.

The recent trend has been to give up the fight altogether and legalize public sector strikes, much to the delight of the unions. The State of Pennsylvania undertook such a course of action in 1971, and in 1972 had the dubious honor of leading the Nation in the number of public sector strikes.

The point being conveniently ignored by the proponents of compulsory public sector collective bargaining is that public sector collective bargaining is the reason for public sector strikes. This fact is inescapable. A union must satisfy its membership. To do this, that union must make demands. This establishes the adversary relationship that unions thrive on. To maintain this adversary relationship and insure the success of their demands, the union must show a willingness to strike, for the strike is their equalizer. The establishment of a willingness to strike necessitates actually going on strike when the situation demands it.

We, as legislators, have a responsibility to our constituents to see that public safety is maintained and that Government services continue uninterrupted. To fulfill this responsibility, we must oppose the injection of compulsory public sector collective bargaining into our society.

Faced with increasing union demands for compulsory public sector collective bargaining, a major concern has to be the question of public sector strikes.

The undesirability of public sector strikes and the reasons for this are obvious.

We have been unable to prevent them. Experts on labor relations and union leaders have declared them unavoidable. Actual experience has echoed this. Strike bans and penalties have been ineffectual.

The reason for public sector strikes is public sector collective bargaining. The rational course is to oppose compulsory public sector collective bargaining.

Mr. President, I was very much interested in the observations of the distinguished junior Senator from Utah. Here is a man who has had firsthand experience in the managing of a great city. He is a man who knows what he is talking about. He is a man who has experienced firsthand what some of the laws that are passed by Congress can do to a city in America. I am a believer in the right of people to join unions. I am well aware, as every interested American must be that unions have moved the standard of living and the welfare of workers forward in a very marked fashion in this country in the last 100 years.

I think the words of the distinguished junior Senator from Utah and others here today who have talked on this subject ought to be listened to by every Member of this body. They ought to be read by every Member of the other body, and before we pass legislation that guarantees public employees the right to strike, we had better see what we are doing. I hope that this Congress will act responsibly in this area and not take a step that, some say, would be a step forward, but, in fact, would be a very sad step backward for America.

This is a great country. The rights of individuals are protected here as they are nowhere else on Earth.

I yield the floor.

Mr. McCLURE. Mr. President.

The PRESIDING OFFICER (Mr. FORD). Under the previous order, the Senator from Idaho (Mr. McCLURE) is recognized for not to exceed 15 minutes.

Mr. McCLURE. Mr. President, I ask unanimous consent that the order of appearance between Mr. BUCKLEY and myself be reversed and that he be recognized at this time.

The PRESIDING OFFICER. Without objection, it is so ordered. The Senator from New York is recognized.

155

Mr. BUCKLEY. I thank the distinguished Senator from Idaho.

Mr. President, I wish to address, in my remarks, one aspect of this discussion, namely, whether or not the Federal Government has any authority or any right to intervene in what is basically the business of the States and their political subdivisions.

Mr. President, I find it disturbing to read predictions in the newspapers that this Congress will soon enact what is described as "a new Federal law granting collective bargaining rights" to the more than 11 million employees of the Nation's States, counties, cities and towns.

During the current session numerous bills have been introduced here for the purpose of mandating collective bargaining at all levels of government. Such legislation was submitted to the 93d Congress and to several of its predecessors.

But somehow, we are seeing steam generated behind them.

I recognize that this legislation has been the subject of public hearings conducted by committees and subcommittees of the Senate and House of Representatives.

It would be a grave mistake, in my view, for the Federal Government to attempt to dictate to the States and their political subdivisions with respect to their own employees.

If a given State bargains, or refuses to bargain, with its own civil servants, that is the State's business and not the business of the Federal Government.

If a given State grants monopoly bargaining privileges to labor unions comprised of its own employees, or without such privileges, that is the State's business and not the business of the Federal Government.

If a given State either prohibits or sanctions the mandatory unionization of State workers who do not want to be represented by labor unions, that also is the State's business and not the business of the Federal Government.

If a given State decides to permit employees of the State and its political subdivisions to engage in strikes, that, too, is the State's business and not the business of the Federal Government.

Several proposals now pending in the Congress would compel all of the 50 States and their political subdivisions to recognize and bargain with unions purporting to represent their employees. These proposals would also extend monopoly bargaining privileges to recognized unions. They would legalize the practice of requiring workers on public payrolls to pay dues or fees to labor unions as a condition of employment. And the measures to which I refer would put the Federal Government's stamp-of-approval on strikes by State,

156

county, and municipal employees—including public school-teachers.

The very fact that serious consideration is likely to be accorded—in fact, is being accorded—these proposals illustrates how far we have strayed from the principles which guided the Nation's Founding Fathers.

The men who established our form of government sought to diffuse sovereign power. George Washington said:

> Government is like fire, a dangerous servant and a fearful master.

Students of our country's history well remember that ratification by the States of our Constitution was assured only by adoption of the first 10 amendments to that document. Throughout our national life those amendments have been popularly known as the "Bill of Rights" and have been deemed to be that body within the Constitution that protects the citizens and protects the States from the kind of domination out of a centralized government that ultimately represents a threat to all our liberties.

> The powers not delegated to the United States by the Constitution, nor prohibited by it to the States, are reserved to the States respectively, or to the people.

Nowhere, Mr. President, do I find in the Constitution anything that remotely suggests that the Federal Government would have the authority to dictate the way in which the individual sovereign States would conduct their own relationships with their own employees.

Mr. President, the imposition by the Congress of a collective bargaining straitjacket of the States and local jurisdictions would be an indefensible violation of the authority reserved to the States by the 10th amendment to the U.S. Constitution.

It would extend still further the already dangerous concentration of power in the Federal Government and would continue the transformation of our once-sovereign States into the status of mere administrative units for the administration of Federal policy. This is precisely the result that the Constitution was designed to prevent, a concentration, namely, of power that would ultimately threaten the freedoms of our people. Such a law would supersede and override constitutional provisions and statutes adopted by a majority of the States in the Union. Within recent years many States have enacted comprehensive collective bargaining laws for the benefit of public sector employees.

A distinct advantage of our form of government is that it

encourages the use of the States as laboratories in which varied ideas and theories can be tested without committing the entire Nation to a certain policy or course of action. The collective bargaining process is now being tested in the public sectors of many of our States, and even if it had the constitutional authority to impose its will, Congress ought not to try to interfere. It would, in fact, be well advised to permit that testing to continue.

To date no less than 34 States have chosen to outlaw compulsory unionism in their public sectors. By what authority will we, as Federal legislators, tell the States they may not prohibit the forced unionization of public employees over whom they exercise jurisdiction?

In 1959 the Congress created the Advisory Commission on Intergovernmental Relations to monitor the operation of the American federal system and also formulate recommendations pertinent to the system's improvement. The Commission periodically chooses specific intergovernmental issues for study and invites review and comment by spokesmen for all affected levels of government, representatives of interested groups, and technical experts. Members of the Commission then debate the selected issue and formulate its policy position on the issue.

In 1970 the Commission published its findings and recommendations after conducting a 1-year study of employer-employee relations in the public sector. In unmistakable language, the Commission's report expressed vigorous opposition to:

> Any Federal effort to mandate a collective bargaining, meet and confer, or any other labor-relations system for the employees of State and local jurisdictions or for any sector thereof. Little would be left of the Federal principle of divided powers were such legislation enacted. No interpretation of the commerce power, of the State as proprietor, or of the "general welfare" clause can, in our opinion, serve as a legitimate constitutional basis for this kind of drastic infringement upon the basic authority of the States and localities as governments in a federal system.

Mr. President, it is germane to observe that agencies of the Federal Government are not yet obligated by law to engage in bargaining with their employees. Under the prevailing circumstances, imposition by the Congress of such an obligation on the States and their political subdivisions would be anomalous—not to say gratuitous.

The failure or refusal of the Congress to apply a labor relations law to its own agencies and departments and their employees was not overlooked by the Advisory Commission on Intergovernmental Relations. Its report concluded:

> In the absence of overwhelming evidence of the unwillingness or inability of State and local governments to act, the Federal Government should refrain from preemptive action. Such evidence clearly is lacking at present. States and localities have developed and are developing their own response to the challenge of employee militancy, especially teacher militancy. Given the nature of this challenge, experimentation and flexibility are needed, not a standardized, Federal, preemptive approach....
>
> The Federal Government clearly has an interest in the development of stable and equitable labor-management relations at the other levels. This interest can be best served, however, by avoiding actions that would exacerbate these relations and by focusing on ways and means of directly encouraging the establishment of strong, innovative personnel systems.

The Commission, whose members represent the public and the executive and legislative branches of Federal, State and local governments, is a respected and permanent bipartisan body. Among its members who fashioned the 1970 report on employer-employee relations in the public sector were Senator MUSKIE of Maine, former Senator Ervin of North Carolina, the late Senator Karl E. Mundt of South Dakota, Congressman ULLMAN of Oregon, Congressman FOUNTAIN of North Carolina, and the former Congresswoman from New Jersey, Mrs. Florence P. Dwyer.

Mr. President, I appeal to my colleagues to heed the Commission's recommendation. We are bound by our oaths to reject all legislation designed to compel the States and localities to bargain with labor unions purporting to represent their employees.

I might add, Mr. President, that only 2 weeks ago, at the National Governors' Conference, the Committee on Executive Management and Fiscal Affairs adopted the following resolution, which I shall read in its entirety. It is headed "Public Employee Relations," and reads as follows:

> The United States Congress is considering legislation which would provide to State and local government employees the right to organize and collectively bargain. This legislation would substantially replace individual state laws and procedures which now regulate these activities with a uniform federal law.
>
> The National Governors' Conference opposes federal intervention in this area. It is the belief of the Nation's Governors that matters relating to the employees of State and local governments are within the sole jurisdiction of these units and are not properly the subject of federal legislation.
>
> The National Governors' Conference, in adopting this state-

ment, takes no position on the principle of collective bargaining for public employees but states its firm commitment to the view that this is an area which should be left to the discretion of the several States.

Mr. President, I know it has become unfashionable in this body to suggest that there are any constitutional limitations remaining to Federal action. The courts have cooperated in a gradual expansion of the commerce clause, so that it bears no conceivable relationship to what our founders intended, and the same thing has been said about the general welfare clause. And although each one of us is sworn to defend the Constitution, I believe we ought to remind ourselves once in a while as to what is in the Constitution.

The PRESIDING OFFICER. The time of the Senator from New York has expired. Under the previous order, the Senator from Idaho (Mr. McCLURE) is recognized.

Mr. McCLURE. Mr. President, let me begin by expressing my commendation to those who have already spoken, particularly to the freshman Senator from Utah (Mr. GARN), the former mayor of the great city of Salt Lake City, and to the Senator from South Carolina (Mr. THURMOND) for his comments, and also to commend the additional comments by the Senators from Arizona, Wyoming, and New York, who have just concluded.

Mr. President, the nature of our discussion here today brings to mind an enduring observation by the 17th century philosopher, Baruch Spinoza, on the role of government in a free society:

> ... The object of government is not to change men from rational beings into beasts or puppets, but to enable them to develop their minds and bodies in security, and to employ their reason unshackled ... in fact, the true aim of government is liberty.

This philosophy quickly found its way into our own national law and discourse.

It is not a long step from Spinoza's ideal government to the Declaration of Independence, in which the Founding Fathers wrote:

> ... That all men are created equal, that they are endowed by their Creator with certain unalienable Rights, that among these are Life, Liberty, and the Pursuit of Happiness—That to secure these Rights, Governments are instituted among Men, deriving their just Powers from the Consent of the Governed.

160

Our society, our Constitution, and supposedly every law and statute enacted by Congress in the past 200 years is built on this concept of government and the governed.

Yet, I am afraid, we have wandered far astray in the field of labor relations law; and, if we are careless in our actions to come, we might not only jeopardize the freedoms we are supposed to protect, we might even jeopardize the Government itself.

As we have already noted, union professionals are trying to build a case for Federal legislation affecting labor relations in the public sector—in the Federal Government, as well as every State, county and borough across the country.

They will undoubtedly attempt to sell these proposals to us in the name of liberty and worker rights.

They will discuss the right to join a union—and it must be noted here that that is a right already protected by the U.S. Constitution—and various other claimed rights, such as the "right" of Government employees to strike against their Government.

But they will ignore other rights, rights which may not seem too important to them, but which in one way or another affect all of us. While it is true that each person has a different focus and perspective on his own and the Nation's needs, there are some insights common to all. Everyone will agree that the protection of his freedom is basic to all other propositions. Most people see that the best way to protect their own freedom is to insist on the protection of freedom for others.

For many, the most precious freedom of those guaranteed by the Constitution is that of religion. They insist that without it any adherence to freedom in other forms is folly. Representatives of several religious groups have come to me explaining that compulsory unionism would force them to violate their religious convictions. Because of this I offered an amendment to the 1970 Postal Reorganization Act providing that:

> No individual who is a member of a religious sect or division thereof, the established and traditional tenets or teachings of which oppose a requirement that a member of such sect or division join or financially support any labor organization as a condition of employment, if such individual pays to the Treasurer of the United States a sum equal to the initiation fees and periodic dues uniformly required as a condition of acquiring and retaining membership in a labor organization which is representative of the employee unless said individual and said labor organization mutually agree upon some other condition of employment.

This amendment was accepted by the House Committee on Post Office and Civil Service. Although the section to which it was amended was ultimately removed from the bill for very different reasons, Congress made it clear that it did not intend to undermine religious beliefs. It seems to me that those people who profess to believe in the separation of church and state ought to be in the forefront of this fight to prevent an incursion by the state into what is for some a religious matter. This will give those people a chance to show that what they really believe in is a separation of church and state—not a separation of church and people.

It is important to stress here again that government, by definition, is unique. It is a uniquely privileged and powerful monopoly, whose very existence is derived from the consent of the governed.

As the distinguished scholar Russell Kirk wrote last year in *Education* magazine:

> By its nature, government is a monopoly. In any community nowadays, ordinarily, there exists but one police force, one fire department, one department of sanitation, one post office system ... one apparatus for the collection of revenue and the disbursing of public funds.
>
> If the people employed in such a monopoly are subject to the will of officers in a union, in some emergency the authority of government might be defied successfully by the men who dominate the union.

Then he warned, even the most essential public services, including the ordinary enforcement of law and keeping of the peace—

> Would depend upon the mood and the ambitions of the people controlling the union.
>
> The real government might be the union itself.

Harsh words, but not unrealistic if we fall into the trap of granting to public sector union officials monopoly control of the public sector workforce through the concession of monopoly representation privileges and compulsory union shop taxing powers, coupled with the right to strike in those unions.

If we grant them monopoly status, we have, as Dr. Kirk has eloquently pointed out, in effect, created a system of dual governments—one legitimate, appointed by the authority of the people, and the other a de facto government, accountable to no one except possibly the political system it feeds on.

The citizen taxpayer, subject to abuse by both governments, could exercise some control over the one, but would be virtually powerless to control the monopoly of the other.

As union officials gain a bigger and mightier foothold, and are able to exercise more control over the selected government, we could be faced with the actual day-to-day operation of vital government services at the whimsy of a union bureaucracy.

Government is unique. Its function is to serve the cause of liberty. We cannot have liberty and compulsory monopoly unions in control of the public service workforce, coupled with the right to strike. The measure of any proposition must be its impact upon a free people. It would be ironic if we were to move into the bicentennial period by inaugurating a program so alien to all that our Founding Fathers fought for.

Mr. President, I yield back the remainder of my time.

The PRESIDING OFFICER. Under the previous order, the Senator from North Carolina (Mr. HELMS) is recognized.

Mr. MANSFIELD. Mr. President, I suggest the absence of a quorum on the time of the Senator from North Carolina.

The PRESIDING OFFICER. The clerk will call the roll.

The assistant legislative clerk proceeded to call the roll.

Mr. McCLURE. Mr. President, I ask unanimous consent that the order for the quorum call be rescinded.

The PRESIDING OFFICER. Without objection, it is so ordered.

The PRESIDING OFFICER. Under the previous order, the Chair will recognize the Senator from North Carolina (Mr. HELMS).

Mr. HELMS. Mr. President, I ask unanimous consent that I will be allowed to yield 2 minutes of my time to the distinguished Senator from Nebraska.

The PRESIDING OFFICER. Without objection, it is so ordered.

Mr. CURTIS. I thank my distinguished friend.

The PRESIDING OFFICER. The Chair might inform the Senator from North Carolina that the quorum call was taken from his time of 15 minutes.

Mr. HELMS. Very well.

The PRESIDING OFFICER. The Senator from Nebraska.

Mr. CURTIS. Mr. President, I wish to join with the distinguished Senator from Utah and others in calling attention to the Senate the problems involved in these efforts for unionization of Government employees at all levels of Government.

Within the last day or two, there was an account that appeared in the *Washington Star* concerning what has happened in the State of Illinois.

I believe in the right of people to join the union, I do not think that should be interfered with. I do not believe in the principle of compulsory unionism either by coercion or by a matter of law.

I also wish to point out that there are certain essential services of Government which by their very nature call for restraint.

So, whatever might be our attitude toward strikes involving nongovernmental activities, I am of the opinion that it is not according to sound public policy that these Government unions should be allowed to strike.

We will be faced with this problem in reference to the postal service before long and I think it is important that we look at all of the problems involved and not permit this to further deteriorate a very poorly administered and run postal service.

In saying that, I want to set the record straight, I am sure that there are just countless honest and dedicated postal workers. Yet there is something wrong somewhere. Our Postal Service continues to deteriorate.

I want to again commend the distinguished Senator from Utah for taking the lead in prompting thought on this important subject.

I thank my distinguished friend from North Carolina.

I yield back the remainder of my time.

### NORTH CAROLINA'S SOLUTION

Mr. HELMS. Mr. President, we have just heard it from our colleagues—about the threat to the basic political institutions of the country posed by the compulsory public-sector bargaining proposals being offered for our consideration.

We have discussed here today, in particular what compulsory public sector bargaining on all levels of Government by Federal legislators would mean.

These proposals would compel through Federal action individual public employees to accept an unwanted union as their "exclusive representative" in dealing with their own government, and most likely—as a consequence of compulsory monopoly representation—would cause workers to pay tribute to union officials in order to keep their jobs.

Antistrike provisions and the myriad other technical details union officials propose really only obscure these basic problems—each of which threatens both individual and government sovereignty.

Mr. President, there are very few among us, I think, who would argue with these other points made here today:

That strikes against the government cannot be tolerated by a free society.

164

That government must—by definition—be responsive to and fully accountable to the people at all times.

That the only true function of government is the preservation of liberty.

And that public sector employees are indeed different from their counterparts in industry, both in terms of the rights and privileges they enjoy and the nature of their noncompetitive employment.

I believe that there is a viable solution without passing Federal laws. We can preserve government sovereignty and individual freedom in the public sector without being unrealistic, and certainly without being "unfair" to public employees.

In fact, in my State of North Carolina we have devised and implemented a viable solution at the State level. All public-sector collective bargaining is prohibited in the State of North Carolina.

We recognize that all public employees—and all Americans—are protected in their right to join lawful employee associations by the first amendment.

We have rejected, however, the notion that governments should be duty bound to recognize and bargain with these associations. Experience has taught us that the one thing which gives growth and strength and pressuring power to a union is to recognize that union, treat with it and enter into exclusive agreements with it. Each such agreement is a prelude to successive negotiations, accommodations, and agreements until the union grows to become uncontrolled and uncontrollable.

Now, Mr. President, the North Carolina General Statutes, section 95–98 reads as follows:

> Contracts between units of government and labor unions, trade unions or labor organizations concerning public employees declared to be illegal.—Any agreement, or contract, between the governing authority of any city, town, county, or other municipality, or between any agency, unit, or instrumentality thereof, or between any agency, instrumentality, or institution of the State of North Carolina, and any labor union, trade union, or labor organization, as bargaining agent for any public employees of such city, town, county or other municipality, or agency or instrumentality of government, is hereby declared illegal, unlawful, void and of no effect.

Mr. President, this North Carolina statute is a good law. It has successfully restrained the growth of public sector union power in North Carolina. Yet it has not led to continuous struggles with public employee disputes and conflict. And the statute has withstood challenges in the courts.

In a September 1974 decision the U.S. District Court for

the middle district of North Carolina held constitutional this North Carolina law which declares invalid any contract between a sovereign government and a union in that State.

The court said, that—

> To the extent that public employees gain power through recognition and collective bargaining, other interest groups with a right to a voice in the running of the government may be left out of vital political decisions. Thus, the granting of collective bargaining rights to public employees involves important matters fundamental to our democratic form of government. The setting of goals and making policy decisions are rights inuring to each citizen. All citizens have the right to associate in groups to advocate their special interests to the government. It is something entirely different to grant any one interest group special status and access to the decision-making process.

Simply put, the court made a very affirmative statement of the rights of all citizens and groups of citizens to have equal access to their own government.

While the North Carolina law puts a statutory prohibition on recognition and contract-making, it does not preclude representatives of employee associations from petitioning their government over conditions in the workplace. What it does preclude is government granting monopoly status to a particular union, trading away its own sovereignty, and depriving individual workers of their precious liberty to deal with their own government.

A strict nonrecognition policy, such as exists in North Carolina, would prevent any compromise of necessary government sovereignty.

Second, as the court found last September, it would keep the channels of redress open to all employees—not just to a monopoly bargaining organization.

Third, it would allow government administrators to create and conduct responsible, humane, and effective public employee personnel policies—a responsibility which, when subject to adversary collective bargaining, is less imaginative, and less progressive.

The attention of government administrators would thereby be focused—as it should be—on dealing effectively with the employees and their interests, rather than dealing with the union and its interest.

Among the most important considerations, however, is the fact that nonrecognition would prevent the abuses of human liberty which have been created by the National Labor Relations Act's "exclusive recognition" and compulsory unionism policies.

The North Carolina experience seems to be a good place to

start. It shows that the States can handle the problem on their own without Federal intervention. I commend this law to my colleagues as the way to go in the States which they represent.

Mr. President, the decision of the U.S. district court on the North Carolina law, provides further insights into its working and value, and I ask unanimous consent that the decision be printed in the RECORD.

There being no objection, the decision was ordered to be printed in the RECORD, as follows:

[No. C-286-WS-72]

IN THE U.S. DISTRICT COURT FOR THE MIDDLE DISTRICT OF NORTH CAROLINA, WINSTON-SALEM DIVISION

Winston-Salem/Forsyth County Unit of the North Carolina Association of Educators, an unincorporated association, and Jacqueline A. Ballentine, individually and on behalf of other similarly situated teachers in the Winston-Salem/Forsyth County School System, Plaintiffs, *v.* A. Craig Phillips, State Superintendent of Public Instruction; Frank Crane, Commissioner of Labor for the State of North Carolina; Robert B. Morgan, Attorney General of the State of North Carolina; and John C. Kiger, Omeda Brewer, Eunice Burge, Richard Janeway, Mary Lauerman, William F. Maready, Alan R. Perry, Carol G. Thompson, As Members of the Winston-Salem/Forsyth County School Board, and the Winston-Salem/Forsyth County School Board, and David W. Darr, Henry L. Crotts, G. P. Swisher, Dr. W. L. Thompson, Jr., and Leonard Warner as Members of the Forsyth County Board of Commissioners and the County of Forsyth, Defendants.

Before Craven, Circuit Judge, Gordon, Chief Judge, and Ward, District Judge.

Argued July 12, 1974, decided September 17, 1974.

William G. Pfefferkorn of Winston-Salem, North Carolina, for the plaintiff.

Edwin M. Speas, Jr., Assistant Attorney General, North Carolina Department of Justice, Raleigh, North Carolina, for defendants. A. Craig Phillips, Frank Crane, and Robert B. Morgan; William F. Womble, Jr., of Womble, Carlyle, Sandridge & Rice, Winston-Salem, North Carolina, for Winston-Salem/Forsyth County School Board; and P. Eugene Price, Jr., County Attorney, Winston-Salem, North Carolina, for Forsyth County Board of Commissioners, and the County of Forsyth.

OPINION OF THE COURT

Ward, District Judge:

This case presents a renewed attack on North Carolina General Statute 95–98 which provides that contracts between state governmental units and public employee labor organizations shall be void.[1] Previously, in *Atkins v. City of Charlotte*, 269 F. Supp. 1068 (W.D.N.C. 1969), a three-judge court upheld the constitutionality of that statute while declaring related sections to be unconstitutional.[2]

In the instant case, plaintiffs request injunctive and declaratory relief against the statute on the grounds that it operates to violate their rights of freedom of association guaranteed by the First Amendment of the United States Constitution and of equal protection and due process guaranteed by the Fourteenth Amendment. Jurisdiction is premised upon 28 U.S.C. §§ 2201 and 1343 and 42 U.S.C. § 1983. A three-judge court has been properly convened pursuant to 28 U.S.C. §§ 2281 and 2284.

Plaintiff Winston-Salem/Forsyth County Unit of the North Carolina Association of Educators is an unincorporated labor association representing professional employees, including teachers and administrators. The individual plaintiff is a teacher in Forsyth County and a member of the association. She wishes to represent all teachers in the Winston-Salem/Forsyth County School System. The defendants are State officials, the Winston-Salem/Forsyth County School Board, the Forsyth County Board of Commissioners, and the County of Forsyth.

The discontinuation of a salary supplement plan in 1972 supplied the irritant which caused plaintiffs to bring this action. In 1967, the school officials proposed the plan whereby the teachers in the Winston-Salem/Forsyth County school district would receive a portion of a school tax as part of their salary supplement. Since the supplement was tied to a county tax, it would increase along with the tax base of the county. The school board approved the plan. In 1972, the County Commissioners terminated the plan when they adopted the final budget for the county. Plaintiffs admit that no one source can be blamed for the discontinuation of the plan. They say that the determination of local school salaries results from input by the State Board of Education and the local units composed of the school board and county commissioners. Plaintiffs suggest that one of

---

[1]N.C.G.S. 95–98 reads as follows:

*"Contracts between units of government and labor unions, trade unions or labor organizations concerning public employees declared to be illegal.*—Any agreement, or contract, between the governing authority of any city, town, county, or other municipality, or between any agency, unit, or instrumentality thereof, or between any agency, instrumentality, or institution of the State of North Carolina, and any labor union, trade union, or labor organization, as bargaining agent for any public employees of such city, town, county or other municipality, or agency or instrumentality of government, is hereby declared to be against the public policy of the State, illegal, unlawful, void and of no effect."

[2]The statutes declared unconstitutional in *Atkins, supra*, were N.C.G.S. 95–97, which prohibited firefighting employees of a governmental unit from becoming members of or from assisting a labor organization which was affiliated with a national or international labor organization that had collective bargaining as one of its purposes, and N.C.G.S. 95–99, which provided a criminal penalty for violation of the related sections of the chapter.

the reasons for the termination of the salary supplement was the discovery of the statute, N.C.G.S. 95–98, by the governmental officials between 1967 and 1969. Plaintiffs claim that upon this discovery, the school officials became increasingly intransigent in their discussions with the teachers' association. They would like to blame a drop in their membership to their claimed growing ineffectiveness in discussions with the school officials after the purported discovery of N.C.G.S. 95–98.

In this case, there never was a signed contract between the teachers' organization and the school board. Defendants suggest that plaintiffs lack standing because there is no contract which is rendered void by N.C.G.S. 95–98. We agree that the plaintiffs never had a contract or agreement with the school. However, we read that fact as the basis of their complaint. They say that the school refuses to enter into a contract with them, or even engage in meaningful discussion, because of the statute. Viewed in this light, the question before this court is not moot and plaintiffs have standing to litigate the issue.

Plaintiffs allege that the statute is unconstitutional because of the detrimental effect it has on their ability to associate in a labor organizaion. They contend the statute renders nugatory their right to associate since it voids any contract obtained by the association. Thus, they say, it becomes fruitless for the organization to discuss matters with the school, and the individual teachers in turn become disenchanted with their organization.

Accepting those consequences as true, we cannot accept the premise that plaintiffs' alleged right of association requires that state governmental units negotiate and enter into contracts with them. The Constitution does not mandate that anyone, either the government or private parties, be compelled to talk to or contract with an organization. What Judge Craven wrote in *Atkins, supra,* at 1077, is controlling and bears repeating:

"We find nothing unconstitutional in G.S. § 95–98. It simply voids contracts between units of government within North Carolina and labor unions and expresses the public policy of North Carolina to be against such collective bargaining contracts. There is nothing in the United States Constitution which entitles one to have a contract with another who does not want it. It is but a step further to hold that the state may lawfully forbid such contracts with its instrumentalities. The solution, if there be one, from the viewpoint of the firemen, is that labor unions may someday persuade state government of the asserted value of collective bargaining agreements, but this is a political matter and does not yield to judicial solution. The right to a collective bargaining agreement, so firmly entrenched in American labor-management relations, rests upon national legislation and not upon the federal Constitution. The State is within the powers reserved to it to refuse to enter into such agreements and so to declare by statute."

The other cases considering the problem raised here have likewise rejected plaintiffs' argument. *Newport News F.F.A. Loc. 794* v. *City of Newport News, Va.,* 339 F. Supp. 13 (E.D. Va. 1972); *Hanover Tp. Fed. of Teach. L. 1954* v.

*Hanover Com. Sch. Corp.*, 457 F.2d 456 (7th Cir. 1972). While the First Amendment may protect the right of plaintiffs to associate and advocate, not all of their associational activities have the protection of that amendment. The State is not required to provide plaintiffs with a special forum in order to advocate their views. It is under no duty to provide a "guarantee that a speech will persuade or that advocacy will be effective." *Hanover Com. Sch. Corp.*, 457 F.2d 456 (7th Cir. 1972). *Corp., supra,* at 461.

Plaintiffs' reliance on *Healy v. James*, 408 U.E. 169, 92 S.Ct. 2338,33 L.Ed.2d 266 (1972), in support of the request for reconsideration of *Atkins* is misplaced. *Healy* concerned a college's denial of recognition to a student group. The Court held that the nonrecognition abridged the student group's First Amendment rights. The college had denied the group a formal meeting place, and the use of college bulletin boards and the college newspaper. Significantly, it had granted those rights to other student groups. The court noted that "the group's possible ability to exist outside the campus community does not ameliorate significantly the disabilities imposed by the President's action" (408 U.S. at 183, 33 LdEd.2d at 280). Thus the restriction in *Healy, supra,* directly affected the student group's right of advocacy and ability to organize in a situation where the college had granted those rights to other groups. In the present case the statute we are concerned with does not differentiate between public employee labor associations, nor does it restrict in any material way the ability to organize.

In *Healy, supra,* the college's action materially and discriminatorily affected the student group's right to speak and advocate. Here the statute has no such effect. All that it does is to render void contracts between the labor association and the State. As stated previously, the First Amendment does not guarantee that an organization's advocacy will be effective; it only protects the right to speak.[3]

The State, as a matter of public policy, has chosen not to enter into enforceable contracts with public employee organizations. That policy decision cannot be regarded lightly, or as

---

[3]*In Aurora Ed. Ass'n E. v. Board of Ed., Etc. Kane County, Ill.,* 490 F.2d 431 (7th Cir. 1973), the court distinguished *Hanover Tp. Fed. of Teach L. 1954 v. Hanover Com. Sch. Corp., supra,* from the issue before it concerning whether a school could penalize a teacher who merely *believed* that teachers should be given the right to strike. It said at 434:

"Whatever else may be said about the case, it dealt with the question whether a public body is under a constitutional duty, apart from statute, to bargain collectively with the labor representative of its employees. There was no occasion to consider in that case, and the court did not consider, the problem of this case, that is, whether a public body may interfere with its employees' freedoms to think and to speak—which from the beginning of time have been recognized as wholly different from the freedom to associate and to seek to use the strength which comes from union in assembly and action. See Wyzanski, "The Open Window and the Open Door," 35 *Cal.L.Rev.* 336 (1947)."

merely the result of antiunion animus. The decision of whether to permit public employees to engage in collective bargaining with the government involves far greater interests than the mere right to association claimed by the plaintiffs here. Professor Sylvester Petro in "Sovereignty and Compulsory Public-Professor Bargaining," 10 *Wake Forest Law Review* 25 (1974), ably and thoroughly discusses the case against the recognition of public employee labor organizations and bargaining with them. Even in an article more sympathetic to plaintiffs' position, Professor Summers discusses serious problems which cannot be avoided if collective bargaining is permitted. *See* Summers, "Public Employee Bargaining: A Political Perspective," 83 *Yale Law Journal* 1156 (1974). There the author views collective bargaining by public employees as part of the political decision-making process. As such it cannot be fairly compared with collective bargaining in the private sector. While he sees collective bargaining in the public sector as giving the public employees a chance to give unity, clarity, and persuasion in discussing their views with a governmental body, he also notes that, at present, permitting public employee collective bargaining might well over-shift the balance of power because of the inability, in some instances, of present governmental structure to effectively deal with a collective bargaining situation. Moreover, to the extent that the public employees gain power through recognition and collective bargaining, other interest groups with a right to a voice in the running of the government may be left out of vital political decisions. Thus the granting of collective bargaining rights to public employees involves important matters fundamental to our democratic form of government. The setting of goals and making policy decisions are rights inuring to each citizen. All citizens have the right to associate in groups in order to advocate their special interests to the government. It is something entirely different to grant any one interest group special status and access to the decision-making process. As Professor Summers notes at 1193–94:

"In the private sector the parties may agree at the bargaining table to expand the subjects of bargaining, but a public employee union and a public official do not have the same freedom to agree that certain decisions should be removed from the ordinary political processes and be decided by them in a special forum. The private employer's prerogatives are his to share as he sees fit, but the citizen's right to participate in governmental decisions cannot be bargained away by any public official.

"In legal terms the principal question in the private sector is what the *mandatory* subjects of bargaining are, *i.e.*, what decisions the employer *must* share with his employees. The principal question in the public sector is what the *permissible* subjects of bargaining are, *i.e.*, what decions *may* be made through the specially structured political process."

Viewed in this context, plaintiffs' purported right to associate via collective bargaining must compete with equally, if not more, important rights belonging to the citizenry.

171

The actual decision of how to accommodate public employees in the decision-making process without denying the right of association to others is a legislative decision.[4] Both legally and logically that decision is the prerogative of the legislature, which is much better suited to make it than are the federal courts, whose many duties cannot, under our system of government, include those of legislation. In North Carolina, the legislature has decided to resolve the competing interests by voiding contracts between the state and public employee labor organizations.

Plaintiffs also urge that N.C.G.S. 95–98 violates equal protection and due process. We disagree. While an unwarranted or unjustified interference with a First Amendment right may also be a violation of a Fourteenth Amendment right, *McLaughlin v. Tilendis*, 398 F.2d 287 (7th Cir. 1968); *Shelton v. Tucker*, 364 U.S. 479, 81 S.Ct. 247, 5 L.Ed.2d 231 (1960), we have concluded that the statute in question does not violate plaintiffs' right of freedom of association under the First Amendment. From our previous discussion it follows, and we so hold, that plaintiffs' Fourteenth Amendment rights are not violated.

Plaintiff's request for injunctive and declaratory relief is, therefore, denied.

[No. C-286-WS-72]

In the U.S. District Court for the Middle District of North Carolina, Winston-Salem Division

Winston-Salem/Forsyth County Unit of the North Carolina Association of Educators, an Unincorporated Association, and Jacqueline A. Ballentine, Individually and on Behalf of Other Similarly Situated Teachers in the Winston-Salem/Forsyth County School System, Plaintiffs, v. A. Craig Phillips, State Superintendent of Public Instruction; Frank Crane, Commissioner of Labor for the State of North Carolina; Robert B. Morgan, Attorney General of the State of North Carolina; and John C. Kiger, Omeda Brewer, Eunice Burge, Richard Janeway, Mary Lauerman, William F. Maready, Alan R. Perry, Carol G. Thompson, As Members of the Winston-Salem/Forsyth County School Board, and the Win-

---

[4]The Tenth Amendment of the United States Constitution reserves to the states those powers not delegated to the federal government. The Amendment is a clear expression of the desire that the states would retain their sovereignty within our federal form of government. The decision by the State of North Carolina to void contracts between public employee organizations and governmental units is a matter entrusted to the state's sovereign discretion. See *Atkins, supra,* as quoted above. It cannot be emphasized enough that in speaking of a state's sovereignty, the term means more than prerogatives belonging to some inanimate object, rather it signifies the right of the people of a state to govern themselves under the form of government of their choosing. Therefore, since the prospect of public employee collective bargaining impinges upon those rights, it truly is important that the legislature, elected by the people, determine whether to permit such collective bargaining, and if so; on what terms.

ston-Salem/Forsyth County School Board, and David W. Darr, Henry L. Crotts, G. P. Swisher, Dr. W. L. Thompson, Jr., and Leonard Warner as Members of the Forsyth County Boa Commissioners, and the County of Forsyth, Defendants

## ORDER

For the reasons set forth in an Opinion of the Court entered contemporaneously herewith,

It is ordered that the relief requested by the plaintiffs in the prayer for relief be and the same hereby is denied, and the action is dismissed.

For the Court:

HIRAM H. WARD,
*U.S. District Judge.*

SEPTEMBER 17, 1974.

# Appendix V

Public-Employee Union Statutes According to States

## FREEDOM OF CHOICE GUARANTEED

States forbidding the forced
unionization of public employees

| State | Employees Affected | Citations |
|---|---|---|
| Alabama | All public employees | Code of Alabama, Title 26, § 375(1) |
| | Firemen | Code of Alabama, Title 37, § 450(3)(2) |
| Arizona | All public employees | Article XXV, Arizona Constitution, Arizona Revised Statutes Annotated, § 23-1302 |
| Arkansas | All public employees | Amendment No. 34, § 1, Arkansas Constitution |
| California | All public employees Teachers | Deerings California Government Code Annotated, §§ 3502 and 3527 |
| | Teachers | Deerings California Education Code Annotated, § 13082 |
| Connecticut | Teachers | Connecticut General Statutes Annotated, § 10-153(a) |
| Delaware | Public school employees | Delaware Code Annotated, Title 14, § 4003 |
| Florida | All public employees | Florida State Constitution, Art. 1, § 6 |
| Illinois | State employees | Executive Order #6 (1973) |
| Iowa | All public employees | Iowa Code Annotated, § 736A.1. |
| Kansas | All public employees | Kansas Constitution, Art. 15, Section 12 |
| Louisiana | All public employees | Louisiana Constitution, enacted April 20, 1974 |
| Maine | State employees | State Employment Labor Relations Act, adopted March 1974 |
| Maryland | Teachers | Annotated Code of Maryland, Art. 77, § 160 |
| Mississippi | All public employees | Mississippi Constitution, Art. 7, Sec. 198-A |
| | | Mississippi Code Annotated, Section 6984.5(a) |

| Missouri | All public employees except policemen | Missouri Revised Statutes, Chapter 105, § 510 |
|---|---|---|
| Nebraska | All public employees | Nebraska Constitution, Article XV, §§ 13, 14, and 15 |
| Nevada | All public employees | Nevada Revised Statutes, § 613.250 |
| New Hampshire | All state employees except teachers | New Hampshire Revised Statutes, § 98-C:2 |
| | Policemen | New Hampshire Revised Statutes, 1972, § 105-B:3 |
| New Jersey | All public employees | New Jersey Statutes Annotated, Section 34:1 3A-5:3 |
| New Mexico | State employees | State Personnel Board Regulations Revised May 9, 1972 II and VII |
| New York | All public employees | McKinney's Consolidated Laws of New York Annotated, Civil Service Law, §§ 202 and 208 |
| North Carolina | All public employees | North Carolina Statutes, § 95-98 |
| North Dakota | All public employees | North Dakota Century Code Annotated, § 34-01-14 |
| Ohio | All public employees | *Foltz v. City of Dayton,* 75 LRRM 2331 (Ohio Ct. of App. 1970) |
| | | *CSEA v. AFSCME,* 405 GERR B-9 (Ohio 1971) |
| | | *Sheehy, et al. v. Ensign, et al.,* 395 GERR B-3 (Common Pleas Court 1971) |
| | | *Hagerman v. City of Dayton, et al.,* 71 N. E. 2d 247 (Ohio 1947) |
| Oklahoma | Firemen and policemen | Oklahoma Statutes, Title 11, § 548.2 |
| | Teachers | Oklahoma Statutes, Title 70, § 509.9 |
| | Municipal employees | Oklahoma Statutes, Title 11, § 548.3-1 |
| Pennsylvania* | All public employees except policemen and firemen | 43 Purdon's Pennsylvania Statutes Annotated, § 1101.705 |
| | Policemen and firemen | *IAFF Local 1038 v. Allegheny Co.,* 490 GERR B-4 (Comm. Ct. of Pa. 1973) |
| Rhode Island | Municipal employees | General Laws of Rhode Island, § 28-9.4-8 |
| | Teachers | General Laws of Rhode Island, § 28-9.3-7 |
| South Carolina | All public employees | South Carolina Code Annotated, Title 40, § 46 |

---

*Public employees in Pennsylvania who *voluntarily* join labor unions or employee associations can legally be required to maintain their memberships "for the duration of a collective bargaining agreement . . ."

| | | |
|---|---|---|
| South Dakota | All public employees | South Dakota Compiled Laws Annotated, §§ 3-8-2 and 60-8-3 |
| Texas | All public employees | Vernon's Annotated Civil Statutes, Art. 5154 g. § 1 |
| Utah | All public employees | Utah Code Annotated, Title 34, § 34-2 |
| Vermont | State employees | Vermont Statutes Annotated Title 3, Chapter 27, §§ 903, 941(2) and 962(6)(a) |
| Virginia | All public employees | Code of Virginia Annotated, § 40.1-58.1 |
| Wyoming | All public employees | Wyoming Statutes Annotated, Title 27, § 245.3 |

# FREEDOM OF CHOICE DENIED

### States authorizing the forced unionization of public employees

| States | Employees Affected | Citations |
|---|---|---|
| Alaska | All public employees except teachers | Alaska Statutes Annotated, § 23.40.11 and § 23.40.110(b) |
| Hawaii | All public employees | Hawaii Revised Statutes, Chapter 89, §§ 2 and 4 |
| Kentucky | Firemen | Kentucky Revised Statutes, § 345.050(1)(c) |
| Massachusetts | All public employees | Senate Bill 1929 effective 7/1/74 |
| Michigan | All public employees | Michigan Compiled Laws Annotated, § 423.210(10) |
| Minnesota | All public employees | Minnesota Statutes Annotated, § 179.65, Subd. (2) and (4) |
| Montana | All public employees | Revised Code of Montana Annotated, Title 59, § 1605(c) and § 1612 |
| Oregon | All public employees | Oregon Revised Statutes, §§ 243.711 and 243.730 |
| Rhode Island | State employees | General Laws of Rhode Island, § 36-11-2 |
| Vermont* | Municipal employees | Vermont Statutes Annotated, Title 21, Chapter 22 §§ 1722 and 1726 |
| Washington | All public employees | Revised Code of Washington, § 41.56.110 |
| Wisconsin | State employees | Wisconsin Statutes, Subchapter V, §§ 111.81(6) and 111.84 (1)(f) |
| | Municipal employees | Wisconsin Statutes, Subchapter IV, §§ 111.70(1)h and 111.70 (3)(a)3 |

*Although the Vermont statute authorizes "agency shop" agreements, it provides: "No municipal employer shall discharge or discriminate against any employee for nonpayment of an agency service fee or for nonmembership in an employee organization."

# LAWS SILENT

States whose laws are silent on the question of voluntary
or compulsory unionism for public employees

Colorado
Georgia
Idaho
Indiana
Tennessee
West Virginia

# Index

Aaron, Benjamin, 77
AAUP (American Association of University Professors), 76, 77
*ABC's of the G-E Strike—A Teaching Unit for Secondary School Teachers, The* (Di Lorenzo), 57–59
Abernathy, Ralph, 64
ACLU. *See* American Civil Liberties Union
Acton, Lord, 115
Advisory Commission on Intergovernmental Relations, 147–48, 157, 158
AFL, 9, 10
AFL-CIO, 14, 21–22, 23, 27–28, 34, 41, 44, 59, 84, 87–89, 146
AFL-CIO Executive Council, 21, 41, 87
AFSCME (American Federation of State, County, and Municipal Employees), 16, 21, 26–27, 30, 36–44, 49, 61, 85–86, 104, 118, 140
AFT, 30, 56, 61–68, 76, 77
Alexander, Herbert E., 21, 88 n
Alien and Sedition Acts, 32
Alioto, Joseph, 50–53
Allis-Chalmers strike, 23
Amalgamated Clothing Workers, 19
Amalgamated Transit Union, 44
American Association for Public Opinion Research: Code of Ethics of, 121
American Association of University Professors. *See* AAUP
American Civil Liberties Union, 117
American Federation of Government Employees, 44, 148
American Federation of Labor. *See* AFL
American Federation of State, County, and Municipal Employees. *See* AFSCME
American Federation of Teach-

ers. *See* AFT
Andrews, Ike, 104, 133
Applegate, Carol, 70–71
Ashbrook, John, 134
Associated Press, 39, 96
*Atkins* v. *City of Charlotte,* 83

*Ball* v. *City of Detroit and the American Federation of State, County and Municipal Employees,* 18
Baltimore police strike, 36–40, 152
Barkan, Alexander, 87, 88
*Barnette* decision, 29
Barrett, Catherine, 75
Bayh, Birch, 22, 89
Beard, Edward, 104, 133
Bell, Alphonzo, 133
Biaggi, Mario, 104, 133
"Bill Moyers Journal," 60
Bill of Rights (AFT), 65–66
Bill of Rights (U.S. Constitution), 29, 32, 83, 157
Black Panthers, 63
Blouin, Michael, 103, 133
*Boston Globe,* 52
Boston police strike, 9–14
Boulware, Lemuel, 58
Boulwarism, 58
Brademas, John, 104, 133
Bradley, Tom, 149
Brandeis (justice), 101
Braun, R. J., 63
Brinkley, David, 22
Brown, Edmund (Jerry), 35, 51
Buchanan, John, 134
Buckley, James L., 137, 156
Burton, Phillip, 26, 104, 133

Carnegie Commission on Higher Education, 76
Central Intelligence Agency. *See* CIA
Chavez, Cesar, 19
Chisholm, Shirley, 26, 104, 133
*Chisholm* v. *Georgia,* 107
Chrysler Corporation, 24

CIA, 22, 32
*City of Springfield* v. *Clouse*, 108
Civil Service Commission, 15, 44
Clark, Joseph, 89
Clay bill. *See* "National Public Employment Relations Act"
Clay, William, 17, 26, 103, 133
Clayton Act, 115
Committee on Political Education. *See* COPE
Condon-Wadlin Act, 45, 46
Connecticut Supreme Court, 108
*Constitution of Liberty, The* (Hayek), 90, 115
Coolidge, Calvin, 10–12, 21
COPE, 21, 87–88
Cornell, Robert, 104, 133
Corrupt Practices Act, 14, 21, 41, 103
Cox, Archibald, 20, 117
Crowley, Gerald, 51
Curtis, Carl T., 137, 163
Curtis, Edwin U., 11, 12

Daniels, Dominick, 104, 133
Declaration of Independence, 160
*Declaration of Purpose and Policy, The* (Clay bill preamble), 29, 30
*Decline of the West, The* (Spengler), 120
DeLury, John J., 47, 48
Dent, John, 104, 133
Dicey, A. V., 115
Di Lorenzo, Jeannette, 57
Drewes, Robert, 50
Dubinsky, David, 20
Dwyer, Florence P., 159

Economic Development Council of New York, 87, 93
*Economics of Trade Unionism, The* (Rees), 79
Education and Labor Committee, House, 26, 103
Elisburg, Donald, 151
Erlenborn, John, 134
Ervin, Sam, 159
Esch, Marvin, 133
Eshleman, Edwin, 134
Executive Order 10988, of President Kennedy, 14–16, 18, 28, 36, 148

Fair Labor Standards Act, 149–150, 152
Fannin, Paul J., 137, 145
Farah (manufacturer), 19
Farmer, Guy, 23
FBI, 32
Federal Bureau of Investigation. *See* FBI
Federal Mediation and Conciliation Service, 79
*Final Recommendations on a Statewide Bargaining Strategy* (Michigan Education Association), 72
*Financing the 1968 Election* (Alexander), 88 n
Fire and Police Protective League, of Los Angeles, 85
First Amendment, 32, 71 n
Ford, Gerald, 35
Ford Motor Company, 24, 100
Ford, William, 104, 133
Fountain (congressman), 159
Franklin County (Pa.) labor dispute, 90–92

Garn, Jake, 137, 149, 160
Gay Activist movement, 63
Gaydos, Joseph, 104, 133
General Electric strike, 59–62
General Motors, 24
George III (king of England), 22, 23
Gilligan, John, 89
Goldberg, Arthur, 148
Gompers, Samuel, 12, 101, 105
Goodling, Bill, 134
Gotbaum, Victor, 61, 112
Government Printing Office, 43
*Government Work Stoppages, 1960, 1969, and 1970* (Bureau of Labor Statistics), 80
Great Depression, 56
Griesbach, Rick, 97
Griffin, Robert P., 23

Hall, Tim, 104, 133
Hansen, Clifford P., 137, 152
Hanslowe, Kurt L., 113 n, 117
Hanson, Ole, 9
Harper, Timothy, 96
Harvard Law School, 30
Hatch Act, 118
Hawaii State Teacher's Association, 67
Hawkins, Augustus, 134

179

Hayakawa, S. I., 75
Hayek, F. A., 90, 115
Hechinger, Fred, 61
Helms, Jesse A., 137, 163, 164
Henderson, David, 35
Hill, Herbert, 65 n
Hillman, Robert, 153
Holmes, Oliver Wendell, 12
Holmquist, Albert, 71 n
Hortonville (Wis.) teachers' strike, 96–97
Humphrey, Hubert H., 21, 64

Imperiale, Anthony, 63
Industrial Workers of the World (IWW), 9
International Ladies Garment Workers, 20

Jackson (Justice), 116 n
Jefferson, Thomas, 32 n
Jeffords, James, 134
Johnson, Haynes, 27–28
Johnson, Lyndon, 46

Kadish, Sanford, 76
Kansas City Firemen's strike, 53, 54
Kansas City Times, 53
Kennedy, John F., 14–15, 16, 18, 28, 36, 117, 148
Kheel, Theodore W., 47 n, 153
Kilpatrick, James Jackson, 16 n
King, Martin Luther, 44
King, Owen, 39
Kirk, Russell, 162
Kirkland, Lane, 28
Kotz, Nick, 27–28

Ladd, Everett Carll, Jr., 76
LaFortune, Robert, 151
Landrum-Griffin Act, 23
Lebanon (Ohio) Correctional Institution, 38
Lehman, William, 104, 133
Lejeune, Anthony, 106 n
Lenin, 44
Lindsay, John V., 45, 46, 47, 48, 49, 85
Lipsett, Seymour, 76
Locke, John, 107
Los Angeles Federation of Labor, 86

McAullife v. City of New Bedford, 12

McAvoy, Joan Zeldon, 113 n
McClure, James A., 137, 149, 155, 160
McGovern, George, 21
Machinists (union), 27
Madison, James, 32 n, 84
Maki, Margaret, 71
Mandel, Marvin, 36, 38, 39, 152
Mansfield, Mike, 163
MEA. See Michigan Education Association
Meany, George, 14, 21, 22, 27, 33, 64, 108, 116, 117, 146, 153
Meeds, Lloyd, 104, 133
Michigan Education Association, 70–74
Michigan Teacher Tenure Commission, 70
Middle South Broadcasting, 24
Miller, Clyde C., 71
Miller, George, 104, 133
Mills, C. Wright, 115
Mink, Patsy, 26, 104, 133
Minnesota State Capital Employees Union (MSCEU), 118
Mises, Ludwig von, 116 n
Missouri Supreme Court, 108
Morrison, Donald E., 67
Moss, Robert, 151
Mottl, Ron, 104, 133
Moyers, Bill, 60
Mundt, Karl E., 159
Murphy, James W., 38
Muskie, Ed, 159

National Association for the Advancement of Colored People, 118
National Association of Letter Carriers, 44
National Education Association. See NEA
National Federation of Federal Employees, 16
National Governors' Conference, 1975, 119, 159
National Guard, 11, 48
National Labor Relations Act (NLRA), 21, 22, 25, 28, 33, 61, 79, 80, 140, 166
National Labor Relations Board. See NLRB
National League of Cities, 150; Board of Directors of, 149
National Maritime Union, 35

180

"National Public Employment Relations Act" (Clay bill), 26, 28, 29, 31, 33–34

National Public Employment Relations Commission. *See* NPERC

National Right to Work Committee, 34, 119

National Right to Work Legal Defense Foundation, 70, 118

NEA, 30, 63, 67–71, 74–77, 104, 140

Nelson, Gaylord, 89

New Deal, 28

New York Central Labor Council, 45

New York City Board of Education, 56, 60, 62, 93

New York City Board of Higher Education, 93

New York Civil Liberties Union, 62 n

*New York Daily News,* 146

New York State Supreme Court, 46

*New York Times,* 37 n, 38, 44, 85, 86, 146

New York Transit Authority, 45–46, 93

*Newsweek,* 53, 65 n

NFFE. *See* National Federation of Federal Employees

Nixon, Richard, 22

NLRB, 21, 24, 28, 31, 32, 99, 100

Norris-LaGuardia Act, 21, 24, 116

*Norwalk Teachers Association v. Board of Education,* 108

NPERC, 31, 32

O'Hara, James, 26, 104, 133

Ohio General Assembly, 39

Ohio Youth Commission, 39

Opinion Research Corporation (Princeton, N.J.), 18, 102; Caravan Survey of, 121–32, 135–36

Parrish, Richard, 65 n

Patrolmen's Benevolent Association, of New York City, 85, 86

Pell, Claiborne, 69

Perkins, Carl, 104, 134

Peters, Andrew, 11

Petro, Sylvester, 106, 110, 120, 141

Peyser, Peter, 104 n, 133

Phillips, Jennings, Jr., 151

Police Officers Association of San Francisco, 50, 51

Politburo, 65 n

Pomerleau, Donald, 38

Postal Reorganization Act, 148, 161

Pound, Roscoe, 116 n

Pressler, Larry, 134

*Professors, Unions, and American Higher Education* (Ladd; Lipsett), 76

*Progressive,* 43

*Public Employee,* 86

Public Service Railway, 9

Public Service Research Council, 34, 35, 81

Quie, Al, 133

Quill, Michael J., 44, 45, 46

Raftery, S. Frank, 28

Rees, Albert, 79

Reilly, Gerald D., 24

Reuther, Walter, 20, 44, 64, 84, 111

Riesel, Victor, 96

Risenhoover, Ted, 104, 133

Rockefeller, Nelson, 46, 47, 48, 85

"Role of Politics in Local Labor Relations, The" (UCLA *Law Review*), 84

Roosevelt, Franklin Delano, 13–14, 25, 137

Roybal, Edward, 34

*Sacramento Bee,* 54

*St. Louis Globe Democrat,* 72 n

St. Louis Education Association, 71

San Francisco General Hospital, 152

San Francisco police strike, 50–54

San Francisco State College, 63

Sape, George P., 151

Sarasin, Ronald, 133

Schumpeter, J. A., 115 n

*Second Treatise of Government, The* (Locke), 107

Seidman, Joel, 100, 101, 105

Shanker, Albert, 56–57, 60–62, 66, 84, 105
Sherman Act, 116
Simon, Henry C., 90
Simon, Paul, 103, 133
Smith, Mortimer, 60 n
Smith, Virginia, 134
Spengler, Oswald, 120
Spinoza, Baruch, 160
Stalin, 65 n
Steel Workers, 27
Steinert, Paul, 97
Steward, L. C., 13, 137
Stock, J. Stevens, 128
Streit, Saul S., 48, 49
Subcommittee on Separation of Powers, Senate, 22
Summers, Clyde, 99

Taft-Hartley Act, 14, 20, 135
Tammany Hall, 56
Taylor, George W., 47
Taylor Law, 47, 48
Teacher Tenure Act, of Michigan, 70
*Teachers and Power* (Braun), 63
Teamsters union, 71
Tenth Amendment, 29–30, 157
Thompson, Frank, 34, 104, 133
Thoreau, Henry, 41
Thurmond, Strom, 137, 142, 160
*Time*, 44, 53
Trade Dispute Act, of 1960 (Great Britain), 115
Trades Union Council (England), 25
Transit Workers Union, 85
Transport Workers Union, 44
Trenton (N.J.) City Council, 119

UFT, 56–57, 59–62, 65 n
Ullman (congressman), 159
Uniformed Sanitation Men's Association, 47, 49, 85
*Unions and the Cities, The* (Wellington, Winter), 80 n
"Unions, The" (Johnson, Kotz), 27
United Auto Workers, 23, 44, 100

United Farm Workers, 19
United Federation of Postal Clerks, 44
United Federation of Teachers. *See* UFT
*United Teacher*, 59
United Teachers of Los Angeles, 69
U.S. Conference of Mayors, 150
U.S. Constitution, 30, 32 n, 34, 84, 116, 120, 157, 160, 161, 172 n
U.S. Department of Labor, 57, 58
*U.S. News & World Report*, 41–43
U.S. Postal Service, 98
U.S. Supreme Court, 107, 116, 118
Usery, W. J., 53

Van Arsdale, Harry, 45
Vietnam war, 31, 36

Wagner Act. *See* National Labor Relations Act (NLRA)
Walcoff, Victor, 119
War of 1812, 117 n
Warren Court, 22
Washington, George, 109, 157
*Washington Monthly*, 98
*Washington Post*, 27, 37, 153
Wellington, Harry K., 80 n
Wheeler, Charles B. (Jr.), 54
White, William Allen, 10, 11
Wilson, Charles, 34
Wilson (Prime Minister), 106 n
Wilson, Woodrow, 12, 107
Winter, Ralph K., Jr., 80 n
Wisconsin Education Association, 97
Wise, Helen D., 68, 75
Wootton, Barbara, 115
Wurf, Jerry, 21, 26, 30, 33, 36–37, 38–39, 40–44, 49, 61, 79 n, 83, 105, 111, 118

Zander, Arnold, 42
Zeferetti, Leo, 104, 133

**National Right to Work Committee**
8316 Arlington Boulevard Dept.100
Fairfax, Virginia 22038

I agree that union membership should be voluntary, not compulsory. Please send me additional information on how I can help.

Name_____

Address_____

City_____State_____Zip_____

"The National Right to Work Committee . . . correctly interpreted the situs bill as a further intrusion into the individual liberties of American workers . . . led the fight (against it) . . . and deserves considerable credit," Sen. Paul Fannin, R-Ariz., after President Gerald Ford's veto of legislation to legalize coercive picketing at construction sites, January 1976.

"Outstanding service to the Nation and to the cause of personal freedom," Rep. David Henderson, D-N.C., in June, 1970, after the National Right to Work Committee led a successful grassroots campaign which resulted in a strong Right to Work provision being included in the postal reorganization act.

"The successful defense of 14(b) proved that, provided the leadership, millions of Americans . . . will take the time to stand up for freedom," nationally syndicated columnist James J. Kilpatrick, May 1966, following the year-long fight to preserve the Taft-Hartley labor act provision which authorizes state Right to Work Laws.

With nearly a million active supporters, the National Right to Work Committee is one of the largest public interest lobbies in the United States. For more than 20 years the Committee has provided vital leadership in the fight to protect working people against compulsory unionism. While the Committee supports the right of every citizen to voluntarily join a union, it also believes no one should be forced to do so in order to get or keep a job.

# What Really Causes Strikes Against Government?

The union bosses want us to believe that it is the lack of public sector collective bargaining.

All the logical evidence points to the conclusion that, rather than the solution, compulsory public sector collective bargaining is the cause of strikes.

What do you think?

For more information, send this coupon to Americans Against Union Control of Government to get your free copy of "Questions and Answers about Compulsory Public Sector Collective Bargaining."

Americans Against Union Control of Government is a division of the Public Service Research Council.

**Americans Against Union Control of Government**
8320 Old Courthouse Road
Suite 430
Vienna, Virginia 22180

Please send me my free copy of "Questions and Answers about Compulsory Public Sector Collective Bargaining."

Mr•Mrs•Miss _____

Street _____

City _____ State _____ Zip _____

# A Free Book

with every four books you order!

1. HOW TO START YOUR OWN SCHOOL, Robert Love. Everything a parent or principal needs to know, by someone who did it himself. "An important and readable book that tells you how to do it"—*Human Events*. **$1.95**

2. THE REGULATED CONSUMER, Mary B. Peterson. *The Wall Street Journal* contributor shows how seven Federal regulatory agencies have been captured by the businesses they were supposed to regulate! How this hurts consumers everywhere, and what can be done about it. "This thoughtful, challenging book can perform a great service" —*Fortune*. **$2.95**

3. THE DEFENSELESS SOCIETY, Frank Carrington and William Lambie. A scathing look at how the Courts and Congress have tilted the battle against crime in favor of the criminal and against society, with proposals for restoring the balance. Frank Carrington is the author of *The Victims*, executive director of Americans for Effective Law Enforcement. **$1.95**

4. THE CASE AGAINST THE RECKLESS CONGRESS, Hon. Marjorie Holt, ed. Nineteen Republican congressmen contribute chapters on the major issues before Congress. All 435 Representatives' votes are recorded. "Not merely a naysayers political bible. The authors do offer alternative programs. Moreover, the book provides us with a chance to examine 'the conservative side' whether or not one agrees with it."—*CBS Radio*. **$1.95**

5. THE MAKING OF THE NEW MAJORITY PARTY, William Rusher. "If anyone can invigorate the ideological comradeship of economic and social conservatives, it is William Rusher. This is a well-written and thoughtful book." —*The Wall Street Journal*. **$1.95**

6. THE SUM OF GOOD GOVERNMENT, Hon Philip M. Crane. Often mentioned as a 1976 vice-presidential candidate, the brilliant conservative Illinois congressman offers a positive program for solving the problems of American government in our country's 200th year. (September.) **$1.95**

7. THE GUN OWNER'S POLITICAL ACTION MANUAL, Alan Gottlieb. Everything a gun owner needs to know to be politically effective in the firearms freedom fight. Includes voting records of all Congressmen on every pro-/anti-gun vote, how to use the media, and a large reference section on publications and organizations. (September.) **$1.95**

# A Free Book

with every
four books
you order!

8. SINCERELY, RONALD REAGAN, Helene von Damm. The personal correspondence of Ronald Reagan as Governor of California. Covers his views on almost every national issue. "There is much in these letters that sheds new light on the man."—*Saturday Evening Post* **$1.25**

9. THE HUNDRED MILLION DOLLAR PAYOFF: HOW BIG LABOR BUYS ITS DEMOCRATS, Douglas Caddy. "An extensively documented exposé of big labor's illegal largesse."—*Newsweek* **$2.95**

10. A NEW DAWN FOR AMERICA: THE LIBERTARIAN CHALLENGE, Roger MacBride. The Libertarian Party presidential candidate calls for a return to first principles. **$ .95**

11. THE MUNICIPAL DOOMSDAY MACHINE, Ralph de Toledano. "Forced unionization of public employees threatens American democracy. Toledano's book is must reading" —*Ronald Reagan.* **$1.95**

12. REFLECTIONS ON ECONOMIC ADVISING, Paul W. McCracken. The former Chairman of the President's Council of Economic Advisers shows how our economy is managed. (*Booklet.*) **$ .95**

13. THE POLITICIZATION OF ECONOMIC DECISIONS, Alan Walters, introduction by Harry Johnson. The economies of the West are being ruined by the substitution of politics for economics; the author shows how, and why. (*Booklet.*) **$ .95**

---

Green Hill Publishers, Inc.
Post Office Box 738
Ottawa, Illinois 61350

Please send me postpaid the following books:
(*Circle numbers*)   1  2  3  4  5  6  7  8  9  10  11  12  13
I understand that if I order four books, I get No.____FREE.

I enclose $_____*

_____

_____

_____

_____Zip code_____

*Illinois residents please add 5% sales tax.

**NOTE:** Free book offer applies only when all books are shipped together. If not-yet-published books are ordered, entire order will be held until all books are available.

*"America must come to grips with the issue of public employee unions. We need an open, thoughtful debate. Ralph de Toledano has taken a giant first step in this direction."*—Senator Jesse Helms (R-N.C.)

## QUANTITY DISCOUNTS

# The Municipal Doomsday Machine

### by

### Ralph de Toledano

### QUANTITY PRICES*

| | | | | | |
|---|---|---|---|---|---|
| 1 copy | $1.95 | 10 copies | $12.50 | 100 copies | $ 60.00 |
| 3 copies | $5.00 | 25 copies | $25.00 | 500 copies | $275.00 |
| 5 copies | $7.50 | 50 copies | $35.00 | 1000 copies | $500.00 |

\* Illinois residents please add 5% sales tax.

GREEN HILL PUBLISHERS, INC.
Post Office Box 738
Ottawa, Illinois 61350

Please send me postpaid_____copies of THE MUNICIPAL DOOMSDAY MACHINE by Ralph de Toledano. I enclose

$_____

_____

_____

_____

_____Zip Code_____

*"America must come to grips with the issue of public employee unions. We need an open, thoughtful debate. Ralph de Toledano has taken a giant first step in this direction."*—Senator Jesse Helms (R-N.C.)

## QUANTITY DISCOUNTS

# The Municipal Doomsday Machine

## by

## Ralph de Toledano

### QUANTITY PRICES*

| | | | | | |
|---|---|---|---|---|---|
| 1 copy | $1.95 | 10 copies | $12.50 | 100 copies | $ 60.00 |
| 3 copies | $5.00 | 25 copies | $25.00 | 500 copies | $275.00 |
| 5 copies | $7.50 | 50 copies | $35.00 | 1000 copies | $500.00 |

* Illinois residents please add 5% sales tax.

GREEN HILL PUBLISHERS, INC.
Post Office Box 738
Ottawa, Illinois 61350

Please send me postpaid_____copies of THE MUNICIPAL DOOMSDAY MACHINE by Ralph de Toledano. I enclose

$_____.

_____

_____

_____

_____Zip Code_____